Professional DotNetNuke® Module Programming

Professional
DotNetNuke® Module Programming

Mitchel Sellers

Wiley Publishing, Inc.

Professional DotNetNuke® Module Programming

Published by
Wiley Publishing, Inc.
10475 Crosspoint Boulevard
Indianapolis, IN 46256
www.wiley.com

Copyright © 2009 by Wiley Publishing, Inc., Indianapolis, Indiana

Published simultaneously in Canada

ISBN: 978-0-470-17116-5

Manufactured in the United States of America

10 9 8 7 6 5 4 3 2 1

Library of Congress Cataloging-in-Publication Data is available from the publisher.

*I dedicate this book to my dad,
who has had a profound impact on who I am today,
and who introduced me to computers and
software development at a young age.
Without his support over the years,
this book would not be possible.*

About the Author

Mitchel Sellers is CEO/Director of Development for IowaComputerGurus, Inc., a .NET and DotNetNuke consulting firm based in Des Moines, Iowa. IowaComputerGurus has a special collection of partnerships that enables the company to offer full-solution services to handle all IT needs — from planning and development to implementation and long-term support. Sellers is a Microsoft-certified Professional with nine individual areas of specialization, including Microsoft Certified IT Professional (MCITP), Microsoft Certified Professional Developer (MCPD), and Microsoft Certified Technology Specialist (MCTS), with all certifications on .NET 2.0 and later, as well as SQL Server 2005 and later. He has also presented at various public events, including OpenForce '07. Sellers maintains a blog at `www.mitchelsellers.com/blogs.aspx` that provides helpful information about DotNetNuke development.

Credits

Acquisitions Editor
Scott Meyers

Development Editor
Kevin Shafer

Technical Editor
Jon Henning

Production Editor
Kathleen Wisor

Copy Editor
Luann Rouff

Editorial Manager
Mary Beth Wakefield

Production Manager
Tim Tate

Vice President and Executive Group Publisher
Richard Swadley

Vice President and Executive Publisher
Barry Pruett

Associate Publisher
Jim Minatel

Project Coordinator, Cover
Lynsey Stanford

Proofreader
Nancy Bell

Indexer
Robert Swanson

Acknowledgments

To start out, I would like to thank the individuals at John Wiley & Sons for the opportunity to write this book. It has been an enjoyable learning experience, and has really opened my eyes as to what goes into a book. It is hoped that this also opens a door for future writing projects.

I would like to thank Jim Minatel, Scott Meyers, Kevin Shafer, Kathleen Wisor, and the rest of the editorial staff that was involved in the writing of this book. Because this is my first book, I greatly appreciate how very cordial they have been in communications, and they were more than understanding when I didn't know how the process worked — not to mention that their editing has transformed this book into a great overall package. It wouldn't have been possible without them.

Jon Henning, the technical editor, deserves special acknowledgment because he took great care when reviewing the book to ensure that all the topics discussed were covered in detail, and properly worded his comments and queries to avoid any potential communication issues. His invaluable feedback helped to create the final result.

Charles Nurse and the rest of the DotNetNuke core team also deserve acknowledgment here because they have also provided useful feedback and validation about many of the items included in the book. This has been especially important because this book was written while DotNetNuke 5 was still under major development.

I would also like to take a moment to thank the DotNetNuke community for their support over the past few years — reading my blog, posting suggestions for content in this book, and encouraging me to complete it.

Lastly, I would like to thank my family, friends, and clients, all of whom have been supportive of me during the time I spent writing this book. With a busy schedule already, and this book taking a big chunk out of my remaining available time, everyone has been incredibly supportive — and that means a lot to me.

Contents

Contents

Contents

Contents

Foreword

A book on professional module development would not make much sense without a fundamental understanding and appreciation of why a modern software developer should use a modular approach to building web software rather relying on the historical practice of constructing a monolithic web application from scratch.

The fact is that the majority of web applications in existence today share a common set of business requirements and technical characteristics. This is true regardless of industry, environment, or audience. These common underpinnings represent the foundation for all production web applications. Therefore, rather than implement a brand new foundation for each new web application, it makes practical sense to re-use some of the mature functionality created for previous applications. Abstracting these components into comprehensive library, results in a robust application framework which can be used as the basis for new web applications. Over time a framework will evolve to support new technology innovations and business requirements, and benefits from broader developer usage and mission critical run-time experience.

Since it is not possible for a piece of software to solve every customer problem, a web application framework needs to be flexible so that it can be easily extended to accommodate additional functionality. Essentially a web application framework must be a platform; an operating environment where third party applications, plug-ins, add-ons, and designs can be seamlessly integrated. Most popular web application frameworks support a concept known as Modules, which are essentially mini-applications that leverage capabilities of the framework to expose custom business functionality. At run-time, modules are instantiated within the context of the web application framework and offer advanced security, consistent behavior, and a seamless user experience.

It could be said that a web application framework is essentially a collection of modules, and, for the most part, this is true. Modules are designed for a specific business purpose and are usually comprised of a user interface, business logic, and data access methodology. In technical terms this approach closely resembles the Model-View-Controller (MVC) pattern which has become synonymous with web application architecture. Simple modules may only require a very minimal implementation; whereas more advanced modules may in fact be larger and more sophisticated than the web application framework itself. Regardless of the functionality provided by modules, it is also essential that there is a packaging and distribution capability within the framework which allows for simple installation and configuration of modules at run-time.

DotNetNuke® is a web application framework designed specifically for the Microsoft technology platform. It is mature, enterprise-grade, full-featured, and freely available as an open source distribution licensed under a liberal MIT license. The framework contains a robust API and full source code, providing developers with the greatest productivity benefit and maximum flexibility. The framework is coupled with a content management system (CMS) which allows end-users to easily install and configure modules and host them in a fully functional web environment.

Over the past five years, a commercial ecosystem has emerged around the DotNetNuke platform. This ecosystem has allowed software developers from all over the world to create powerful modules and make them available for sale to users of the platform. A variety of organizations and individuals now derive all, or a substantial portion of, their revenue from this module ecosystem. In the years ahead we expect the market demand for high quality, functional modules to increase exponentially as the platform continues to gain greater business adoption.

In this book, Mitchel has done an exceptional job of explaining the various aspects of module development from a practical business perspective. His in-depth experience and knowledge of the DotNetNuke web application framework provides the reader with a powerful combination of software development principles as well as in depth guidance on how to use the DotNetNuke software platform productively and effectively. This makes *Professional DotNetNuke Module Programming* a must-have book for all developers of the DNN® platform, regardless of their background or past development experience.

Shaun Walker
Project Creator & Chief Architect
DotNetNuke Corporation

Introduction

This book was written to provide insight into the development techniques needed (and the options available) to work within the DotNetNuke framework. I have placed an emphasis on the available methods to extend the framework, as well as the situations and rules governing when each respective extension model should be used. Along with this emphasis on selecting the right extension method, the book stresses the importance of leveraging the framework in as many areas as possible, and ultimately using the framework to the advantage of the developer, rather than merely working with it.

As an active developer in the DotNetNuke community for a number of years, I have found that although existing books cover DotNetNuke concepts, no book focuses primarily on developing DotNetNuke. Most books on the market today cover development topics with a few relatively small chapters toward the tail end of the book, after spending a majority of the time on general conceptual information about how to administer the framework. This approach precludes a focus on development.

In addition to this, one current weakness of the DotNetNuke framework is developer documentation. The framework provides developers with numerous amazing methods to extend the framework and build truly robust applications, but as of this writing, minimal API documentation exists, and overall development topics are scattered all over the Internet. Many community members have helped to supplement this lack of developer content by writing blog articles and technical tutorials to help teach the individual concepts, but because there is no central repository, it can be tedious and difficult to find just what you need.

I wrote this book to help truly identify and document some excellent new features that are supported starting with DotNetNuke 5.0. The inclusion of jQuery exposes developers to a great JavaScript library that will enable interactive and animated interfaces to be created easily. The new Module Packaging system (discussed in detail in Appendix D) provides module developers and skin designers with many much-needed options when it comes to deploying applications. This book was written to expose this information, and to function as a key resource for the development community.

This book would not be what it is today without the great support and feedback that I have received from the DotNetNuke community and especially the regular readers of my blog. This community has spoken and provided their perspective as to what this book should include. I tried to listen as closely as possible because ultimately this book was written for you, the module developer.

Who This Book Is For

This book assumes that the reader has a working knowledge of standard ASP.NET development techniques and terminologies. Samples in the book are provided in both C# and Visual Basic (VB) to enable readers with diverse backgrounds to fully understand the concepts presented. Users do not need to have a comprehensive understanding of DotNetNuke prior to using this book because the early chapters discuss the configuration of both DotNetNuke and the development environment, and careful consideration has been taken to ensure that DotNetNuke-specific terminology is explained as the book progresses.

Readers already familiar with DotNetNuke 4.x development will find this book valuable because it introduces many of the new features of the latest software version, although some of the beginning chapters for these readers will be redundant because the overall concepts of environment configuration and basic interface elements have not changed from 4.x to 5.x. Differences between versions 4.x and 5.x are pointed out as appropriate.

This book does *not* discuss design principals in detail. If you are a designer, I strongly recommend looking at other titles available from Wrox Press that are geared toward the creation of skins and overall designs.

What This Book Covers

As the title implies, this book primarily covers development techniques within the DotNetNuke 5.x platform. However, because DotNetNuke 5.x does not yet have a firm release date (as of this writing), the chapters point out similarities and differences between the 4.x and 5.x platforms, enabling readers to apply some newer concepts to the older technology. Although this book primarily focuses on the concept of module development, it discusses other extension models as well, such as skin objects and authentication providers. Also covered in this book are recommended practices for successful integration with the framework.

How This Book Is Structured

This book begins with an introduction to development within DotNetNuke. The discussions walk you through DotNetNuke setup, terminology, development environment setup, and options for .NET project setup.

The book then presents a scenario-based model to introduce basic concepts of module development. This is accomplished by building a simple guestbook module that demonstrates how individual portions interact with one another. The discussion lays the foundation for the most basic elements of development within DotNetNuke. Later in the book, you learn about the more advanced module programming concepts, such as optional interfaces and DotNetNuke user controls. This discussion additionally introduces other extension methods, such as authentication providers and skin objects, as well as best practices.

In short, the main content of the book creates a working model that guides you through the most common development scenarios; at the same time, it provides the detail needed to tightly integrate custom code with the framework.

The appendixes provide supplemental information to what is contained in the chapters. This is material that, while not critical to an understanding of the individual chapters, is nonetheless important. The appendixes include items such as community resources and general DotNetNuke configuration items, as well as a detailed look at the new module manifest and a few key integration API points that are not well documented overall.

What You Need to Use This Book

In order to work through the examples in this book, you need either Visual Studio 2005/2008 Standard Edition or higher, with Service Pack 1 (SP1) installed; *or* you need Visual Studio 2008 Visual Web Developer Express SP1. This is because of the needed support of the Web Application Project (WAP) template that is only available in the listed versions of Visual Studio. In addition, it is necessary to either have SQL Server installed locally or have access to a remote server that can be used to create and retain the DotNetNuke database.

To follow along with all examples in the exact manner listed, it is also necessary for Internet Information Services (IIS) to be installed on the machine for the configuration of the development installation of DotNetNuke. It is possible to use various versions of Windows, with the exception of Windows XP Home Edition.

All samples and screen captures in the book were taken from either Visual Studio 2005 Standard running on 32-bit Windows Vista, or Visual Studio 2008 Pro running on 64-bit Windows Vista.

Other dependencies include Visual Studio templates and a DotNetNuke installation, although the beginning chapters of the book will walk you through their installation. However, make sure you are using a system that can have additional software elements installed.

Conventions

To help you get the most from the text and keep track of what's happening, a number of conventions have been used throughout the book.

> **Boxes like this one hold important, not-to-be forgotten information that is directly relevant to the surrounding text.**

Tips, hints, tricks, and asides to the current discussion are offset and placed in italics *like this.*

As for styles in the text:

❑ New terms and important words are *highlighted* in italics when introduced.

❑ Keyboard strokes are shown like this: Ctrl+A.

❑ Filenames, URLs, and code within the text are shown like this: `persistence.properties`.

❑ Code is presented in the following two ways:

```
In code examples we highlight new and important code with a gray background.
The gray highlighting is not used for code that's less important in the present
    context, or has been shown before.
```

Source Code

As you work through the examples in this book, you may choose either to type in all the code manually, or use the source code files that accompany the book. All of the source code used in this book is available for download at www.wrox.com. Once at the site, simply locate the book's title (either by using the Search box or by using one of the title lists), and click the Download Code link on the book's detail page to obtain all the source code for the book.

> *Because many books have similar titles, you may find it easiest to search by ISBN; the ISBN for this book is 978-0-470-17116-5.*

Once you download the code, just decompress it with your favorite compression tool. Alternately, you can go to the main Wrox code download page at www.wrox.com/dynamic/books/download.aspx to see the code available for this book and all other Wrox books.

When extracting the code samples, it is important to place all extracted files into the /DesktopModules/ folder of your DotNetNuke installation to ensure that all projects open successfully. Source code download projects have all been created using Visual Studio 2008.

Errata

We make every effort to ensure that there are no errors in the text or in the code. However, no one is perfect, and mistakes do occur. If you find an error in one of our books (such as a spelling mistake or a faulty piece of code), we would be very grateful for your feedback. By sending in errata, you may save another reader hours of frustration, and at the same time you will be helping us provide even higher quality information.

To find the errata page for this book, go to www.wrox.com and locate the title using the Search box or one of the title lists. Then, on the book details page, click the Book Errata link. On this page, you can view all errata that has been submitted for this book and posted by Wrox editors. A complete book list, including links to each book's errata, is also available at www.wrox.com/misc-pages/booklist.shtml.

If you don't spot "your" error on the Book Errata page, go to www.wrox.com/contact/techsupport .shtml and complete the form there to send us the error you have found. We'll check the information and, if appropriate, post a message to the book's errata page and fix the problem in subsequent editions of the book.

p2p.wrox.com

For author and peer discussion, join the P2P forums at p2p.wrox.com. The forums are a Web-based system for you to post messages relating to Wrox books and related technologies and to interact with other readers and technology users. The forums offer a subscription feature to e-mail you topics of interest of your choosing when new posts are made to the forums. Wrox authors, editors, other industry experts, and your fellow readers are present on these forums.

At http://p2p.wrox.com, you will find a number of different forums that will help you not only as you read this book, but also as you develop your own applications. To join the forums, just follow these steps:

1. Go to p2p.wrox.com and click the Register link.
2. Read the terms of use and click Agree.
3. Complete the required information to join, as well as any optional information you wish to provide, and click Submit.
4. You will receive an e-mail with information describing how to verify your account and complete the joining process.

You can read messages in the forums without joining P2P, but in order to post your own messages, you must join.

Once you join, you can post new messages and respond to messages other users post. You can read messages at any time on the Web. If you would like to have new messages from a particular forum e-mailed to you, click the "Subscribe to this Forum" icon by the forum name in the forum listing.

For more information about how to use the Wrox P2P, be sure to read the P2P FAQs for answers to questions about how the forum software works, as well as many common questions specific to P2P and Wrox books. To read the FAQs, click the FAQ link on any P2P page.

Introduction to DotNetNuke and Resources

Anyone can visit `DotNetNuke.com` and download a copy of the DotNetNuke development framework, but it is a very daunting task to fully understand the different versions, packages, and resources available. This chapter provides an overview of DotNetNuke versions, packages, and resources — those available via `DotNetNuke.com` and other community sites.

This chapter begins with an examination of the three major DotNetNuke versions available, and details a bit of the history surrounding how DotNetNuke has evolved to the framework that it is today. Technology and other requirements are discussed for key releases in recent DotNetNuke history. The discussion then examines the various download packages available from `DotNetNuke.com`, and the process for obtaining legacy versions, should the need arise for a noncurrent version. The chapter concludes with a quick overview of community resources available for more information on DotNetNuke and module development with DotNetNuke.

Versions Explained

A first-time visitor to the DotNetNuke website can easily be confused by all the versions of DotNetNuke. As of this writing, the `DotNetNuke.com` website has published links for downloading versions 4.8.4, 4.70, 4.62, and 3.3.7. This alone can be very confusing to many, as identifying the proper starting point can be a bit unclear. The following sections examine the 3.x, 4.x, and 5.x versions of DotNetNuke, with key milestones identified and details on when and why the downloads are available.

The DotNetNuke Corporation provides *all* historical versions for download, but they can be a bit complicated to locate. All historical version downloads can be found via the "Legacy Releases" section of the Downloads page, which can direct you to the SourceForge listings for all DotNetNuke downloads.

3.x Versions

The 3.x DotNetNuke platform is a legacy platform that is designed to work with ASP.NET 1.1. The final release of the 3.x platform was version 3.3.7, released November 30, 2006. The new use of this platform is not recommended because many security and performance enhancements have been completed in subsequent releases.

Users currently on the DotNetNuke 3.x platform can follow standard upgrade processes to upgrade installations to the most current DotNetNuke releases. In many cases, this is recommended via a multi-step upgrade process. The exact process for upgrading is beyond the scope of this book, but Appendix A provides community resources with upgrade guides.

4.x Versions

The 4.x DotNetNuke platform was the first version to be built for the .NET 2.0 framework. Releases prior to 4.3.7 were done in parallel to the 3.x platform to allow the option of running .NET 1.1 or 2.0. Starting with version 4.4.0, the 4.x version was the only supported version. During the 4.x life cycle, DotNetNuke issued many releases with greatly improved core functionality.

Following are some highlighted versions:

❑   **Version 4.4.0:** Released in December 2006, Version 4.4.0 provided major performance and scalability improvements. After upgrading, many users noticed dramatic performance improvements. With this being the first .NET 2.0–only release, many 3.x users were encouraged to upgrade to this version to attain the performance benefits.

❑   **Version 4.5.0:** Released in April 2007, version 4.5.0 provided many usability and performance enhancements to the framework. The most notable enhancement with this release was the inclusion of ASP.NET Ajax integration into the core framework. This integration enables module developers to implement Ajax functionality with actions as simple as checking a box to have controls automatically wrapped in an update panel.

❑   **Version 4.6.0:** Released in September 2007, version 4.6.0 was announced as a stabilization release. However, it included a few somewhat hidden enhancements that enabled developers to produce more efficient modules. Most notable was the inclusion of the IHydratable interface for object hydration. (IHydratable is discussed in detail in Chapter 10.) Another key enhancement with this release was the default inclusion of the FCK editor that replaced the older FreeTextBox editor for all rich text editing inside a DotNetNuke portal.

❑   **Version 4.6.2:** Released September 2007, version 4.6.2 is worth noting because it contains a mostly unknown feature, `XMLMerge`, which enables individuals to upgrade to any future version of DotNetNuke without manually merging `web.config` files. This is a major administrative benefit because the risk for failed upgrades is dramatically reduced when manual `web.config` changes are no longer required.

❑   **Version 4.8.0:** Released December 2007, version 4.8.0 provided support for Visual Studio 2008 and Internet Information Server (IIS) 7.0 compatibility for the entire framework. The versions released between 4.5.0 and 4.8.0 were stabilization releases that helped to solidify the DotNetNuke core, and created the solid base needed to create DotNetNuke 5.0.

❑ **Security Releases:** As of this writing, a number of security point releases (for example, 4.8.3 and 4.8.4) where completed to resolve security issues identified in prior versions of the framework. Because of the security issues resolved in these versions, DotNetNuke Corporation strongly recommended that users upgrade to the most current point version to resolve any potential security concerns. For detailed information regarding security notices and other security concerns, visit the DotNetNuke Security Policy page at www.dotnetnuke.com/News/SecurityPolicy/tabid/940/Default.aspx.

❑ **Version 4.9.0:** Released September 2008, version 4.9.0 provided a few additional security fixes, as well as a few back-ported features from the upcoming 5.0 release. Special items to note in this release include a new default skin and an updated version of the FCK editor control providing support for the Safari browser.

5.x Versions

The DotNetNuke 5.x platform includes many major enhancements to the core DotNetNuke system. This includes a unified package system for modules, skin objects, skins, and more, as well as separation of core administration modules to provide users with greater flexibility in site management than was possible in prior versions.

> As of this writing, the exact date of the first 5.x release is unknown, but it is likely to be available by the time you read this. All topics covered in this book relate to the 5.x version. Differences between the 5.x version and previous versions are pointed out where appropriate.

Packages Explained

Each version of DotNetNuke contains four different packages that may be downloaded for use. Knowing the differences between the packages and which one to use is key to successfully working with and developing for DotNetNuke. The following sections explain the differences between the packages, as well as the factors governing when each should be used.

Starter Kit

The Starter Kit is a Visual Studio Installer Package (.vsi) used to add DotNetNuke-specific templates to your Visual Studio installation. You can find more detailed information on Visual Studio Installer packages at the Microsoft Developers Network (MSDN) at http://msdn.microsoft.com/en-us/library/ms185314(VS.80).aspx.

The following template types are included with the Starter Kit:

> **The following descriptions discuss multiple project types and are provided for reference only. Chapter 2 provides a deeper look at the differences between project types.**

❑ **DotNetNuke Web Application Framework:** This template is the entire DotNetNuke solution that can be used to set up a website for development. This template should not be used because development can more easily be completed via manual installations using the Install package.

❑ **DotNetNuke Compiled Module (VB):** This template will create a Web Application Project (WAP)-compiled Visual Basic (VB) module. This template creates all standard DotNetNuke module elements, including the data access layer (DAL) and multiple view controls. This is the template that is used in this book for all VB examples. It creates a module that will be compiled into a single .dll for distribution via standard build processes.

❑ **DotNetNuke Dynamic Module (VB):** This template will create a Web Site Project (WSP) VB module that utilizes the app_code folder for all classes. This template creates a complete module with similar contents to the Compiled Module template, including full DAL classes. This template is recommended for users with Visual Studio Express, which prior to Visual Studio 2008 Service Pack 1 cannot support the WAP development model. Chapter 2 provides full information on Visual Studio versions and project types.

This template is implemented as an item template, and may only be added to a DotNetNuke Web Application Framework solution created via the template discussed previously.

❑ **DotNetNuke Dynamic Module (C#):** This template will create a Web Site Project (WSP) C# module that utilizes the app_code folder for all classes. The created project will be exactly like that of the Dynamic VB Module, but translated to the C# language. This project template is recommended for developers who prefer C# and are using Visual Studio Express.

This template is implemented as an item template and may only be added to a DotNetNuke Web Application Framework solution created via the template discussed previously.

❑ **DotNetNuke Simple Dynamic Module (VB):** This template will create a dynamic VB.NET module, but the module created will only have a single view control and the .dnn manifest. This is designed for individuals looking for a custom implementation, or those looking for a clean project to start with.

This template is implemented as an item template and may only be added to a DotNetNuke Web Application Framework solution created via the template discussed previously.

❑ **DotNetNuke Skin:** The final template included in the Starter Kit creates all files needed to create a single skin and container for a DotNetNuke website. Chapter 3 discusses skins and containers in more detail.

This template is implemented as an item template and may only be added to a DotNetNuke Web Application Framework solution created via the template discussed previously.

Source Package

The source package of DotNetNuke contains all source code for the DotNetNuke framework in a fashion that can be modified right out of the box. The downloaded ZIP file contains two folders: Web site and library. The Web site portion is the same as that provided with the Install version. The library section provides all additional source code used to create the compiled DotNetNuke.*.dll files that are included in installation and upgrade versions.

Recommended Uses

The use of this package of DotNetNuke is recommended only for individuals who are interested in customizing the DotNetNuke core. Note here that modifications to the DotNetNuke core will remove an installation from the upgrade path, and all changes must be managed on a case-by-case basis during upgrade.

> In my experience, I have found that it is much easier to find other ways around a core modification that enable my sites to stay on the standard upgrade path.

Benefits

Regardless of customizations to the core framework, this version will provide you with *all* source code for the DotNetNuke framework. Many organizations view this as a great benefit, as you have all source code available for review and/or modification, should business needs arise that require the code to be available.

Install Package

The Install package of DotNetNuke is exactly that: the minimal collection of files needed to run the DotNetNuke framework, including all core DotNetNuke modules (not all are installed by default), and compiled library assemblies. This package is used in Chapter 2 to create the development environment used throughout the remainder of the book.

Recommended Uses

This package of DotNetNuke is recommended for all production installations and all development environments that will *not* require modifications to the core DotNetNuke framework. Some individuals additionally use this version for upgrade purposes to ensure that core modules are upgraded at the same time as the core.

Benefits

Using this package has a number of benefits, but one of the best is that it is simply a less cluttered download. Because you only get the core files needed to install and use DotNetNuke, you are not bothered by other files that you will not modify.

Upgrade Package

The final DotNetNuke package available is the Upgrade package. This package is optimized to include *only* the files needed to upgrade to the specific version. This package does not contain a few key files that would cause problems with upgrades. The most notable difference is that this package does *not* contain a `web.config` file, although you do have a `release.config` file for reference, if needed, which is essentially a copy of the `web.config` file. It is named differently to avoid the accidental overwriting of an existing configuration.

Recommended Uses

The only recommended use for this package is to perform an upgrade to an existing DotNetNuke site. Note that depending on your existing DotNetNuke version, the upgrade process might not be as simple as overwriting files with the Upgrade package. See the available DotNetNuke documentation and community resources for complete information regarding DotNetNuke upgrades.

Benefits

The major benefit of this package is that it is a simple package that can be used to quickly update the core DotNetNuke framework, and associated items that need to be upgraded — namely, the Text/HTML module because it is part of the core. You will not be bothered with the extra overhead of updated core modules and install-only files. Along these same lines, this package will prevent many common errors that often occur when individuals upgrade using the Install package.

Resources

A project as large of DotNetNuke has many resources available — those provided by DotNetNuke Corporation and those provided by community members. Abundant though this information is for many people starting to develop in DotNetNuke, you may find yourself in a vexing cat-and-mouse game looking for the information specific to your needs. The following sections introduce many DotNetNuke and community resources that contain valuable tutorials and/or documentation.

DotNetNuke.com

The `DotNetNuke.com` website, shown in Figure 1-1, is the most commonly overlooked community resource. There is so much information on this site that many people give up before finding exactly what they need. The material presented here can help you zero in on the information you are looking for, and perhaps other items of interest.

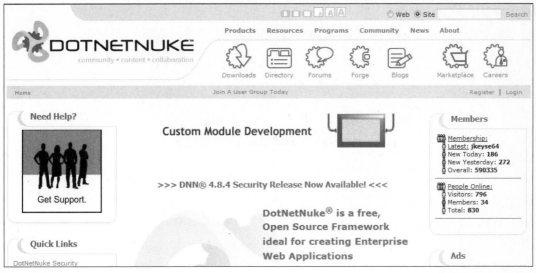

Figure 1-1

From the home page, you can see that the navigational structure is clearly laid out for quickly getting to key items.

Downloads

Obviously, the Downloads link shown at the top of Figure 1-1 is one of the most active pages of the DotNetNuke website. Using this link, you can access downloads for all current and past versions of the DotNetNuke core and core modules. You must be registered and logged into the DotNetNuke. com website in order to view the downloads. Once you are logged in, you will notice that the downloads are divided into multiple sections:

❑ **Core Framework:** You can use the Core Framework download section to locate the different versions and packages referenced earlier in this chapter. Notes regarding the specifics of each version and package are also provided to ensure that the most appropriate package is downloaded.

❑ **Supplementary Downloads:** These components are downloads that are part of the core, but not part of the DotNetNuke Projects program. Items downloaded here are developed for use in the core framework, but do not have any other place for download.

❑ **DotNetNuke Projects (New Releases):** Downloads in this section include the most current releases of various core DotNetNuke module projects. The key thing to note about this section is that not all module downloads are found here; only the most current releases (for modules that have had recent releases) are found here. For modules not listed here, the module's project page is the place to go for downloads.

❑ **Legacy Releases:** The Legacy Releases section contains a single link to the SourceForge.net repository for all DotNetNuke downloads. Clicking this link brings up the window shown in Figure 1-2. Following links from this page, you can drill down to find any legacy release of any DotNetNuke project. This function is a very commonly overlooked aspect of the DotNetNuke downloads section.

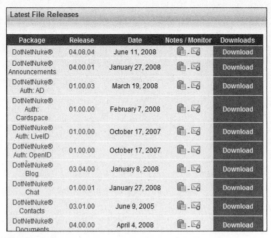

Figure 1-2

Forums

The DotNetNuke forums are a great technical resource. Many community members and core team members monitor the forums on a very regular basis to answer various questions and share information about numerous aspects of DotNetNuke. Typically, if you are encountering an issue when you are starting out with module development or any other task within the DotNetNuke framework, you can get a response within a day. The amount of information shared via this communication channel is quite amazing, and many new users can benefit greatly simply by reviewing past threads to learn the various tips and tricks shared.

Blogs

Blogs on DotNetNuke.com are written by core team members and project team leads. Typically, this communication channel is where you can get an idea of when the next module release is going to be, or what new features are going to be included in the next core release. Many helpful tutorials are posted, such as those from Michael Washington, Charles Nurse, and many others, which help expose the development community to sometimes little-known benefits of the DotNetNuke core.

Documentation

Documentation is available via the DotNetNuke.com website. However, as of this writing, the information contained in this section is a bit out of date, especially from a development standpoint. Nonetheless, much of it can be very helpful for those looking to understand how the core framework is put together. A few key documents include "Module Localization Guide," "Security: Hardening Installations," and "Security: Module Development." These documents address three key DotNetNuke areas of concern, and provide a great deal of information in a compact and easy-to-read format.

Online Help

Another great resource, available at `www.dotnetnuke.com/Resources/Knowledge/DotNetNukeOnlineHelp/tabid/787/Default.aspx`, is the online help documentation for the most current DotNetNuke version. This documentation is directed more toward site administrators and content management, but many advanced topics are covered to help answer questions regarding core DotNetNuke functionality. The DotNetNuke Corporation also offers a PDF version of this documentation for those looking for an offline solution.

Sponsorship Program

The DotNetNuke sponsorship program is one final resource that is worth mentioning. This sponsorship program enables individuals to attain community recognition for supporting the DotNetNuke project, as well as attain more direct access to DotNetNuke core team members for assistance via a private discussion forum. For individuals who want a more direct communication channel for questions and answers, while supporting the open-source initiative, this is the way to participate with mutual benefits.

Community Resources

There are many community resources that provide more focused DotNetNuke tutorials, videos, training, and other general help. Some resources are available free, while others have membership costs associated with them.

Following are a few resources that are key for an individual starting with development in DotNetNuke:

- ❑ `dnncreative.com`: This website is a subscription service that provides video tutorials related to site configuration, administration, troubleshooting, and development. Many individuals find the information contained on this site to be an invaluable resource. Membership to DNN Creative grants a user access to more than 300 historical tutorials, reviews, and more, as well as access to all upcoming content for the next year.

- ❑ `dotnetnuke.adefwebserver.com`: This website is maintained by Michael Washington, a long-standing DotNetNuke core team member. On this site you will find guided module development tutorials, each focusing on one key element. These quick-to-read tutorials are great for refreshers, or to quickly learn how to complete a specific task.

- ❑ `mitchelsellers.com`: This is my website, where I maintain a mostly DotNetNuke-focused blog. Any updates to this book after publication will also be included here. You will find detailed installation, upgrade, migration, backup, and development tutorials mixed in with relevant blog postings.

Appendix A contains a more comprehensive listing of available community resources.

Summary

This chapter has introduced the different versions and packages of DotNetNuke, as well as a few community resources that might help greatly along the way. Understanding the differences between the DotNetNuke versions is key to understanding dependencies and capabilities, which is a key component when distributing custom modules.

Now that you have a firm base knowledge of the DotNetNuke package options, you are ready to progress to the installation and configuration of the development environment, as well as a discussion about the available project types, all of which is covered in detail in Chapter 2.

2

Creating the Development Environment

Creating the proper development environment for DotNetNuke module development requires administration within Microsoft Windows, Microsoft SQL Server, Microsoft Visual Studio, and DotNetNuke itself. For many people, this is a very complex task, because most developers do not play the role of systems administrator, database administrator, and integration specialist. This chapter demystifies the installation process and provides the information needed to create a proper development environment, regardless of your level of experience.

The chapter starts with a brief discussion about the two different Web development project models supported by Visual Studio 2005 and 2008, including additional information references for in-depth comparisons. The discussion then examines any limitations imposed by different versions of Visual Studio and how they might affect module development. After discussing the different project models and Visual Studio limitations, this chapter provides an examination of a guided installation of DotNetNuke, including all external configuration elements. The chapter concludes with the installation of development templates for Visual Basic and C# DotNetNuke modules.

Development Models

With the introduction of .NET 2.0 and later versions, developers now have two distinct methods by which Web applications and modules are created. Because there are major differences between the two models regarding compilation, project structure, and module creation, this section provides a very high-level comparison. A general knowledge of the differences between .NET 1.1 and 2.0 is assumed for complete understanding.

Web Site Projects (WSP)

The Web Site Projects (WSP) development model is the default development project module in .NET 2.0 and later. Using WSP, developers place common coding elements inside the App_Code folder and do not need to recompile the application to view the effects of changes to individual .cs and .vb files. This dynamic compilation module is considered by many to be a very significant benefit because you can quickly develop and test your application.

WSP with DotNetNuke involves creating all custom DotNetNuke modules inside the main DotNetNuke solution, because the WSP model does not provide any project files (.vbproj or .csproj) to manage the list of files inside the project. This enables developers to complete simple debugging using the familiar Debug ➪ Start With Debugging option from the Visual Studio menus.

However, for many, the advantages of WSP at development time are outweighed by the disadvantages at deployment. By default, with the WSP model, a custom development module must be deployed with all .vb or .cs source files to the production environment. The dynamic compilation model of WSP will then compile the source files for the first Web request, and then use the dynamically created assemblies for all future requests. Typically, two issues are associated with this model. Primarily, the deployment of source files to a production system can make it difficult for individuals to protect the intellectual property of their modules. The second issue with dynamic compilation is that any WSP module will add slightly to the application startup time because the module is compiled into an assembly.

There are ways to create compiled assemblies from WSP projects, but that is a subject beyond the scope of this book, and, overall, they are very complex to complete.

Web Application Projects (WAP)

The Web Application Projects (WAP) model was introduced for Visual Studio 2005 as part of the Service Pack 1 release. Microsoft added this project module to give developers a familiar project module that can create compiled assemblies. The WAP model is very similar to that of the project structure used in .NET 1.0 and 1.1, whereby you have solution and project files to manage the projects. The developer has the capability to specify pre- and post-build events, as well as specific assembly names.

Using this project model for DotNetNuke module development provides developers with a much greater degree of development and deployment control. Using the WAP model, developers can create complex modules that reference other WAP modules, and obtain a single assembly for deployment. This enables you to protect your code, and helps to reduce the amount of dynamic compilation needed on application startup.

> **Although WSP modules can reference other modules (including WAP modules), there are difficulties associated with referencing modules written in different languages, or installed in different orders.**

Along with its benefits, this development model also has its own complications. They are not exactly disadvantages, because they are easily resolved, but they simply add a step for debugging and impose limitations on which versions of Visual Studio can be used.

Differences between the debugging processes are discussed in detail in Chapter 9.

The WAP model does impose a Visual Studio version limitation because Visual Studio 2005 Express and Visual Studio 2008 Express (prior to SP 1) editions cannot work with WAP. This limitation is discussed later in this chapter in the section "Selecting a Visual Studio Edition."

Because of the benefits of compiled assemblies and individual project files, this book uses the WAP module as the framework for all development examples. In my experience, I have found that professional development projects are simplified when using the WAP model — specifically when working with individual projects that are easy to add to source control, and the post-build events module packages can also be created with ease.

WSP Versus WAP Features

The previous discussion provides a very brief overview of the differences between WSP and WAP. Table 2-1 provides a short list of the respective features based on the default configurations of each model.

Table 2-1

	WSP	WAP
Dynamic compilation	Yes	No
Production deployment requires .cs/.vb files	Yes	No
Ability to add pre-build and post-build events	No	Yes
Allows references from other projects	No	Yes
Ability to debug via standard Debug ⇨ Start with Debugging option	Yes	No
Ability to develop with Express Editions of Visual Studio	Yes	No (Yes with VS 2008 Express SP 1)

For more detailed information regarding WSP and WAP project modules, you can view the "Introduction to Web Application Projects" article on MSDN at http://msdn.microsoft.com/en-us/ library/aa730880(VS.80).aspx. This article provides a number of comparison charts, scenarios, and other helpful information. There is also a very helpful article posted by Rich Strahl at http://west-wind.com/weblog/posts/5601.aspx that provides a detailed comparison of the two models.

Selecting a Visual Studio Edition

Selecting the appropriate version of Visual Studio for overall .NET development is a topic beyond the scope of this book, but the following sections examine the differences between two key editions of Visual Studio and explain how version selection affects development activities related to DotNetNuke module development.

Express Editions

Visual Studio Express editions were new offerings by Microsoft starting with Visual Studio 2005. These editions were released to enable a broad user group to start with .NET development, enabling hobbyist developers to use an integrated development environment (IDE) with no costs associated. Of course, because they are free editions of Visual Studio, they do have some functionality limitations when compared to the full editions. There are three key limitations that impact DotNetNuke module development.

The first issue only applies to Visual Studio 2005 Express and Visual Studio 2008 Express (prior to Service Pack 1). With this limitation, the Web Developer edition of Visual Studio Express only supports the WSP template. This limitation will prevent the modification of any project using the WAP development model, which includes a majority of the core modules provided by DotNetNuke Corporation.

The second limitation with Visual Studio Express editions is that they do not offer support for source control integration. As you progress in development activities, it becomes important to keep version history information. Other editions of Visual Studio provide integration options that enable check-in and check-out via integrated controls within the IDE. Source control is possible with an Express edition, but manual intervention using an external source control application is needed to check in and check out files.

The third limitation of Visual Studio Express editions is one with limited effect on individuals working exclusively with DotNetNuke, as it relates to working with different languages and environments. Within the standard Visual Studio IDE, users can work on projects of any language and any project type from the same IDE. The Express editions of Visual Studio provide separate IDEs for each language, and can be slightly more difficult to work with if multiple project types are used.

Other Editions

Microsoft offers many other editions of Visual Studio to support the development needs of all individuals and organizations. With Visual Studio 2005, you will find four additional versions to the Express editions: Standard, Professional, Tools for Office, and Team System. Each version has a distinct set of features, limitations, and benefits that must be balanced to identify the right selection. Microsoft provides a very helpful product line overview at `http://msdn.microsoft.com/en-us/vs2005/aa700921.aspx`.

With Visual Studio 2008, Microsoft has simplified things a little by providing Standard, Professional, and Team System editions. Visual Studio 2008 Team System is implemented with multiple editions geared toward different types of development groups. Full information on the product offerings for Visual Studio 2008 Team System can be found on Microsoft's website at `http://msdn.microsoft.com/en-us/vsts2008/products/bb933734.aspx`. One major benefit of Visual Studio 2008 for use with DotNetNuke development is its capability for design-time support of common DotNetNuke controls in WAP projects.

This book assumes the use of a Visual Studio edition that supports the WAP development model. All examples provided in future chapters are presented with default displays from Visual Studio 2005 Professional or Visual Studio 2008 Professional.

Installing DotNetNuke

Installing DotNetNuke on a local machine involves the coordination of multiple applications and system components, and can be considered quite complicated for many first-time users of DotNetNuke. The following five steps approach DotNetNuke installation in an easy-to-follow manner for installation on a local system. For DotNetNuke installation instructions to another environment (such as a remote production server), see the links provided in Appendix A.

Configuring SQL Server

DotNetNuke is a dynamic Web application, and a SQL Server database is used to store the information needed for display. It is possible to use a streamlined approach for DotNetNuke database configuration if you are using SQL Server 2005 with dynamically attached databases. I personally do not recommend this practice because future maintenance of the database may become complicated, and the proper configuration does not take much additional time. The following steps will create a new database for use by DotNetNuke, using SQL Server 2005 and SQL Server Management Studio (SSMS). DotNetNuke still offers support for SQL Server 2000 if needed, in which case the configuration steps vary slightly from the examples provided here.

> **Before continuing with this part of the setup, note that this book assumes that SQL Server has been configured to allow both remote connections and mixed-mode authentication. For assistance with these portions of SQL Server configuration, refer to Microsoft's documentation on server configuration.**

The first step of the SQL Server configuration process is to open SQL Server Management Studio. When SQL Server Management Studio starts, you will see the Connect to Server dialog shown in Figure 2-1, which presents the default connection information. If you are connecting to the default server, then simply click the Connect button; otherwise, modify the values as necessary to properly connect.

Figure 2-1

> **Be sure to note the "Server Name" value for later use.**

After successful connection to a server instance, the Object Explorer window appears, shown in Figure 2-2. Right-click on the `Databases` folder and select New Database. A dialog similar to the one shown in Figure 2-3 is displayed. Simply specify a name for the database (in this example, `DotNetNuke5`) and click OK.

Figure 2-2

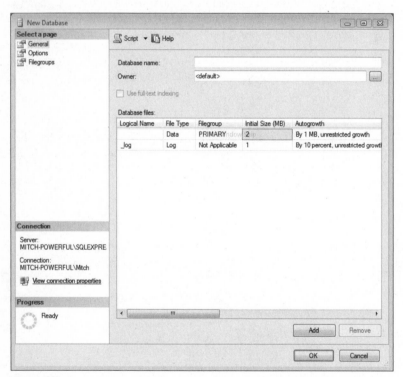

Figure 2-3

> Be sure to note the selected database name for later use.

Once the database has been created, you must create a database user for the application. To complete this step, expand the Security node in SQL Server Management Studio, and then right-click on Logins. Select New Login. A dialog similar to the one shown in Figure 2-4 should be displayed. To properly configure a login user, four configuration items are needed: login name, authentication type, login password, and database permissions. Click the SQL Server Authentication button for the authentication mode, and enter the username **DotNetNuke5User** and the password **password1!**.

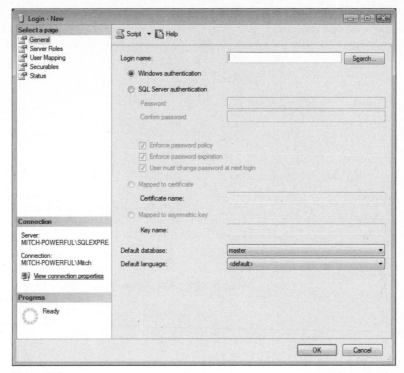

Figure 2-4

> **Be sure to note the selected username and password information, because it will be needed for DotNetNuke configuration.**

The username and password provided in this step of configuration do not have to match the values in this book. However, it is imperative that the "User must change password at next login" option is *not* selected. If this option is selected, then the user account will not be able to properly log in to the server.

Once the needed "general" information has been provided for the user, you are now ready to configure the permissions to grant the account full access to the DotNetNuke5 database created earlier. Select User Mapping from the option area in the left pane of the Login-New window. You will see a dialog similar to the one shown in Figure 2-5. Ensure that you check the box next to your database in the top pane, and that the db_owner option is elected in the lower pane, as shown in the figure. After this is completed, simply click OK.

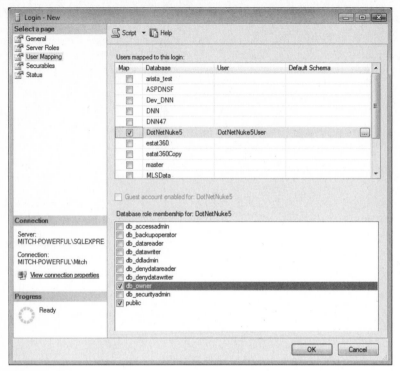

Figure 2-5

This completes the SQL Server configuration portion of the DotNetNuke installation.

Configuring DotNetNuke Files

The next key piece of the installation process is to prepare the needed DotNetNuke files — those found in the Install package downloaded from the DotNetNuke.com website. After downloading and opening the ZIP file provided for the Install package, the Extract function of the Windows ZIP utility can be used to extract all files to the proper location. The recommended file location for a local installation is inside the C:\inetpub\wwwroot\DotNetNuke folder. (The DotNetNuke folder is created at the time of extraction.) This is a recommendation only; files can be stored in any location on your local machine.

> If you use a different file location, be sure to note the install location for future use.

Most individuals will be able to continue the DotNetNuke installation process without any additional configuration. However, a number of different settings can be configured within the DotNetNuke web.config file. Appendix B examines the additional configuration options in full detail.

Configuring File Permissions

After placing the DotNetNuke installation files in the proper location, you must configure the file permissions for all files inside the DotNetNuke directory. Because of the dynamic nature of DotNetNuke and the capability to add and remove modules and other content, you must give the ASP.NET worker process full permissions over the entire directory. This enables DotNetNuke to successfully create folders and copy any and all files needed.

This permission setup is quite easy. However, note that in Windows 2000 and XP, the ASP.NET worker process account is ASPNET. In Windows 2003, Windows 2008, and Windows Vista, it is NETWORK SERVICE.

In Windows Explorer, open to the C:\inetpub\wwwroot folder. As in the previous steps, right-click on the DotNetNuke folder to reveal a menu similar to the one shown in Figure 2-6. Select Properties from this menu. From the new window that appears, select the Security tab at the top. You should then see a dialog similar to the one shown in Figure 2-7.

Figure 2-6

Figure 2-7

19

> If you are using Windows Vista with User Access Control enabled, it might be necessary to select an Edit option to get the view shown in Figure 2-7.

This dialog is where permissions can be established for the ASP.NET worker process. Click Add at the bottom of the top pane to bring up a final dialog. In the input box, type **NETWORK SERVICE** (2003, 2008 and Vista) or **ASPNET** (2000 and XP), and then click OK at the bottom of the dialog. The previous screen will appear. The newly added user will be selected and the permissions for this account will be displayed. Select the Allow option for Full Control to grant all permissions needed to run DotNetNuke.

With the permissions configured properly for DotNetNuke to execute and run, you are now ready to configure Internet Information Services (IIS). This configuration is what grants DotNetNuke the capability to host on your machine.

Configuring Internet Information Services (IIS)

The configuration of IIS is a very important step, because incorrect settings in these areas can cause a DotNetNuke installation to fail immediately. The discussion of this configuration is divided into the following two groups:

❑   IIS7 (Windows 2008 and Vista)

❑   Previous versions of IIS

This delineation is necessary because of the large number of changes that have occurred within the IIS utility.

IIS7 Configuration (Windows 2008 and Vista)

IIS configuration for Windows 2008 and Vista has been greatly simplified with the modifications presented in IIS7. In addition, with versions 4.8.0 and later, DotNetNuke provides full support for operation inside IIS7. These two factors combined provide for an easy-to-complete DotNetNuke installation when using IIS7.

To start IIS configuration, open the Windows Control Panel and select Administrative Tools. Inside this view, you will see an option for Internet Information Services (IIS) Manager. If this option is not available, then IIS must be installed via the Windows Component setup process.

You can find instructions for installing IIS7 on Windows Vista at `http://learn.iis.net/page.aspx/365/installing-necessary-iis7-components-on-windows-vista/`.

Once you locate the IIS Manager option, double-click it and a dialog similar to the one shown in Figure 2-8 appears.

Figure 2-8

On the left pane of this window is a section called Connections. All configuration will be completed using options from this section. Expand the Web Sites and Default Web Site nodes to see the website configuration. The DotNetNuke folder created previously should appear under the Default Web Site section. Right-click this folder to produce an option called Convert to Application. When you select this option, you will see the Add Application dialog shown in Figure 2-9. The information from this dialog is used to create the virtual directory and other isolation items necessary for proper operation of DotNetNuke. Simply click OK to complete the setup of IIS.

Figure 2-9

This is a much more streamlined process than the process used for previous versions of IIS, or previous versions of DotNetNuke when used inside of IIS7.

IIS5 and IIS6 Configuration (Windows 2000 and XP)

The configuration of IIS5/6 is a bit more involved than the configuration process for IIS7, but it is still fairly straightforward. To get started, you follow a process similar to that used in the IIS7 configuration. Open the Control Panel and select the Administrative Tools option. In the list of administrative tools is an option called Internet Information Services. Double-click this entry to produce a window similar to that shown in Figure 2-10.

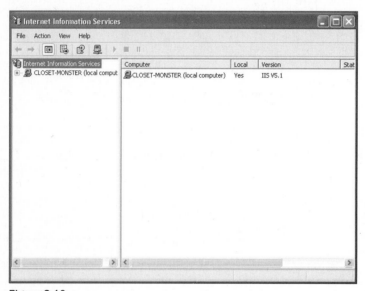

Figure 2-10

If the Internet Information Services option is not available, IIS must be installed. You can find instructions at www.webwizguide.com/kb/asp_tutorials/installing_iis_winXP_pro.asp.

Similar to the process followed with IIS7, start the configuration process by expanding the nodes on the left side of the screen until the Web Sites and Default Web Site nodes are fully expanded. Inside the list of folders, you should seen an entry for the DotNetNuke folder created previously.

Right-click the DotNetNuke folder and select Properties. A dialog similar to the one shown in Figure 2-11 appears. On the main view page of the Directory tab, click the Create button. The Application Name field should list DotNetNuke as the application name.

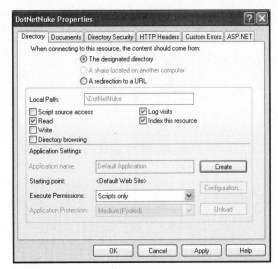

Figure 2-11

Clicking through the tabs in this window, it is important to validate a few additional configuration points:

❑ Under the Documents tab, an entry in the list of documents should exist for `default.aspx`. Without this setting enabled, it is highly possible that when it comes time to install DotNetNuke, you will experience a "page cannot be found" error.

❑ Under the ASP.NET tab, the ASP.NET version should indicate a *minimum* of 2.0.50727. It is possible for DotNetNuke 5.x to run under .NET 3.5, but it will *not* run on .NET 1.1.

After all of these configuration items have been validated, click OK to save all the changes. This completes the IIS configuration for IIS5/6 machines.

If you have configuration problems, check out the appendixes for recommended community resources available to troubleshoot installation.

Executing DotNetNuke Installation

With all external elements configured and ready to go, you are now ready to complete the DotNetNuke installation process using the DotNetNuke Installation Wizard. Begin by opening Internet Explorer (or your browser of choice) and type the following URL in the address bar:

```
http://localhost/DotNetNuke/
```

Click Go. It may take a while to build and load the DotNetNuke system. Depending on the specifications of the system, this time can be anywhere from 15 seconds to a few minutes. Once this loading is complete, the welcome screen of the DotNetNuke Installation Wizard will appear, as shown in Figure 2-12. Click Next to continue installation using the Typical installation method.

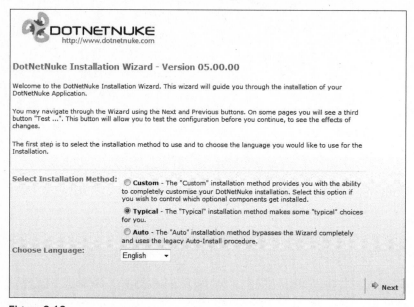

Figure 2-12

The next step of the DotNetNuke Installation Wizard is designed to ensure that file permissions have been set correctly. Click the Test Permissions button to begin executing a series of permissions tests to ensure that sufficient permissions have been set. Once you click this button, a message stating "Your site passed the permissions check" should be displayed. If you see this message, click Next to continue the installation. If you do not see this message, revisit the section "Configuring File Permissions" earlier in this chapter to see how to validate the configuration. Then, return to the Installation Wizard. Continuing past this step with incorrect file permissions will result in an incorrect DotNetNuke installation.

Following a successful file permissions test, you are ready to configure the database connection. This configuration is very important, and requires that the information from the SQL Server configuration be input correctly into all data input fields.

The first step is to select SQL Server 2000/2005 Database from the Select Database option. This indicates that installation is to be completed against a SQL Server database on the server, and not with a dynamically attached database. After this is complete, input the Server and Database names noted from previous installation steps.

With the general server and database information populated, it is time to provide the username and password to connect to the database. To complete this step, uncheck the box next to Integrated Security. A user ID and password input area will appear. After inputting all the necessary configuration information, the wizard page should look similar to the one shown in Figure 2-13. Click the Test

Database Connection option to validate the configuration. If the connection was successful, click Next to continue the installation.

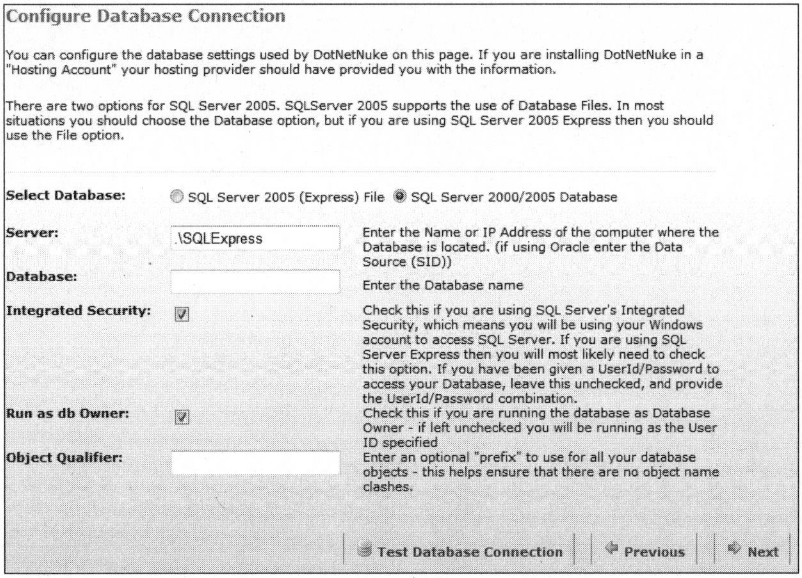

Configure Database Connection

You can configure the database settings used by DotNetNuke on this page. If you are installing DotNetNuke in a "Hosting Account" your hosting provider should have provided you with the information.

There are two options for SQL Server 2005. SQLServer 2005 supports the use of Database Files. In most situations you should choose the Database option, but if you are using SQL Server 2005 Express then you should use the File option.

Select Database: ○ SQL Server 2005 (Express) File ● SQL Server 2000/2005 Database

Server: `.\SQLExpress`
Enter the Name or IP Address of the computer where the Database is located. (if using Oracle enter the Data Source (SID))

Database:
Enter the Database name

Integrated Security: ☑
Check this if you are using SQL Server's Integrated Security, which means you will be using your Windows account to access SQL Server. If you are using SQL Server Express then you will most likely need to check this option. If you have been given a UserId/Password to access your Database, leave this unchecked, and provide the UserId/Password combination.

Run as db Owner: ☑
Check this if you are running the database as Database Owner - if left unchecked you will be running as the User ID specified

Object Qualifier:
Enter an optional "prefix" to use for all your database objects - this helps ensure that there are no object name clashes.

🔲 Test Database Connection | ⬅ Previous | ➡ Next

Figure 2-13

> **Although the Object Qualifier option can be used to install multiple DotNetNuke installations inside a single database, I do *not* recommend using this option.**

After clicking Next to continue, DotNetNuke will begin installing all the needed database scripts. Depending on the configuration of the target machine, this process can take anywhere from a few seconds to a few minutes. Once the configuration is complete, a message stating "Completed Installing Database Scripts" will be shown. Ensure that no errors are reported inside the list box, and then click Next to continue installation.

The next screen prompts you to confirm the details for the host account, which is the SuperUser account that can maintain all aspects of a DotNetNuke installation. Be sure to pick a strong password for this account, and to pick something that is not easily forgotten because host passwords *cannot* be sent via e-mail. After supplying the needed information for the host account, click Next to continue.

The Portal Configuration screen appears, which enables configuration of the main portal to be used. On this page, an administrator will be created who has Edit rights to the created portal but will not have permission to change overall DotNetNuke configuration elements. A portal tile will also be specified that names the created portal. After clicking Next, you will see a message indicating "Completed," with an option of Finished (Go to Site). Click Finished to be directed to the newly created DotNetNuke site.

The default DNN installation should look similar to what is shown in Figure 2-14. Upon complete installation, login will be possible using the credentials identified during the installation process. It is important to note that although DotNetNuke installs with default content elements, you can quickly and easily remove any elements that are not appropriate for a new site design.

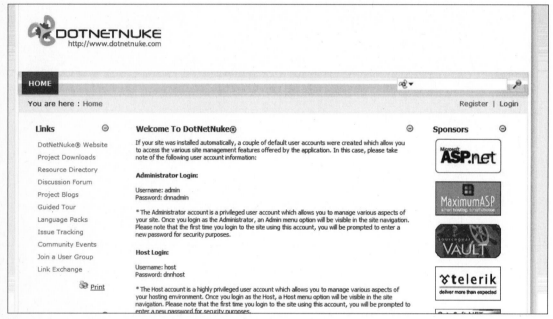

Figure 2-14

> The screen captures and Wizard text elements have been captured from a DotNetNuke 5.0 Beta 6 build. The final release version of 5.0 may contain slightly different skin designs and/or instructional text.

Installing Development Templates

With a local installation of DotNetNuke complete, you are now ready to install the templates required for module development. As mentioned previously in this chapter, the WAP development model is used for all of the examples. Module development using WAP templates is sourced from two different locations:

❑   The first set of templates (for use with VB.NET) can be obtained from DotNetNuke Corporation.

❑   The second set of templates, for the C# language, can be found from my company website.

DotNetNuke Corporation has not elected to include a C# WAP module template with the DotNetNuke installations. All examples in this book are provided in both C# and VB, so it is not necessary to install both sets of templates.

Installing VB.NET Templates

The VB.NET WAP project template is included as part of the DotNetNuke Starter Kit, which can be downloaded from DotNetNuke.com at any time. After selecting the download, a .vsi file will be downloaded. Save this file to a location that can be easily found. After the download is complete, simply double-click the .vsi file and a dialog similar to the one shown in Figure 2-15 should be displayed. The only template that must be installed is the DotNetNuke Compiled Module (VB). All of the others are optional, depending on specific needs.

Figure 2-15

Clicking next will reveal a signature warning message box, similar to the one shown in Figure 2-16. Simply click Yes to continue the installation process. This message appears as most templates provided are not digitally signed by the creator. You will then see a summary box. Click Finish to complete the installation. At this point, all the required VB.NET templates have been installed.

Figure 2-16

Installing C#.NET Templates

The installation procedure for C#.NET templates is nearly identical to the process used for VB.NET. The only difference is that third parties must be used to supply the compiled module templates. I have a compiled module template that can be downloaded from www.iowacomputergurus.com/ free-products/visual-studio-add-ons.aspx. Once the file has been downloaded, follow the instructions provided earlier for installation of .vsi packages.

> As of this writing, the only templates available are for 4.x and later modules. Manual modification of the .dnn file must be completed in order to use the new 5.x module manifest. Differences are discussed in later chapters of this book.

Summary

This chapter focused on the development environment and how to create a safe workspace for all DotNetNuke module development. SQL Server, IIS, and Windows configuration elements were discussed, and their importance within a DotNetNuke environment was examined.

Chapter 3 takes a deeper technical dive into the DotNetNuke world, and discusses the various data types and elements that affect the day-to-day development of DotNetNuke.

3

Under the DotNetNuke Hood

The first two chapters of this book provided a history of DotNetNuke, explained DotNetNuke packages, and established a development environment. The discussion in this chapter starts to peek into the inner workings of the DotNetNuke system, exploring the different elements, their common names, and why they are important to developers using the DotNetNuke framework. The chapter specifically looks at the terminology, the data elements, and the potential integration points to build the needed foundation for the examples provided in the rest of the book.

This chapter begins with explanations of tabs, modules, skins, and users as they relate to the DotNetNuke system, and custom-developed modules. The chapter continues the investigation of core DotNetNuke functionality by investigating portals and how they can affect development effort, and provides a brief summary of differences between parent and child portals. Although you will find a brief discussion about DotNetNuke localization, this topic is covered in more detail in Chapter 8. This chapter concludes with a discussion of common administration elements, including scheduled tasks and settings. By the end of this chapter, common DotNetNuke lingo should be more familiar to you, and the foundation established here will enable you to follow subsequent chapters without difficulty.

Tabs

The *tab* is a very important item when it comes to DotNetNuke architecture. A tab inside of DotNetNuke is what many people would refer to as a *page*. A tab is implemented as a specific collection of content. It contains one or more modules, and it has a distinct URL for accessing its content. References to tabs or the `TabId` are found in almost all areas of documentation of DotNetNuke. It also appears in almost every standard DotNetNuke URL. Many DotNetNuke URLs look like the following:

```
http://www.mysite.com/home/tabid/36/default.aspx
```

The TabId portion is a query string value that has been rewritten into the URL. The internal DotNetNuke system uses this ID to load the specific content needed.

Tabs themselves provide users with multiple configuration options. Figure 3-1 shows the standard options available when editing an individual tab. This figure shows only a subset of the customizations that can be completed at the tab level, but it does reflect the most important elements as they relate to development in DotNetNuke.

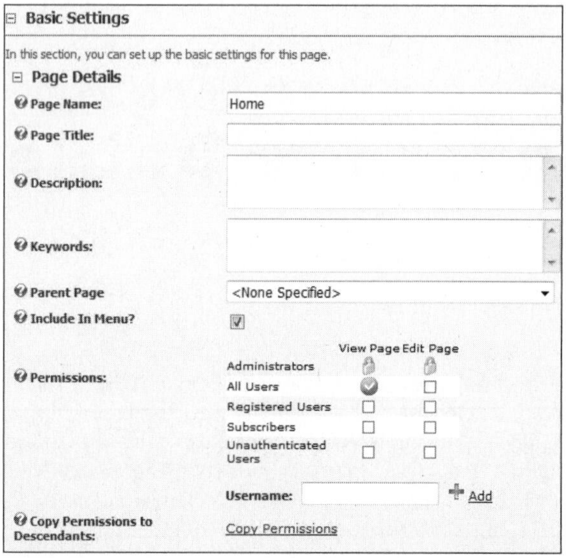

Figure 3-1

The first section of settings specifies the details for the current page/tab:

❑ The Page Name option reflects what is shown to the user in the menu.

❑ The Page Title option is the title value that is loaded to the browser window's title bar.

❑ The Descriptions and Keywords values are used to populate the metatags for the generated page. If these two options are left blank, DotNetNuke will inject the default values set inside the Site Settings for the current portal.

❑ The Parent Page option enables an administrator to select the parent page or create a page hierarchy that essentially builds the dynamic menu shown to the user.

❑ The Include in Menu? option enables administrators to hide a page from showing in the menu for the site. If this option is unchecked, the page exists but a navigation link to the page will *not* be placed in the site's menu.

The lower section of the Basic Settings window reflects the permissions set. Permissions within a DotNetNuke site can be set at many different levels. Tab-level settings apply to the tab itself (as well as any of its settings) and the settings/administration of all controls on the page, unless they are specifically overwritten. To ensure that a page is visible to all users, the View Page column must have a check next to

All Users. The Edit Page permission options grant users the capability to edit the layout and information on a specific page. Additionally, modules can be added by anyone with edit permissions.

Key Data Elements

When it comes to working with DotNetNuke modules (and other custom DotNetNuke components), only two key data-level items must be remembered: TabId and TabName. These values are commonly used to integrate with other modules and to navigate to different sections of a DotNetNuke site. The DotNetNuke framework provides methods that enable you to generate a link to a specific page based on the TabId or TabName of the current page. This process is very simple and can be completed as described here.

In C#, you would use the following:

```
DotNetNuke.Common.Globals.NavigateUrl(this.tabId);
```

In Visual Basic (VB), you would use this:

```
DotNetNuke.Common.Globals.NavigateUrl(Me.tabId)
```

Any time a developer works with linking to another page, or with obtaining information on the current page, the TabId or TabName are required to generate the link.

Integration Points

Custom modules will integrate with tabs and tab data in a few specific ways. The primary method is similar to the example provided previously to obtain proper links to other pages, or even the current page. The second most common integration is used when working with rewriting a URL or with custom URL schemes, although these topics are beyond the scope of this text.

Additionally, tab-specific data is typically not an integration point for storing individual module data. For example, if a tab were deleted, associated records would be removed as well. Content integration is discussed later in this chapter.

Modules

Modules are the key pieces of functionality that exist inside a DotNetNuke installation. Tabs create the page structures needed to house the functionality; and, in the end, modules actually implement the desired result. DotNetNuke has many core modules available that provide specific functions for site administrators to build their sites. Core module offerings include the following:

- ❑ Documents
- ❑ Links
- ❑ Forums
- ❑ FAQ
- ❑ Text

Another way to look at modules is to see them as building blocks that create the content of a site. Without individual modules (whether they are core, third party, or custom), you will not have any content to display.

This book covers the general module development techniques for creating general content. Different flavors of extensions to DotNetNuke modules are briefly discussed in upcoming sections. The key point to keep in mind about modules is that a module provides a specific set of functions, a forum, a list of links, or, in the case of the example in this book, a guestbook.

Key Data Elements

Modules themselves have many data elements that are helpful to a developer. However, two specific data elements are used in this book, and they are the basis for all module development.

ModuleId

The `ModuleId` is the unique identifier from the `Modules` table within a DotNetNuke database. This identifier can be used to identify a particular module instance. Each time a module is added to a page in DotNetNuke, an entry is added to the `Modules` table.

TabModuleId

The `TabModuleId` is the unique identifier for the specific placement of a module instance. This differs from the `ModuleId` in that with DotNetNuke, it is possible for an administrator to copy a module from one page to another. When performing this operation, the `ModuleId` will be the same. However, the `TabModuleId` will differ. This is another bit of granularity that can be used to associate custom data elements to a module after it is published to a page.

Integration Points

As discussed in the previous section, `ModuleId` and `TabModuleId` values are a couple of the most common integration points for module development. Using `ModuleId` and `TabModuleId` values, a developer can associate content with specific instances of a module to ensure that the proper content is displayed and stored, thus allowing for multiple instances of a module inside a single portal.

Integration with the `ModuleId` and/or `TabModuleId` values is the only way to isolate module content between different instances while inside the same portal, unless a custom separation system is created.

Skins

A *skin* inside of DotNetNuke relates to the various files needed to create the look and feel of a DotNetNuke website. In the DNN 4.x days, two default skins were provided: DNN-Gray and DNN-Blue (shown in Figure 3-2). Skins can be swapped out at any time by the site administrator; and, depending on permissions, new skins can be uploaded by host or admin users. (These types of users are discussed in more detail later in this chapter in the section "Default User Types.") This book does not provide any skin-creation information. For more details about how to create and work with skins, see the reference listing in Appendix A.

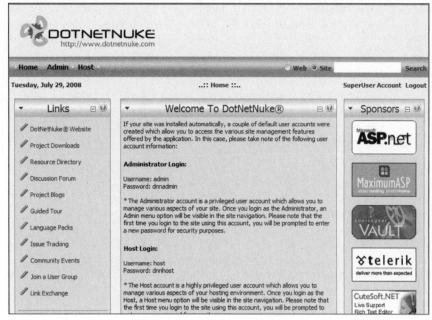

Figure 3-2

Skin Objects

Skin objects are items that are placed on a site via the *skin file*. However, the actual "object" is created in a very similar manner to a module. A skin object provides a common piece of functionality that should exist on all pages of a portal — something that is not optional, or that should not be able to be removed. Examples of core DotNetNuke skin objects include Login, Registration, Copyright, Breadcrumb, and Logo. These are very specific implementations and are packaged in a manner similar to that of a module. The actual creation of skin objects is outside the scope of this book, but Appendix A has a great reference listing with tutorials on skin object creation.

Containers

Containers are the final element of a DotNetNuke skin. They are the holders in which each module is placed. Site administrators have a great amount of flexibility when designing a site. For example, they can assign containers on a module-by-module basis to achieve the look and feel they want. It is also possible for site administrators to decide to not display the container if they have content that they would like to display without surrounding styles. It is very common for skins to contain multiple container designs. The default DotNetNuke skins contain at least three individual container designs for each skin package.

Users

DotNetNuke has a full-featured user-management system that is built from the standard ASP.NET 2.0 membership system. This enables DotNetNuke to rely on the tried-and-true ASP.NET model but still extend it in a manner that will work with the multi-portal nature of a DotNetNuke website.

DotNetNuke provides a number of different user security levels out of the box; and as a DotNetNuke module developer, it important to know the limitations of each individual access level. It is also important to know how site administrators can customize the environment with their own security roles and custom permissions.

The following sections examine the different standard user types that are created with a default DotNetNuke installation. The discussion then continues with a quick examination of roles, permissions, and how they relate to module development.

Default User Types

With a default installation of DotNetNuke, a module developer has four different groups of users who can be presented content. Each of these users has different capabilities and restrictions within the DotNetNuke system.

The first two types of users are *unauthenticated users* and *registered users*. These are general users of the system. Unauthenticated users are those users who are not currently logged into the DotNetNuke site, and they are typically the users with the least capabilities. By default, any user who has an account in DotNetNuke is given the registered users role, which creates the first level of granular permissions — allowing those users who have accounts to potentially be able to see different or more content than those who have not logged in or registered.

The next type of user is the *site administrator*. This user has full administrative permissions for a specific portal. These users can edit all pages and all modules, as well as control access to the site via the user accounts. However, this user cannot administer higher-level functions such as scheduled tasks, performance settings, or performing module installations.

The final type of user is the *host user*. This user has full administrative permissions to the entire DotNetNuke installation. Host users are also commonly known as *super users*, as they have super permissions over all site functionality. This user will appear as a member in any/all custom roles, as well as have permissions to change any settings. Custom module developers can leverage this user level to provide specific host settings that are global to a specific site implementation.

DotNetNuke Roles/Permissions

In addition to the standard DotNetNuke configuration, site administrators can add, edit, and delete system roles, which provides a robust collection of options for building a site that meets specific needs. By default, the establishment of a new role will not grant that role any additional power. A site administrator must delegate permissions to the specified role by modifying permissions. Permissions for viewing and editing can be specified on two specific levels: tabs and modules. This can allow users to create page-level and module-level editor roles.

This administration is completed in a simple fashion. Figure 3-3 shows an example of the permission grid in action for a page-level configuration.

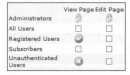

Figure 3-3

It is important to understand the effects of this default permissions set because it can be beneficial for a developer to restrict views to edit permissions, and simply ensure that users are given the capability to delegate this permission set to other users. A very common example of this delegation is for individuals to be given "moderation" permissions in a forum. This is a very common "edit" operation that, on a module-specific basis, can be delegated to another user/group.

As you can see from Figure 3-3, administrators can select from three different states: allowed (green check), denied (red x), and no status. This is a new feature set included in DotNetNuke 5.x. In previous versions, users were not able to explicitly deny permissions to a module or page.

Key Data Elements

The key data element when working with user-specific information or configuration inside of DotNetNuke is the UserId value obtained from the DotNetNuke users table. Integration into other aspects of the permission system can be completed in various ways, which are discussed in more detail in later chapters when discussing module-level security.

Portals

Another key benefit that is often touted when discussing the use of DotNetNuke is the fact that it is *multi-portal*. What does this truly mean? Well, at the most basic level, it reflects DotNetNuke's capability to host more than one site on the same DotNetNuke installation. For site administrators, this is a great feature because it enables multiple sites to be maintained with a single code base.

For developers, this poses a very interesting issue. By default, DotNetNuke separates all data on a portal-by-portal basis, making information-sharing impossible between portals. This is the DotNetNuke-recommended best practice. However, business requirements often require a different level of integration.

Portal administrators can create two different types of portals. The following two sections briefly explain the differences and their potential impact on a module developer.

Parent Portals

Parent portals are the easiest of the portal types to understand. A parent portal is simply a portal that has its own unique URL. An example of a parent portal installation would be the way in which my website is hosted. My main DotNetNuke installation has been completed on http://www.icgportals.com, but my website was created as a parent portal inside the DotNetNuke installation and responds to the URL http://www.mitchelsellers.com. From a module development perspective, nothing needs to be handled differently when working with a parent portal installation.

Child Portals

Child portals are implemented by adding a specific folder to an existing site and treating it as a separate site. For example, if the default DotNetNuke installation is completed at http://www.mysite.com, then it would be possible to create a child portal that responds to http://www.mysite.com/

`childportal`. In this case, DotNetNuke physically creates the folder and adds a `default.aspx` page that redirects back to the root site. This specific action is nothing that a module developer needs to be concerned about.

Conversely, one action that can be greatly affected when working with child portals is file linking that starts with a single `backslash (\)´ to try to indicate a site root. Because of the way in which multi-portal systems are created, when using child portals it is not possible to build links in this manner.

Key Data Elements

From a module development perspective, the most important data element to be used when working with portals is the `PortalId` value. This is the unique identifier value from the DotNetNuke `portals` table. It can be used as a key value in module data models to associate content with a specific portal, and it is needed when looking for user accounts and other administration functions that might be accessed via code.

Localization

Content localization is another major aspect of all DotNetNuke development. Providing a module that is localizable is a very big benefit to global audiences that want to convert text elements to their native languages. DotNetNuke provides a robust static text localization engine that enables developers to quickly create resource files that can localize common static text elements. Chapter 7 examines the full localization process in detail.

> **As of this writing, DotNetNuke does not yet support dynamic content localization. This is a slated item for future releases on the 5.x platform.**

Scheduled Tasks

DotNetNuke at the host user level provides a scheduled task engine that developers can utilize to create processes that run on a fairly regular schedule. The terminology "fairly regular" is used because the scheduler system is managed inside the ASP.NET application. Therefore, if the application shuts down because of inactivity, tasks will not be executed. Regardless, this is a very helpful extension point if routine actions are needed, such as automatic content updates, e-mail queuing, or other similar tasks.

The appendixes of this book contain helpful resources for information regarding scheduled task creation.

Settings

DotNetNuke has a plethora of configuration and other settings that can be used by portal administrators to configure the framework for their specific implementations. It is important for module developers to understand the various general settings areas in order to know where they might need to look for specific data elements required for proper module integration. The following sections examine three basic settings areas that can affect module developers and their custom applications.

Host Settings

The host settings section is only accessible by the host user account, and supplies settings that apply across the entire DotNetNuke installation. This settings section (available via Host ⇨ Module Definitions from the menu) is where Simple Mail Transfer Protocol (SMTP) mail and performance settings are configured on a portal-by-portal basis. It is very common for module developers to reference the SMTP information stored in this section in order to be able to send e-mail notifications or other messages from the DotNetNuke system.

For complete information on what settings are included in this section, as well as how to properly configure them, see my blog article "DotNetNuke Host Settings Explained!" at www.mitchelsellers .com/blogs/articletype/articleview/articleid/189/dotnetnuke-host-settings-explained.aspx.

Portal Settings

The portal-level settings (also known as Admin settings) are available to administrators and host users to configure information that is specific to a particular portal. Primarily, these settings specify the user registration type, portal name, copyright, skin setup, and default pages. The values in this section have a dramatic effect on your module. However, they are less often used as integration elements for custom module development — typically, only when working with custom registration modules.

Module Settings

Module settings are available at each module installation, and they encompass all settings that relate to a specific module's display. This section is where module permissions are set. It is also the default integration point for a custom module's settings control. This integration point is discussed in more detail as the module is built during the course of this book.

When leveraged properly, these settings can help users manage module display by allowing them to disable containers and/or show a module on all pages. It is important for module developers to understand how these settings can help their module be more useful to the user. For example, a developer creating a Google AdSense module would want to specifically put into module documentation in the proper configuration items needed to show the module on all pages.

Summary

This chapter briefly introduced many DotNetNuke-specific terms and supplied supporting information to help explain the link between DotNetNuke specifics and module development tasks.

Now that you have a working understanding of the DotNetNuke architecture and terminology, Chapter 4 presents the Guestbook module specifications that will be used as the programming exercise for the remainder of this book. This discussion includes a brief section at the end of the chapter that provides an overview of three key areas of consideration when preparing DotNetNuke requirements.

Guestbook Module Requirements

Previous chapters in this book have provided overviews of DotNetNuke, packages, installation, and general terminology. With that base knowledge, you are now ready to dive into the specific requirements of the module that will be built in the remaining chapters of this book. This chapter begins with a basic listing of the requirements of the module that will be created. It then progresses into a discussion regarding the database table structure that will be used to store module information.

After discussing the specifics of the Guestbook module, the remaining sections of the chapter examine a few key items that are helpful when creating requirements for future module development projects. This includes discussions regarding data isolation and key elements to investigate during the requirements process.

Guestbook Module Requirements

Over the course of the remaining chapters of this book, you will create a simple Guestbook module. Certain requirements for the example module are less extensive than a true "for profit" module would require. This is done to ensure that the examples contained in the book are an appropriate size, as they are designed to provide a module that can be used as a base and extended for future requirements.

Overview

The created Guestbook module should provide a few basic bits of functionality for a robust and customizable user interface, leveraging as many core features of DotNetNuke as possible. The module should be created with two distinct view controls: a sign guestbook control and a view guestbook control. These two controls should be displayed on the same page as the DotNetNuke portal. However, these should be separate units in order to provide site administrators with flexible layout options. In addition to the view controls, a settings control will be created to enable administrators to enable/disable options within the module. Specific requirements for each control are provided in the following sections. This will serve to outline the key functionality introduced in each element.

Guestbook Settings Control

Because the Guestbook module will contain two different view controls, an association between the "Sign Guestbook" definition and the "View Guestbook" definition is needed. This is a very simple settings control. It simply lists the other modules on the current tab and enables the administrator to create a link to reference the other control for content.

View Guestbook Control

This primary view of the guestbook is where user submissions to the guestbook will be displayed. Consideration will be taken to ensure that administrators can customize the look and feel of the display, and to ensure that the content integrates successfully with the existing site layout and skin. Following are the specifics:

❑ **Template-driven display:** The module will employ a template-driven design, with templates stored inside localization files to ensure usability in multiple languages. A token-based replacement system will be used to enable users to place user-specified information.

❑ **Administration options for edit users:** Users with edit permissions for the module should be given the capability to "delete" any entry that has been added to the guestbook. Additionally, if the users are configured for moderation, they should be able to "approve" any pending entries that are not currently publicly visible.

❑ **Non-postback based paging:** A paging system will be implemented that accomplishes paging in a search-engine-friendly manner that does not rely on page postbacks to move to the next page.

Sign Guestbook Settings Control

This control is the primary configuration control for the administrative site users. It will provide users with the capability to configure the module to meet their needs. These settings will be security-related, and will allow users to quickly enable options to prevent spamming. Following is a list of the settings that will be available, each of which is implemented using a checkbox for Yes or No selection:

❑ **Allow Anonymous User Posting:** Selecting this option will allow users to post entries to the guestbook even if they are not logged into the site.

❑ **Enable DotNetNuke CAPTCHA control:** Selecting this option will require that users input the secret code from the DotNetNuke CAPTCHA control before they are able to sign the guestbook. Full details regarding the CAPTCHA option, as well as a general description of the option, are explored later in this chapter in the discussion about working with the sign guestbook control.

❑ **Moderate All Postings:** Selecting this option will require that all postings be approved by an individual with edit permissions to the module. Additionally, each new post to the guestbook will result in an e-mail being sent to the administrator, notifying him or her of an entry that is pending approval.

Sign Guestbook Control

The secondary view control for the guestbook module will accept user input. This control should focus on security implementations to avoid any type of script injection, because guestbooks and other publicly available interfaces are common starting points for such misuse. The following list describes the key features of the sign guestbook control to be created:

❑ **Common user input fields:** For simplicity, this module should prompt a user for three specific inputs: name, website, and comment.

❑ **CAPTCHA for spam prevention:** If enabled inside the settings control, the DotNetNuke CAPTCHA should be enabled to help reduce the possibility of spam submissions to the module. A CAPTCHA is an image with text elements that are morphed in a human-readable manner; it is designed to prevent automatic form submission by bots. Figure 4-1 shows an example of the DotNetNuke CAPTCHA.

❑ **HTML encode elements for protection:** For security purposes, all user input elements should be HTML encoded to ensure that if malicious content is provided, it will not be executed. This is a simple form of protection from common attack methods.

❑ **Store comments at the module level:** All submitted comments should be stored with the specific module instance, which enables a site administrator to place multiple instances of the module in a single site for different purposes.

Figure 4-1

Database Structure

Given the simple nature of the example module being created in this book, a simple single database will be used to store all content for the module. Figure 4-2 shows the DNNModuleProgramming_Guestbook table that will be created in future chapters to store the record information.

DNNModuleProgramming_Guestbook		
Column Name	Data Type	Allow Nulls
EntryId	int	☐
ModuleId	int	☐
SubmitterName	nvarchar(255)	☐
SubmitterWebsite	nvarchar(255)	☑
SubmitterComment	ntext	☑
SubmissionDate	datetime	☑
IsApproved	bit	☐
		☐

Figure 4-2

To coincide with the requirements set forth previously in this chapter, three columns will store the submitter's name, website, and comment. Additionally, because all content for this module is to be stored on a module basis, a data column, `ModuleId`, will hold a reference to the individual module. This is the key integration point to the DotNetNuke data structures. When the actual table is created, a foreign key will be created to ensure that module data and DotNetNuke data remain synchronized.

A few additional columns will be included to provide a unique identifier, time tracking, and approval status (if moderation is used). This creates a very simple base module data structure. It provides enough data interactions to enable you to become familiar with the DotNetNuke data provider model, and it is simple enough to avoid bogging down future examples with unnecessary SQL-specific examples and code.

Requirements Summary

The preceding sections have painted the high-level picture of the module that will be created in the remaining chapters of this book. As the book progresses, all code samples are provided in both VB.NET and C#.NET to enable users to follow the samples. A staged implementation process is demonstrated to lead up to the final functionality. Any deviations from the requirements are noted as the functionality is created.

Data Isolation

The Guestbook module requirements presented in this chapter have revisited the data-isolation topic that was introduced briefly in Chapter 3. Now that a real-life example of module-level data isolation has been provided, let's take a quick look at the three most common data-isolation levels, and when it might be a good idea to use each.

Portal-Level Isolation

Data that is isolated at the portal level is data stored at the highest level, commonly used by third-party developers. Information stored with portal-level isolation is available to all module instances inside a given portal, allowing administrative users to add and/or remove modules from pages at will, without the risk of data loss.

Portal-level data isolation is typically used when information truly applies to a site level. A typical example of portal-level isolation is a Forums module. For example, you might have a need to show different portions of a forum within a site, but the data for each individual forum should still show in the main forum page, essentially shared across all module instances.

When storing module at the portal level, a relation is created between custom module data tables and the `PortalId` value stored inside the DotNetNuke `Portals` table.

Module-Level Isolation

Data that is isolated at the module level is the most commonly used data-isolation method for third-party developers. Information stored with module-level isolation is only available to the current module instance. If the module is removed from the page, then the information no longer has any association that will allow visible display. It is a common practice for modules that implement module-level data isolation to remove data upon successful module deletion to ensure strong data integrity.

Module-level data isolation is used for most modules, as the content is truly specific to that given instance. The core Text/HTML module and Links modules are prime examples of modules that need to store different data for each individual instance of the module.

Module-level data isolation is accomplished by retaining the `ModuleId` of the current module and linking it to the value stored inside the `Modules` table inside the DotNetNuke database. As explained in Chapter 3, each module instance will have an entry in the `Modules` table with a unique `ModuleId` value. Isolating data in this manner enables site administrators to copy a module to another location, with the capability to still share the same `ModuleId`, even though the copied module will contain a new `TabModuleId`.

User-Data Isolation

The final data-isolation level (which until recently has not been a common isolation point) is user-level data isolation. Typically, user-level data isolation is used when working with modules that are geared toward presenting user-specific information, or for creating social-networking-style modules. The most common scenario for user-level data isolation is when working with user profile information.

One important item to note is that data isolation at the user level is different from storing the user information with a specific record. Many modules (such as the core forum module) retain user ID values with entries to associate them with a user. However, the record is isolated at the portal level because all users are able to see it. User isolation involves restricting view to the specific user or users in question. An example of a module that utilizes user-level isolation is a private messaging module that enables users to send communication to one another via the website.

User-level data isolation is accomplished by not only retaining the `UserId` value from the `Users` table, but also creating references to it, and then restricting display based on the value.

Key Requirements-Gathering Information

The final key element of this chapter is to briefly outline the common requirements-gathering items that should be considered for all DotNetNuke development projects. These are items that are fundamental to any implementation, and they should serve as a starting point for creating a requirements-gathering system:

- ❏ **Data isolation/sharing:** The data isolation discussion earlier in this chapter contains one of the most important considerations that must be investigated as part of the module requirements process. Making changes to data-isolation strategies after module development should be avoided, as it can be costly and very tedious to successfully modify existing data.

- ❏ **Security levels:** Important consideration should be given to the core DotNetNuke security permissions schema. Specifically, can it provide the needed controls? Understanding control visibility and permissions for View, Edit, Admin, and Host are important elements for developers to understand. If at all possible, you should build a module that can operate inside the standard confines of the DotNetNuke security controls. If deviations are made, they must be fully documented, and integration to the core system must be closely monitored to ensure that the desired effect is attained.

❑ **Display formats:** DotNetNuke has an almost unlimited number of display options that can be leveraged by module developers. During the design portion of a development project, it is important to identify the various views and display formats, and when each should be visible. This is a key consideration because special processes must be followed when working with multiple view controls that must be displayed at the same time.

These points reflect the key elements that should always be considered when working with a DotNetNuke development project. These elements, in combination with the elements presented in the remaining chapters, should provide the needed foundation to properly architect a DotNetNuke module.

Summary

This chapter discussed the specific requirements of the module that will be created in remaining chapters. You have learned about a framework that can be used to build a functional Guestbook module that can be easily extended in the future. You also learned about DotNetNuke data isolation and the requirements-gathering processes, which should serve as food for future thought as the module is built.

Chapter 5 begins the hands-on portion of this book, where the module-creation process is started using the developer templates installed previously. By the end of Chapter 5, you will have created the framework for the Guestbook module, and will have set the stage for the actual development that is demonstrated in subsequent chapters.

Starting the Module
Creation Process

Previous chapters of this book have worked through the basics of DotNetNuke, including historical information and overall system configuration. This chapter introduces the development process and is the first step to creating the Guestbook module that will be fully functional by the end of the book. This chapter focuses on the basic elements of DotNetNuke module creation, including file locations, template limitations, and DotNetNuke manifest files. Also provided is a brief overview of the files included in a default module template.

The chapter begins by creating the module project, and examples are provided for both C# and VB.NET developers. After creating the project, general template limitations for both the C# and the VB.NET templates are discussed. After the project is completed, the overall structure of the project is investigated, including information on all included files, and general changes that will be required. By the end of this chapter, you will have created a full Visual Studio WAP solution that can be used for all development activities in the remaining chapters of the book.

Creating the Module Project

The actual process of setting up the development project is as simple as selecting the project template from within Visual Studio by choosing File ⇨ New Project. However, you should consider a few specific limitations and words of warning before immediately creating the project. The following discussions explain general rules that must be followed by both C# and VB users, as well as the detailed installation process for both languages.

In order for modules to be tested in an adequate manner, they must be created in the proper location. DotNetNuke expects custom modules to reside inside the /desktopmodules/ folder. Each module has its own folder inside the desktopmodules folder. The C# version of the Guestbook will be created in /DesktopModules/GuestbookCS/, and the VB version will be created in /DesktopModules /GuestbookVB. It is important to note this information because if additional folders are introduced, testing will not be possible from the build locations.

In addition to the proper location for module installation, it is also imperative that the proper module solutions be used. If a module is accidentally created with the dynamic module template, then it will be practically impossible for you to modify it to work like the compiled module template.

Creating the GuestbookCS Module

Creating the C# module project is a very simple task that can be completed in two distinct steps. The first involves creating the default project setup using the previously installed C# templates. The second step involves preparing the project by setting items that were not completed successfully by the template system.

Creating the Project

To create the C# version of the Guestbook module, start by opening Visual Studio 2005. From the start page, select File ⇨ New ⇨ Project, as shown in Figure 5-1. From the New Project window that appears under Visual C# ⇨ Web, select the option for C# DNN Module Template. Then specify **GuestbookCS** for the name. Set the Location to C:\inetput\wwwroot\dotnetnuke\desktopmodules and uncheck the "Create directory for solution" option.

Figure 5-1

After selecting all the appropriate options, the New Project dialog should resemble the one shown in Figure 5-2. After this has been completed, click OK to create the project. At this point, Visual Studio will open with very important notes from the template creator about limitations of the template system.

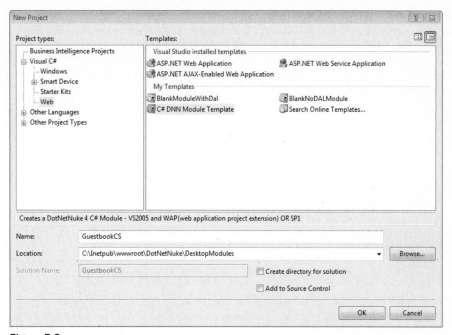

Figure 5-2

> If your default language, as specified in Visual Studio, is not C#, then the navigation
> steps to locate Visual C# might be slightly different from what is shown in Figure 5-2.

This completes the general project setup. Let's now take a look at the additional configuration items
needed because of the limitations in the template system.

Configuring the Project

With the default C# template, you must modify assembly information (as well as other project
configurations) to fully set up the project for development. At this stage of the development process, the
project properties must be updated. However, individual code files will not be updated here, but instead
during the respective discussions appearing in later chapters.

> Because of the additional changes that will be completed in future chapters, trying
> to "build" the project at this time might result in build errors. These errors will be
> resolved in future chapters.

With the project open in Visual Studio, right-click on the GuestbookCS project inside the Solutions Explorer and select Properties. This will open global properties that apply to the entire project, as shown in Figure 5-3. The left side of the dialog indicates the tab displayed. In the first tab, Application, change the values for both Assembly Name and Default Namespace to "WroxModules.GuestbookCS" so that the module is isolated from any other DotNetNuke module. Table 5-1 provides detailed explanations of the Assembly Name and Default Namespace settings.

Figure 5-3

Table 5-1

Setting Name	Setting Purpose
Assembly Name	This setting provides Visual Studio with the information needed to create the final .dll file into which the module will be complied. With the example in this book, using a value of "WroxModules.GuestbookCS" results in the generated .dll file for the Guestbook module to be WroxModules.GuestbookCS.dll. This is an important configuration step, because it ensures that the created modules have unique names.
Default Namespace	This setting in C# projects is used to define the namespace that is applied (by default) to all newly created files, and to any code that does not contain a namespace declaration inside the project. This differs greatly from the "Root Namespace" behavior of a VB.NET project.

The final configuration item needed to complete the project setup is to modify the Project URL setting contained inside the Web section of project settings. Select the Web tab on the left of the project settings page to display a series of options. Scroll to the Use Local IIS Web Server option, as shown in Figure 5-4. After you locate this setting, modify the value to show the proper IIS URL of http://localhost/dotnetnuke. When you are done, click the Save button on the toolbar to complete the project setup.

Figure 5-4

Creating the GuestbookVB Module

Creating the VB.NET module project requires following a similar process to that of the C# version of the module. First you create the project, and then you modify the project settings to ensure that a proper development environment is established.

Creating the Project

To create the VB.NET version of the Guestbook module, start by opening Visual Studio 2005. From the start page, select File ➪ New ➪ Project. The process should look similar to Figure 5-1, as provided for the C# module creation. From the New Project window that appears, locate the DotNetNuke Compiled Module option under Visual Basic ➪ Web. Select this option and specify **GuestbookVB** for the name. Set the Location option to `C:\inetput\wwwroot\dotnetnuke\desktopmodules` and uncheck the "Create directory for solution" option.

After selecting the appropriate options, the New Project dialog should resemble the one shown in Figure 5-5. Click OK to create the project shell.

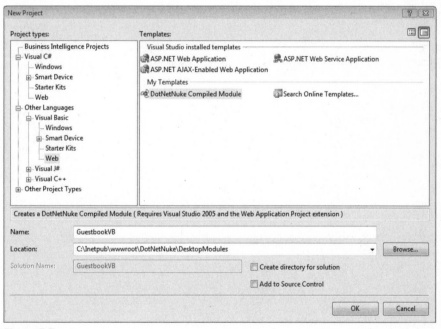

Figure 5-5

> The screen shown in Figure 5-5 was taken from a Visual Studio installation that has C# specified as the default language. If you are creating a new Visual Basic module on an installation with Visual Basic as the default language, the navigational structure under "Project types" will differ from Figure 5-5.

After you click OK to start the module creation process, Visual Studio creates the needed project files and provides you with a few notes about project creation limitations because of the Visual Studio template system. The starting view of Visual Studio should look similar to Figure 5-6. If the error list is displayed and indicates errors, as shown in the bottom of the figure, disregard the errors because the next steps will resolve the issues.

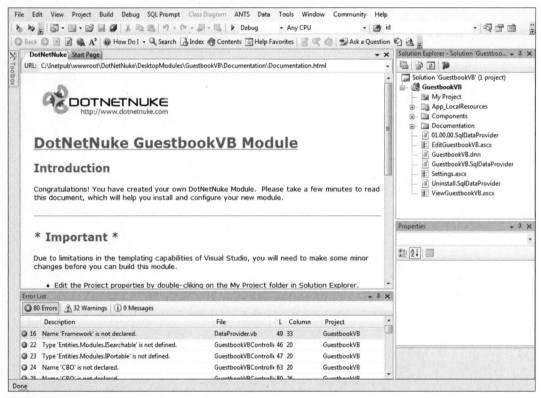

Figure 5-6

Configuring the Project

Similar to the C# project, because of template limitations, additional configuration is needed to ensure that the Visual Basic module is properly configured to continue future module development. All project configurations are located inside the My Project section of the Visual Studio project.

To start, double-click the My Project item in the Solution Explorer window. A dialog similar to the one shown in Figure 5-7 appears and the Application tab at the top of the left side of the page is selected.

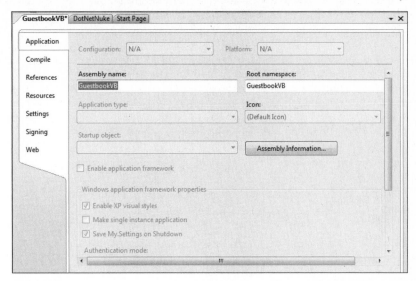

Figure 5-7

Similar to a C# project, Visual Basic projects have two key settings inside the Application section: Assembly Name and Root Namespace. Although these are similar to the settings available for C# projects, there are a few key differences. Table 5-2 provides details for these settings for Visual Basic modules. For the creation of the example module, the Assembly Name option should have a value of `WroxModules.GuestbookVB`, and the Root Namespace should be cleared.

Table 5-2

Setting Name	Setting Purpose
Assembly Name	This setting provides Visual Studio with the information required to create the final `.dll` file into which the module will be compiled. With the example in this book, using a value of `WroxModules.GuestbookVB`, the generated `.dll` file for the Guestbook module will be `WroxModules.GuestbookVB.dll`. This is an important configuration step because it ensures that the created modules have unique names.
Root Namespace	A value specified here will be prefixed to *all* namespaces inside the project. For this reason, it is *not* used in the examples provided in this book because all code files have their own namespace definitions.

The second configuration step needed for Visual Basic projects is to modify the Project Url setting located on the Web tab. On the Web tab, locate the option called "Use Local IIS Web Server," similar to that shown earlier in Figure 5-4. Modify this setting to show the proper IIS URL of `http://localhost/dotnetnuke`. This configuration step completes the most common setup elements for a Visual Basic project. However, let's take a look at one last validation to ensure that all project references are correct. This will resolve any errors that might be displaying in the error list.

Click the References tab inside the project settings to display a list of references, as shown in Figure 5-8. If any references show a Path value of "<The system cannot find the reference specified >," you must remove the reference and add it again to ensure that future project building is successful. In this example, the project is attempting to reference `DotNetNuke.Library`, which is an element only included in the source package of DotNetNuke. Therefore, the reference cannot be located. To resolve this issue, select the DotNetNuke.Library entry and click the Remove button.

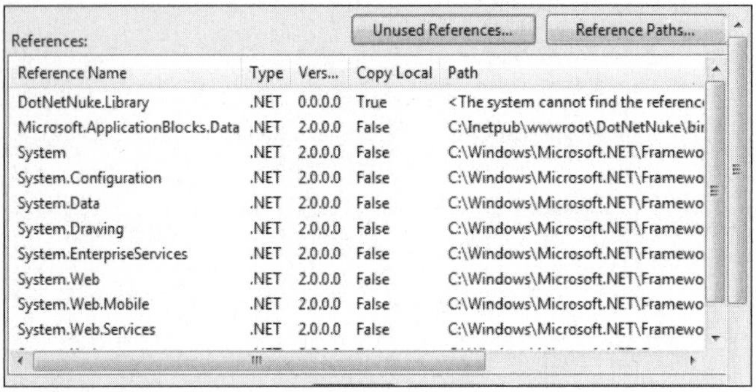

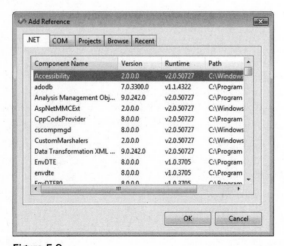

Figure 5-8

After removing the incorrect reference, you can now add the correct reference. This is done by clicking the Add button below the reference listing. The Add Reference dialog will appear, as shown in Figure 5-9. This dialog includes multiple options for locating a project reference. Select the Browse tab to get to a folder browser window. Navigate to the `C:\inetpub\wwwroot\dotnetnuke\bin` folder and select the `DotNetNuke.dll` file. Click OK to add the reference.

Figure 5-9

> As of this writing, the additional reference step listed here is a requirement, but it may no longer be an issue by the time you read this. If you view the project settings and no errors are displayed, then no action for project references is required.

This completes the setup of the default Visual Basic project. Be sure to click the Save button inside Visual Studio to save all project changes.

Now that you have configured both the VB.NET and C# projects for the Guestbook module, let's investigate the newly created elements, and consider the road map for examining each individual code file in detail.

What Was Created?

The default module templates create three subfolders with code files, as well as a few general code files. The following list identifies each of the created folders, and provides information regarding the purpose of the files contained within. The project structures are exactly the same for the Visual Basic and C# modules.

- ❑ `App_LocalResources` **folder:** This folder contains three individual files with a `resx` extension. The files contained within are the individual localization files that are used to support the DotNetNuke Localization scheme. These files are an integral part of creating a module that is accessible to users of all languages. The functions of these files are discussed in detail at the beginning of Chapter 8.

- ❑ `Components` **folder:** This folder is the storage space for all custom code that is not directly tied to the front-end `.ascx` files. Files contained in this folder are discussed in both Chapter 6 and Chapter 7. Chapter 6 focuses on the DotNetNuke data access layer (DAL), and Chapter 7 focuses on the concept of creating information objects and controllers.

- ❑ `Documentation` **folder:** This folder is used for information purposes only, and is not a real part of the DotNetNuke project. Many individuals will remove the files contained in this folder to avoid any confusion between auto-generated information and custom module code.

- ❑ **Root files:** Three types of files are created at the root level of a project. The first type includes the `.SqlDataProvider` files. These files are the scripts that are executed when a module is installed. They are discussed in detail in Chapter 6, and are coded in Chapter 7. The second type of file is the `.dnn` file. This is the manifest file that tells DotNetNuke the needed information about the module. This file is discussed and modified in Chapter 6. The last file type is `.ascx`. These are the user controls that are used to actually display module content to the users. These are discussed in detail in Chapter 8, where the initial project interface is created.

Summary

This chapter has created the module projects needed to move forward with the development of the Guestbook module. Chapter 6 begins by explaining the specifics of the DotNetNuke elements needed to properly build a module, and provides an overview of what is to come when developing the first bits of module code in Chapters 7 and 8.

6

Investigating DotNetNuke Components

The previous chapters of this book have focused on installing DotNetNuke, introducing common terminology, and creating a default project template. This chapter dives into the actual programming behind DotNetNuke module development. It covers three basic elements that make up the main specifics of DotNetNuke module development:

❑   First the chapter investigates the DotNetNuke data access layer (DAL), with brief overviews of the auto-generated code files and the dependencies that exist between each file.

❑   The discussion then examines two key user interface (UI) base classes that will be used to integrate the custom controls created in future chapters with the DotNetNuke system.

❑   The chapter concludes with an investigation of the DotNetNuke module manifest file. The .dnn file is an XML document that defines the module structure so that integration is possible from inside DotNetNuke.

A fully completed module manifest will be created at the end of the chapter. By then, you should have a basic understanding of the DotNetNuke DAL system, which will provide a much easier transition to Chapter 7.

DotNetNuke Data Access Layer (DAL)

The standard DotNetNuke data access layer (DAL) utilizes a provider model to allow for easy migration to different data storage systems. However, because data providers for other data stores are so few and far between, you might find this process to be a bit of overkill for many implementations. I personally still utilize this method to ensure that my development follows the standard coding practices that are employed by the DotNetNuke core team and projects.

The discussion of the DotNetNuke DAL begins with an investigation of the two auto-created code files: DataProvider (.cs/.vb) and SqlDataProvider (.cs/.vb). These two files provide the coding interface to all database actions. The discussion then examines the DotNetNuke-specific .SqlDataProvider files that enable data scripts to be executed during module installation. This discussion focuses on the key elements, and does not delve too deeply into the "weeds" of implementation, just to keep things simple and easier to understand.

DataProvider(.cs/.vb)

The DataProvider (.cs/.vb) code file is a fairly simple piece of code. It is an abstract class that defines the methods that must be implemented by the specific concrete class. The singleton design pattern is used to maintain a single instance of the provider for use by the application. Listing 6-1 (for C# developers) and Listing 6-2 (for VB.NET developers) show the singleton implementation for the data provider as created by the default project templates. For readability, XML comments have been removed from the listings.

Listing 6-1: C# Singleton DataProvider Implementation

```
private static DataProvider instance = null;

static DataProvider()
{
    instance = (DataProvider)Reflection.CreateObject("data",
        "YourCompany.GuestbookCS.Components", "");
}

public static DataProvider Instance()
{
    return instance;
}
```

Listing 6-2: VB.NET Singleton DataProvider Implementation

```
Private Shared objProvider As DataProvider = Nothing

Shared Sub New()
    CreateProvider()
End Sub

Private Shared Sub CreateProvider()
    objProvider = CType(Framework.Reflection.CreateObject("data",
        "YourCompany.Modules.GuestbookVB", ""), DataProvider)
End Sub

Public Shared Shadows Function Instance() As DataProvider
    Return objProvider
End Function
```

This section of the data provider is very simple. A private static variable is created that contains the instance of the data provider. A private constructor is used to instantiate the DataProvider when a new instance is needed. The key thing to remember when looking at this portion of the DotNetNuke DAL is that the private constructor is an assembly reference that is used to dynamically instantiate the concrete implementation. By default, the templates use a namespace that starts with `YourCompany`. When you create the module back end in Chapter 7, you will modify default namespace values and update the `DataProvider` files accordingly to ensure that all configuration elements are correct.

The next section contained inside the `DataProvider` file is the declaration of the abstract data methods. These methods are used to retrieve data from the database. Because the `DataProvider` is an abstract class, all data methods must be defined here to set the contract that all concrete classes must follow. This ensures that all data methods will be supported, even with a different provider implementation. Listing 6-3 (for C# developers) and Listing 6-4 (for VB.NET developers) show the default code listings for the abstract data methods.

Listing 6-3: C# Default Abstract Methods

```
public abstract IDataReader GetGuestbookCSs(int moduleId);
public abstract IDataReader GetGuestbookCS(int moduleId, int itemId);
public abstract void AddGuestbookCS(int moduleId, string content, int userId);
public abstract void UpdateGuestbookCS(int moduleId, int itemId, string content,
    int userId);
public abstract void DeleteGuestbookCS(int moduleId, int itemId);
```

Listing 6-4: VB.NET Default Abstract Methods

```
Public MustOverride Function GetGuestbookVBs(ByVal ModuleId As Integer) As
    IDataReader
Public MustOverride Function GetGuestbookVB(ByVal ModuleId As Integer,ByVal ItemId
    As Integer) As IDataReader
Public MustOverride Sub AddGuestbookVB(ByVal ModuleId As Integer, ByVal Content As
    String, ByVal UserId As Integer)
Public MustOverride Sub UpdateGuestbookVB(ByVal ModuleId As Integer, ByVal ItemId
    As Integer, ByVal Content As String, ByVal UserId As Integer)
Public MustOverride Sub DeleteGuestbookVB(ByVal ModuleId As Integer,ByVal ItemId As
    Integer)
```

These listings provide a few examples of common data functions, some of which will be implemented in Chapter 7 as you build the back-end data storage for the Guestbook module. When working with data methods inside DotNetNuke, note that the return types of functions utilize the common `IDataReader` object. This provides the flexibility needed to support multiple providers. It would be impossible to support multiple providers if functions returned `SqlDataReader` or similar objects.

Now that you've seen the contract defined inside the `DataProvider` file, let's take a look at the `SqlDataProvider(.cs/.vb)` file, which is the concrete implementation for the example module.

SqlDataProvider(.cs/.vb)

The `SqlDataProvider` (`.cs/.vb`) class is a bit more complex than the abstract `DataProvider` class because it actually implements the needed data methods and retrieves settings information from the `web.config` file. The first thing to note is that the class inherits from the base `DataProvider` class. This results in the following public class declarations in C#:

```
public class SqlDataProvider : DataProvider
```

In VB.NET, the following would be true:

```
Public Class SqlDataProvider
        Inherits DataProvider
```

It is very common when manually creating the `SqlDataProvider` to overlook the `Inherits` portion of the class declaration. Doing so will cause many problems later in the development process.

Private Data Members

After the class declaration, the first code region is the private data members area. Here you find the values that are used later to properly communicate with the database, as well as the first stages of settings retrieval. Listing 6-5 (for C# developers) and Listing 6-6 (for VB.NET developers) show the code for property definitions.

Listing 6-5: C# SqlDataProvider Private Data Members

```
private const string providerType = "data";
private const string moduleQualifier = "YourCompany_";
private ProviderConfiguration providerConfiguration =
    ProviderConfiguration.GetProviderConfiguration(providerType);
private string connectionString;
private string providerPath;
private string objectQualifier;
private string databaseOwner;
```

Listing 6-6: VB.NET SqlDataProvider Private Data Memebers

```
Private Const ProviderType As String = "data"
Private Const ModuleQualifier As String = "YourCompany_"
Private _providerConfiguration As ProviderConfiguration =
    ProviderConfiguration.GetProviderConfiguration(ProviderType)
Private _connectionString As String
Private _providerPath As String
Private _objectQualifier As String
Private _databaseOwner As String
```

These data members provide key data elements that are used to identify the database connection to target, the path to the provider, the object qualifier and database owner settings, and any object qualifier specified. Table 6-1 examines each element in detail, as well as the purpose of the element with regard to working with custom modules.

Table 6-1

Name	Purpose
providerType	This constant identifies the provider type so that the DotNetNuke provider configuration class can be used to obtain the configuration that was completed via the web.config file.
ModuleQualifier	This constant is a qualifier that is prefixed to all objects for the module being created. The default value is YourCompany. A different value will be specified for this project in Chapter 7.
ProviderConfiguration	This is a member that contains the DotNetNuke provider configuration elements from the web.config file. These items will be used later to obtain the settings needed for data access.
ConnectionString, ProviderPath, ObjectQualifier, and DatabaseOwner	These are all private members that are used to retain the data obtained from the configuration.

Constructor

After the private data member, you will find the constructor, which actually reads the connection information from the web.config file, processes the information, and retains it in the respective private data members. Listing 6-7 (for C# developers) and Listing 6-8 (for VB.NET developers) show the constructor code.

Listing 6-7: C# SqlDataProvider Constructor

```
public SqlDataProvider()
{
    Provider provider =
      (Provider)providerConfiguration.Providers
      [providerConfiguration.DefaultProvider];
    connectionString = DotNetNuke.Common.Utilities.Config.GetConnectionString();

    if (connectionString == string.Empty)
        connectionString = provider.Attributes["connectionString"];

    providerPath = provider.Attributes["providerPath"];

    objectQualifier = provider.Attributes["objectQualifier"];
    if (objectQualifier != string.Empty && !objectQualifier.EndsWith("_"))
        objectQualifier += "_";

    databaseOwner = provider.Attributes["databaseOwner"];
    if (databaseOwner != string.Empty && !databaseOwner.EndsWith("."))
        databaseOwner += ".";
}
```

Listing 6-8: VB.NET SqlDataProvider Constructor

```
Public Sub New()

    Dim objProvider As Provider =
        CType(_providerConfiguration.Providers(
                        _providerConfiguration.DefaultProvider), Provider)
    _connectionString = Config.GetConnectionString()

    If _connectionString = "" Then
        _connectionString = objProvider.Attributes("connectionString")
    End If

    _providerPath = objProvider.Attributes("providerPath")

    _objectQualifier = objProvider.Attributes("objectQualifier")
    If _objectQualifier <> "" And _objectQualifier.EndsWith("_") = False Then
        _objectQualifier += "_"
    End If

    _databaseOwner = objProvider.Attributes("databaseOwner")
    If _databaseOwner <> "" And _databaseOwner.EndsWith(".") = False Then
        _databaseOwner += "."
    End If
End Sub
```

This section of code obtains the provider information from the provider configuration. It then investigates the code to clean up and store the connection string, object qualifier, and database owner values (if specified from the database).

> Note that because these objects are only created/instantiated once because of the use of the singleton pattern shown earlier, the reads from the web.config file will not have a drastic impact on performance.

Public Properties

Following proper object-oriented (OO) design principles, the template code provides four public read-only properties that expose the connection string, providerPath, object qualifier, and database owner data values. This prevents any outside class from modifying these important values. For brevity, the code for these examples is not shown here.

Private Methods

Both templates include two key private methods that are used to ensure proper execution of all database actions:

❑ The first method, GetFullyQualifiedName, is a simple method that returns an object's name with the full qualification behind it (including database owner, object qualifier, and module qualifier). This avoids the need for repeated typing, and allows for flexibility when working with different site configurations.

❑ The second method, GetNull, provides a method that returns a proper null value if a null value is encountered when working with the module data.

Listing 6-9 (for C# developers) and Listing 6-10 (for VB.NET developers) show the code for these two methods.

Listing 6-9: C# Private Methods

```csharp
private string GetFullyQualifiedName(string name)
{
    return DatabaseOwner + ObjectQualifier + moduleQualifier + name;
}

private object GetNull(object field)
{
    return DotNetNuke.Common.Utilities.Null.GetNull(field, DBNull.Value);
}
```

Listing 6-10: VB.NET Private Methods

```vbnet
Private Function GetFullyQualifiedName(ByVal name As String) As String
    Return DatabaseOwner & ObjectQualifier & ModuleQualifier & name
End Function

Private Function GetNull(ByVal Field As Object) As Object
    Return DotNetNuke.Common.Utilities.Null.GetNull(Field, DBNull.Value)
End Function
```

Public Override Methods

Because the SqlDataProvider class inherits from the DataProvider class, this section is where the required override methods are implemented. The Microsoft Application Blocks Data component is used to streamline data access. Stored procedure execution is completed using the SqlHelper class that is contained within the application blocks. It makes for a very easy process.

Listing 6-11 (for C# developers) and Listing 6-12 (for VB.NET developers) show examples of two different data operations: one that returns data and one that saves data. These are discussed in detail later in this chapter.

Listing 6-11: C# Override Method Examples

```
public override IDataReader GetGuestbookCS(int moduleId, int itemId)
{
    return (IDataReader)SqlHelper.ExecuteReader(connectionString,
            GetFullyQualifiedName("GetGuestbookCS"), moduleId, itemId);
}

public override void AddGuestbookCS(int moduleId, string content, int userId)
{
    SqlHelper.ExecuteNonQuery(connectionString,
            GetFullyQualifiedName("AddGuestbookCS"), moduleId, content, userId);
}
```

Listing 6-12: VB.NET Override Method Examples

```
Public Overrides Function GetGuestbookVB(ByVal ModuleId As Integer, ByVal ItemId As
    Integer) As IDataReader
    Return CType(SqlHelper.ExecuteReader(ConnectionString,
    GetFullyQualifiedName("GetGuestbookVB"), ModuleId, ItemId), IDataReader)
End Function

Public Overrides Sub AddGuestbookVB(ByVal ModuleId As Integer, ByVal Content As
    String, ByVal UserId As Integer)
    SqlHelper.ExecuteNonQuery(ConnectionString,
        GetFullyQualifiedName("AddGuestbookVB"), ModuleId, Content, UserId)
End Sub
```

These examples show that the `SqlHelper.Execute...` methods have a standard syntax that takes the connection string as the first parameter, the stored procedure name as the second parameter, and an optional array of parameter values that should be passed to the stored procedure as the third parameter. Note that any added parameters to be sent to the stored procedure for processing *must* be sent in the same order to the stored procedure as they are listed in the actual procedure code. In the case of data operations that return results, a simple cast converting the `SqlDataReader` to an `IDataReader` is needed to meet the rules defined in the `DataProvider` abstract method definition.

This completes the overview, from a coding perspective, of how the DotNetNuke DAL system works. In Chapter 7, you will modify the generated code to create the actual DAL code needed for the Guestbook modules. Now that you've seen an overview of the .NET side of things, let's take a look at the DotNetNuke-specific `.SqlDataProvider` files.

xx.xx.xx.SqlDataProvider Files

At first, it may seem confusing that two types of `SqlDataProvider` files exist. The ones previously discussed with `.cs` or `.vb` file extensions are the actual .NET coding methods that provide access to the database. The second type of files are named in the format `XX.XX.XX.SqlDataProvider`, where the `XX.XX.XX` values represent the current version of the module being created. These files are used to execute database scripts during the installation or upgrade of a DotNetNuke module, and reflect a specific file setup that is supported by DotNetNuke.

Inside these `SqlDataProvider` files, it is possible to execute any number of SQL scripts needed to make a custom module work. These scripts are joined together, and individual statements are divided with a `GO` statement. The scripts are the same for both Visual Basic modules and C# modules.

To help you fully understand the `SqlDataProvider` files, let's work on three separate aspects: replacements, creating tables, and creating stored procedures. This step-by-step approach will explain each element that makes up a completed `SqlDataProvider` file, and will set the stage for the creation of the Guestbook `SqlDataProvider` file in Chapter 7.

Replacements

Previously in this chapter, you learned about `ObjectQualifier`, which is a user-specified value that is prefixed to all objects in a DotNetNuke database if configured via the `web.config` file. Additionally, there is an option that enables you to customize the `DatabaseOwner`, which, by default, is set to `dbo`. Because of this flexibility, DotNetNuke `SqlDataProvider` files support two replacement tokens: `{databaseOwner}` and `{objectQualifier}`. This enables data scripts to be written in a generic manner that still allows scripts to execute, regardless of the user's configuration.

Anywhere these two replacement token values are found, they will be substituted with the proper values for the target DotNetNuke installation. The database owner token will *always* have a value, whereas the object qualifier is optional and may not exist in a user's installation. In that case, DotNetNuke simply removes the token from the scripts.

Using these replacement tokens is very simple. For example, rather than use the following statement to start a table creation:

```
CREATE TABLE MyCustomTable
```

you can instead simply update the table name portion of the statement to contain the replacement parameters needed, as shown here:

```
CREATE TABLE {databaseOwner} [{objectQualifier}MyCustomTable]
```

This ensures that, regardless of the DotNetNuke installation's configuration, the module installation will follow all configurations specified by the portal administrator. If you are distributing a public module, it is *very* important to have these elements in the data provider scripts. Without them, it is very possible for a module installation to damage a database if a user attempts to install the module on two different installations hosted inside the same database. For more information about `databaseOwner` and `objectQualifier` values, see the information provided in Appendix B.

Creating Tables

Using the replacement rules just discussed, it is very easy to create a table. It is also considered a best practice to ensure that any data script can be re-executed without consequence. Therefore, always check to see whether a table exists before creating it. Listing 6-13 shows an example of a table creation script properly configured with replacements, as well as a check for an existing table.

Listing 6-13: Creating a Table Script for Use in SqlDataProvider

```
if not exists (select * from dbo.sysobjects where id =
    object_id(N'{databaseOwner}[{objectQualifier}YourCompany_SampleTable]') and
    OBJECTPROPERTY(id, N'IsTable') = 1)
  BEGIN
        CREATE TABLE {databaseOwner}[{objectQualifier}YourCompany_SampleTable]
        (
            [ModuleID] [int] NOT NULL,
            [ItemID] [int] NOT NULL IDENTITY(1, 1),
            [Content] [ntext] NOT NULL,
            [CreatedByUser] [int] NOT NULL,
            [CreatedDate] [datetime] NOT NULL
        )

        ALTER TABLE {databaseOwner}[{objectQualifier}YourCompany_SampleTable]
    ADD CONSTRAINT [PK_{objectQualifier}YourCompany_SampleTable]
    PRIMARY KEY CLUSTERED  ([ItemID])
        CREATE NONCLUSTERED INDEX [IX_{objectQualifier}YourCompany_SampleTable]
    ON {databaseOwner}[{objectQualifier}YourCompany_SampleTable] ([ModuleID])

        ALTER TABLE {databaseOwner}[{objectQualifier}YourCompany_SampleTable]
            WITH NOCHECK ADD CONSTRAINT
                [FK_{objectQualifier}YourCompany_SampleTable_{objectQualifier}
                Modules]
    FOREIGN KEY ([ModuleID]) REFERENCES {databaseOwner}[{objectQualifier}Modules]
        ([ModuleID]) ON DELETE CASCADE NOT FOR REPLICATION
        END
GO
```

This listing shows the establishment of a named primary key, a named index, and a foreign key that ties the data at a module level to the Modules table that is part of the DotNetNuke core. This is an example of a best-practice implementation of custom table creation. Replacement tokens have been used with support for all configurations. Named constraints have been added to ensure that naming conflicts are minimal. In addition, data integrity constraints have been used to clean up module data upon module deletion.

Now that you are familiar with the table creation process, let's now take a look at the implementation of creating a stored procedure, again with checks in place to ensure that the object doesn't already exist.

Creating Stored Procedures

Listing 6-14 shows an example of a script to create a stored procedure. Note that this script contains a conditional piece of code indicating that if the procedure is found, then it is dropped just prior to the creation of the new procedure. This method of script writing follows the DotNetNuke development standards because it enables a data script to be executed multiple times without risking the integrity of the data.

Listing 6-14: Creating a Procedure Script for Use in SqlDataProvider

```
IF EXISTS (select * from dbo.sysobjects where id =
    object_id(N'{databaseOwner}[{objectQualifier}YourCompany_GetSamples]') and
    OBJECTPROPERTY(id, N'IsProcedure') = 1)
     drop procedure {databaseOwner}{objectQualifier}YourCompany_GetSamples
GO

CREATE PROCEUDRE {databaseOwner}{objectQualifier}YourCompany_GetSamples
    @ModuleId int
AS
SELECT ModuleId,
      ItemId,
      Content,
      CreatedByUser,
      CreatedDate,
      'CreatedByUserName' = {objectQualifier}Users.FirstName + ' ' +
            {objectQualifier}Users.LastName
from {objectQualifier}YourCompany_Samples
inner join {objectQualifier}Users on
    {objectQualifier}YourCompany_Samples.CreatedByUser
    = {objectQualifier}Users.UserId
where   ModuleId = @ModuleId
GO
```

This is simply a continuation of the previously discussed topics, combining the replacements, data integrity, and other aspects of SqlDataProvider files.

You should now understand how the SqlDataProvider files work. In the end, these files provide a simple method for developers to have scripts execute when modules are installed or upgraded. Naming the SqlDataProvider files in version order enables specific scripts to be executed in a specific order; and if an upgrade is completed, the existing version number is used to prevent old provider files from executing. Over time, many DotNetNuke modules will gain multiple .SqlDataProvider files because changes to the applications dictate changes to the underlying data structures and data access components.

DotNetNuke UI Base Classes

The DotNetNuke API contains multiple base classes that expose specific sets of information to developers. In addition, specific base classes are needed to properly interface with DotNetNuke in certain situations. This section takes a look at the two most common base classes (and those used in the default module templates).

PortalModuleBase

The PortalModuleBase class is used for each standard view control within a DotNetNuke module. The base class is located in the DotNetNuke.Entities.Modules namespace. This base class is not only a requirement to integrate custom user controls within DotNetNuke, but also provides much-needed security, authentication, and system information to module code. This enables configuration and user information to be easily accessed by custom module code.

Table 6-2 shows a few common properties and methods that are provided by `PortalModuleBase` and that may be helpful to module developers.

Table 6-2

Property	Type	Detail
ModuleId	Integer	This is the unique identifier for the current module instance. It is used to uniquely identify a specific module location.
TabModuleId	Integer	This is a unique identifier for the specific module *and* tab. If a module were copied to another tab, then the `ModuleId` for the two instances would be the same. However, the `TabModuleId` will differ.
TabId	Integer	This is the unique identifier for the currently visible tab. This allows for navigation links to be created, or for page-level data association.
IsEditable	Boolean	This property returns a value of `true` if the user viewing the page has edit permissions to the current module instance. This can be used to conditionally display edit/administration options to users based on assigned permissions.
UserInfo	UserInfo	This object holds all of the information contained in DotNetNuke for the currently logged-in user. `DisplayName` and other properties may be accessed via this object — for example, `UserInfo .DisplayName`.
UserId	Integer	This is the unique identifier for the currently logged-in user. This can be used to key information on a user-specific basis. If no user is logged in, then this will return a value of `-1`.
PortalAlias	PortalAliasInfo	This returns a `PortalAliasInfo` record, which contains various information regarding the specific portal alias used to view the current page.
ModuleConfiguration	ModuleInfo	This is an information object containing information about the current module.
PortalSettings	PortalSettings	This is a hash table of portal-specific settings. The most commonly used value from here is the admin e-mail address.
Settings	HashTable	This is the gateway to the custom settings that you can set and store using DotNetNuke methods. The use of this is discussed in detail in Chapter 8.

As the Guestbook module interface is created in Chapter 8, the `PortalModuleBase` class will be used to create the individual standard view controls. Common integration elements listed in Table 6-2 will be used to implement the functional requirements of the Guestbook module.

ModuleSettingsBase

You use the `ModuleSettingsBase` class to create the "settings" control used to configure a DotNetNuke module. As mentioned in previous chapters, the settings control inside a DotNetNuke control is a bit different from other controls within a DotNetNuke module because it is automatically added to the "settings" view for a module that is dynamically created by DotNetNuke. This enables DotNetNuke to provide common functionality in a specific centralized location. Because of this difference from standard controls, the separate base class is needed.

Like the `PortalModuleBase` class, common DotNetNuke data elements and controls are exposed via the base class. Table 6-3 describes a few highlighted public data members provided with the `ModuleSettingsBase` class. The key item to notice here is that inside the settings control, you have two properties for settings: `ModuleSettings` and `TabModuleSettings`. When in the view control using `PortalModuleBase`, you have a specific `Settings` property that accesses the aggregate of these isolation levels.

Table 6-3

Property	Type	Detail
ModuleId	Integer	This is the unique identifier for the current module instance. It is used to uniquely identify a specific module location.
TabModuleId	Integer	This is a unique identifier for the specific module *and* tab. If a module were copied to another tab, the `ModuleId` for the two instances would be the same. However, the `TabModuleId` will differ.
ModuleSettings	HashTable	This is a collection of configuration elements that are associated at the module level.
TabModuleSettings	HashTable	These are settings that apply to a specific instance of a module. They are used to modify views if a module is copied from one location to another.

In addition to the standard public members, `ModuleSettingsBase` also has two public methods that need to be overridden to hook into the common setup, in order to ensure that settings are loaded and saved. These two methods are `LoadSettings` and `SaveSettings`. No parameters or returns are needed. Settings controls do *not* need to have their own Update buttons, because when Update is selected on the overall control, the `UpdateSettings` method is called. These methods will be implemented in Chapter 8 when the module interface is created.

DotNetNuke Module Manifest (.dnn) File

To complete the integration of a custom-developed module, DotNetNuke utilizes an XML document called a *module manifest*, more commonly known as the .dnn file. This file tells DotNetNuke about the custom module and stores all integration points that are needed for later use. There have been two major formats for the .dnn file:

❑ The first format is the one that is used for DNN 3.x and 4.x. This format is the one used by the default module templates as created, and is the only format supported by 3.x and 4.x DNN installations.

❑ The second format was introduced in DNN 5.0. It provides developers with more functionality and control over the installation/upgrade process.

> As of this writing, neither module template contained the DNN 5.0 module manifest format as the default. It is possible that this will have changed by the time of publication.

Given the differences needed, let's first examine the DNN manifest file that will be used with the Guestbook module for both the VB and C# versions. Following the code listings, you will find a discussion about the individual settings.

Guestbook Manifests

Listing 6-15 provides the full text for the base DNN 5.0 manifest file for the C# version of the Guestbook module. For the sake of brevity, this is the only listing included here. To create the VB.NET manifest file, simply replace all occurrences of GuestbookCS with GuestbookVB. This text should be used to entirely replace the text of the GuestbookCS.dnn and GuestbookVB.dnn files as generated by the templates in Chapter 5. This will ensure that the modules can benefit from the new features of the DNN 5 manifest format.

Listing 6-15: DotNetNuke Module Manifest for the C# Guestbook

```xml
<dotnetnuke type="Package" version="5.0">
  <packages>
    <package name="WROX_GuestbookCS" type="Module" version="1.0.0">
      <friendlyName>Guestbook Module CS Version</friendlyName>
      <description>        This example module is being created
                        as an example for the Professional
    DotNetNuke 5 Module Programming book by Wrox Press.
      </description>
      <owner>
        <name>Mitchel Sellers</name>
        <organization>None</organization>
        <url />
        <email>msellers@iowacomputergurus.com</email>
      </owner>
      <license>
```

```
          &lt;p&gt;Permission is hereby granted, free of charge,
                to any person obtaining a copy of this software and
                associated documentation files (the "Software"), to deal in the
                Software without restriction, including without limitation the
                rights to use, copy, modify, merge, publish, distribute, sublicense,
                and/or sell copies of the Software, and to permit persons to whom
                the Software is furnished to do so, subject to the following
                conditions:
   <!--&lt;/p&gt;&lt;p&gt;-->The above copyright notice and this permission notice
                shall be included in all copies or substantial portions of the Software.
                &lt;/p&gt;&lt;p&gt;THE SOFTWARE IS PROVIDED "AS IS", WITHOUT WARRANTY OF
                ANY KIND, EXPRESS OR IMPLIED, INCLUDING BUT NOT LIMITED TO THE WARRANTIES
                OF MERCHANTABILITY, FITNESS FOR A PARTICULAR PURPOSE AND NONINFRINGEMENT.
                IN NO EVENT SHALL THE AUTHORS OR COPYRIGHT HOLDERS BE LIABLE FOR ANY CLAIM,
                DAMAGES OR OTHER LIABILITY, WHETHER IN AN ACTION OF CONTRACT, TORT OR
                OTHERWISE, ARISING FROM, OUT OF OR IN CONNECTION WITH THE SOFTWARE OR THE
                USE OR OTHER DEALINGS IN THE SOFTWARE.
            &lt;/p&gt;
        </license>
        <releaseNotes>
            &lt;/p&gt;
            Example Module
            &lt;/p&gt;
        </releaseNotes>
        <components>
            <component type="Script">
                <scripts>
                    <basePath>DesktopModules\GuestbookCS</basePath>
                    <script type="Install">
                        <name>01.00.00.sqldataprovider</name>
                        <version>01.00.00</version>
                    </script>
                    <script type="UnInstall">
                        <name>uninstall.sqldataprovider</name>
                        <version>01.00.00</version>
                    </script>
                </scripts>
            </component>
            <component type="Module">
                <desktopModule>
                    <moduleName>WROX_GuestbookCS</moduleName>
                    <foldername>GuestbookCS</foldername>
                    <businessControllerClass></businessControllerClass>
                    <moduleDefinitions>
                        <moduleDefinition>
                            <friendlyName>Guestbook CS</friendlyName>
                            <defaultCacheTime>0</defaultCacheTime>
                            <moduleControls>
                                <moduleControl>
                                    <controlKey />
                                <controlSrc>
                                        DesktopModules/GuestbookCS/ViewGuestbookCS.ascx
                                    </controlSrc>
```

(continued)

Listing 6-15 *(continued)*

```xml
            <supportsPartialRendering>True</supportsPartialRendering>
            <controlTitle />
            <controlType>View</controlType>
            <iconFile />
            <helpUrl />
            <viewOrder>0</viewOrder>
          </moduleControl>
          <moduleControl>
            <controlKey>Edit</controlKey>
            <controlSrc>
                DesktopModules/GuestbookCS/EditGuestbookCS.ascx
            </controlSrc>
            <supportsPartialRendering>False</supportsPartialRendering>
            <controlTitle>Edit Guestbook Entry</controlTitle>
            <controlType>Edit</controlType>
            <iconFile />
            <helpUrl />
            <viewOrder>0</viewOrder>
          </moduleControl>
          <moduleControl>
            <controlKey>Settings</controlKey>
            <controlSrc>
                DesktopModules/GuestbookCS/ViewSettings.ascx
            </controlSrc>
            <supportsPartialRendering>False</supportsPartialRendering>
            <controlTitle>View Guestbook CS Settings</controlTitle>
            <controlType>Edit</controlType>
            <iconFile />
            <helpUrl />
            <viewOrder>0</viewOrder>
          </moduleControl>
        </moduleControls>
      </moduleDefinition>
    </moduleDefinitions>
  </desktopModule>
</component>
<component type="Assembly">
  <assemblies>
    <assembly>
      <path>bin</path>
      <name>Wrox.Modules.GuestbookCS.dll</name>
    </assembly>
  </assemblies>
</component>
<component type="File">
  <files>
    <basePath>DesktopModules\GuestbookCS</basePath>
    <file>
      <path>app_localresources</path>
      <name>EditGuestbookCS.ascx.resx</name>
    </file>
```

```
            <file>
              <path>app_localresources</path>
              <name>Settings.aspx.resx</name>
            </file>
            <file>
              <path>app_localresources</path>
              <name>ViewGuestbookCS.ascx.resx</name>
            </file>
            <file>
              <name>EditGuestbookCS.ascx</name>
            </file>
            <file>
              <name>Settings.aspx</name>
            </file>
            <file>
              <name>ViewGuestbookCS.ascx</name>
            </file>
            <file>
              <name>module.css</name>
            </file>
          </files>
        </component>
      </components>
    </package>
  </packages>
</dotnetnuke>
```

> Chapter 8 introduces advanced features and additions to this base manifest file to complete the guestbook implementation.

This manifest file provides full details to DotNetNuke about the module, enabling DotNetNuke to properly create all needed files and folders, and execute the needed scripts when installing the package.

Manifest Components

Although the manifest file presented in the preceding section can be very daunting when you are looking at it for the first time, it is actually a very straightforward document that is easy to follow and maintain once the format is understood.

To that end, the following sections provide a more detailed look at the manifest components:

❑   Manifest Beginning (which includes the opening structure of the manifest)

❑   Package Information

❑   Components (which includes how the package system can be used for multiple types of packages)

Manifest Beginning

The top three lines of the manifest file create the overall XML structure needed to start the manifest definition. The first line presents the `dotnetnuke` node, with attributes for type and version. This indicates that the information contained inside this document is a package based on version 5.0.0. This is the default package information that is valid for DNN 5.0.0 and later versions.

The next node opens the collection of packages, with the third line starting the `package` for the Guestbook module. This package declaration has the following three attributes:

- ❑ `type`: This is a package type from a specific listing of DotNetNuke package types. Table 6-4 shows all the available package types.

- ❑ `name`: This is the unique name for this particular package. It is used to differentiate between new installations and upgrades.

- ❑ `version`: This identifies the unique version of this installation package, and is used to conditionally execute SQL scripts, and so on.

Table 6-4

Type	Detail
Module	A DotNetNuke module
Provider	A provider used to extend default DotNetNuke elements that implement the provider model
Skin	A DotNetNuke skin package
SkinObject	A DotNetNuke skin object, similar to that of the DotNetNuke Breadcrumb
Container	A DotNetNuke container package

Package Information

The elements directly following the start of the package contain general information about the package. This information indicates to an administrator what the individual package being installed contains, and is designed to ensure that accurate information is displayed at all times.

Table 6-5 shows each node inside the package section of the manifest. The Attributes column lists the behavior of the node both with and without attributes.

Table 6-5

Node	Attributes	Detail
friendlyName	None	The friendlyName node contains the friendly name for the module package.
Description	None	The Description node contains text that describes the package. Note that this is an XML document, and any special characters must be properly escaped.
Owner	None	This node has four required child nodes for name, organization, URL, and e-mail address of the package owner. This is the desired contact information for individuals who have questions or concerns about the package.
License	None	With no attributes specified, the License node should contain the full text of the license agreement for the package. The sample modules in this book use the standard DotNetNuke license notice.
License	Src	With the src attribute pointing to a text file included in the installation of the module, the license node should be left blank because the license text will be retrieved from the file.
ReleaseNotes	None	With no attributes specified, the ReleaseNotes node should contain the full text release notes for the current module version. This information is provided to site administrators to enable them to understand any changes to the current version.
ReleaseNotes	Src	With the src attribute pointing to a text file included in the installation of the module, the ReleaseNotes node should be left blank because the content will be retrieved from the text file.

These package elements are mostly new items for the DotNetNuke 5 manifest system, and they are great pieces of information for both administrators and module developers. Ensuring that users agree to the terms of license before installation is an industry standard. This ensures that DotNetNuke components are no different.

Components Node

The components node contains a collection of individual components, each of which is assigned a type value and is used for a specific purpose. Components are used to complete installation procedures for all actions needed for modules, skins, providers, and more.

Following are common components:

❑ **Script component:** This type of component is used to hold individual SqlDataProvider scripts that need to be executed. As discussed previously in this chapter, SqlDataProvider files are individual scripts that, when executed, perform specific database actions. Script components contain a scripts XML node, with one or more child script nodes and a single basePath node. The basePath node sets the path to the folder containing the data scripts to execute.

The script nodes contain subnodes for name and version, and a type attribute that indicates whether the scripts are to be executed on installation or uninstall. Prior to DotNetNuke version 5.0 and this new manifest format, it was only possible for developers to include one uninstall and one install script for each version. This new component structure enables individuals to execute multiple scripts per version, and allows flexibility in file naming.

❑ **Files component:** This type of component is used to hold information on file placement for all files contained inside the package. The component tag contains a child `files` node that contains a `basepath` node and one or more `file` nodes that list each file. This system allows a separate base path to be supplied for the files component, different from what other components use. The format for the listing of files is similar to that of the `files` section of DNN 4.x module manifests.

❑ **Assembly component:** This component type is simply a modified component type that is used specifically to place assembly files. Rather than files and file nodes, the assembly component has assemblies and assembly nodes that list each individual filename. The explicit path of `bin` is specified to ensure proper placement. This process is a welcome change from the DNN 4.x manifests, which simply assumed that if a file ended in `.dll`, then it belonged inside the `bin` folder.

❑ **Cleanup component:** This component type is another modified version of the file component. However, rather than add files, it removes files. It contains a files listing. Each file will be removed upon installation of the proper version of the module. This component type is not illustrated in the Guestbook example.

❑ **Module component:** This component type is the component setup that actually defines a DotNetNuke module. The `desktopModule` node opens the component setup. The first three elements within specify general information about the module: the name, the folder name, and the `businessControllerClass` (which is discussed in detail in Chapter 10). The definition in this book's example lists each component that is included by default. Complete configuration of the module component for the Guestbook module is discussed in Chapter 8 when the user interface is defined.

> Additional component options (as well as full details on each) are discussed in Appendix D.

Summary

This chapter began with an overview of the DotNetNuke DAL, providing you with the specifics of how it functions and how custom modules integrate with it. After reviewing the DAL procedures, you learned about common DotNetNuke UI base classes as key integration points between DotNetNuke modules and the core DNN system. The chapter wrapped up with an examination of DotNetNuke installation packages.

With an understanding of these procedures and packages, you are ready to explore the specifics of DotNetNuke module development, which is explored in greater detail in Chapters 7 and 8. In those chapters, you will put the concepts you have learned into practice as you create the backend and frontend versions of the Guestbook module.

Chapter 7 introduces and builds the database backend portion of the module, working with the DotNetNuke DAL and `SqlDataProvider` files to create an easily accessible and installable module.

7

Creating the Module Back End

Now that you have learned about the components that create a DotNetNuke module and how the DotNetNuke DAL provides the needed development environment, it is time to tackle the creation of the module back end. This chapter starts out by defining the specific data access components that will be needed to facilitate the module's functionality. After providing this listing, you will create the DataProvider(.vb/.cs) and SqlDataProvider(.vb/.cs) files. You will then learn how to create the information objects that will be used to store the data while working inside the application. Specifically, you will create the Controller class, and this chapter concludes with you creating the .SqlDataProvider scripts needed to install the database components referenced by the module code.

By the end of this chapter, you will have created and properly configured the entire module back end to perform all needed data interactions.

Data Methods Needed

Chapter 4 outlined the data structure you use to create this module. It is now time to define the individual methods that are needed to facilitate the communication between the module and the database.

Table 7-1 lists each of the data methods that you must support to provide the desired functionality. The Return Type column shows the return value that will be passed from the DataProvider methods. Later in this chapter, when you create the Controller class, the IDataReader returns will be changed to more usable elements.

Table 7-1: Data Methods Needed

Method Name	Return Type	Purpose
InsertGuestbookEntry	None	Used to insert the user's guestbook entry into the system
ApproveGuestbookEntry	None	Used to approve a guestbook entry for display
DeleteGuestbookEntry	None	Used to delete a guestbook entry
GetApprovedEntries	IDataReader	Gets all approved entries that will be used to display to users of the application
GetAllEntries	IDataReader	Obtains all entries, and will be the data source for administrators

These methods create the backbone needed to support the module. By implementing these five data methods, you will have all the necessary support elements to enable the module to fully function for the users.

Now that you have seen the methods that are needed to support the module, it is time to use the information you learned about the DotNetNuke DAL in Chapter 6 to actually create the various supporting objects.

Creating the DataProvider(.cs/.vb) File

The first step in creating the data portion of the Guestbook module is to create the DataProvider abstract class. This class defines the contract that the SqlDataProvider must follow to provide the needed data elements to the front end of the application. Listing 7-1 shows the full C# version, and Listing 7-2 provides the full VB version of the DataProvider class that is needed. Use the code in the respective listings to replace the code that is included in the default DataProvider files.

Listing 7-1: C# DataProvider.cs File

```
using System;
using System.Data;
using DotNetNuke;
using DotNetNuke.Framework;

namespace WroxModules.GuestbookCS
{
    public abstract class DataProvider
    {
        #region common methods
        /// <summary>
        /// var that is returned in the this singleton
        /// pattern
```

```
        /// </summary>
        private static DataProvider instance = null;

        /// <summary>
        /// private static cstor that is used to init an
        /// instance of this class as a singleton
        /// </summary>
        static DataProvider()
        {
            instance = (DataProvider)Reflection.CreateObject("data",
                "WroxModules.GuestbookCS", "");
        }
        /// <summary>
        /// Exposes the singleton object used to access the database with
        /// the concrete dataprovider
        /// </summary>
        /// <returns></returns>
        public static DataProvider Instance()
        {
            return instance;
        }
        #endregion
        #region Abstract methods
        public abstract void InsertGuestbookEntry(int moduleId, string
            submitterName, string submitterWebsite, string submitterComment,
            DateTime submissionDate, bool isApproved);
        public abstract void ApproveGuestbookEntry(int moduleId, int entryId);
        public abstract void DeleteGuestbookEntry(int moduleId, int entryId);
        public abstract IDataReader GetApprovedEntries(int moduleId);
        public abstract IDataReader GetAllEntries(int moduleId);
        #endregion

    }
}
```

Listing 7-2: VB DataProvider.vb File

```
Imports System
Imports DotNetNuke

Namespace WroxModules.GuestbookVB

    ''' -----------------------------------------------------------------------------
    ''' <summary>
    ''' An abstract class for the data access layer
    ''' </summary>
    ''' <remarks>
    ''' </remarks>
    ''' <history>
    ''' </history>
    ''' -----------------------------------------------------------------------------
    Public MustInherit Class DataProvider

#Region "Shared/Static Methods"
```

(continued)

Listing 7-2 *(continued)*

```vb
        ' singleton reference to the instantiated object
        Private Shared objProvider As DataProvider = Nothing

        ' constructor
        Shared Sub New()
            CreateProvider()
        End Sub

        ' dynamically create provider
        Private Shared Sub CreateProvider()
            objProvider = CType(Framework.Reflection.CreateObject("data",
                "WroxModules.GuestbookVB", ""), DataProvider)
        End Sub

        ' return the provider
        Public Shared Shadows Function Instance() As DataProvider
            Return objProvider
        End Function

#End Region

#Region "Abstract methods"

        Public MustOverride Sub InsertGuestbookEntry(ByVal moduleId As Integer,
            ByVal submitterName As String, ByVal submitterWebsite As String, _
            ByVal submitterComment As String, ByVal submissionDate As DateTime,
            ByVal isApproved As Boolean)
        Public MustOverride Sub ApproveGuestbookEntry(ByVal moduleId As Integer,
            ByVal entryId As Integer)
        Public MustOverride Sub DeleteGuestbookEntry(ByVal moduleId As Integer,
            ByVal entryId As Integer)
        Public MustOverride Function GetApprovedEntries(ByVal moduleId As Integer)
            As IDataReader
        Public MustOverride Function GetAllEntries(ByVal moduleId As Integer)
            As IDataReader


#End Region

    End Class

End Namespace
```

These code listings show the three areas in the DataProvider file that are modified from the standard template layout:

- **Namespace definitions:** The namespace declaration has been modified to match the values specified in the project configuration that was completed in Chapter 5. Listing 7-3 and Listing 7-4 show, respectively, the C# code and the VB code illustrating the changes in namespace values, with the changed item indicated with a bold font.

❑ DataProvider **constructor:** The DataProvider constructor has been modified to reflect the use of the new assembly name that was specified for the respective projects in Chapter 5. Listing 7-5 (C#) and Listing 7-6 (VB) highlight the individual changes.

❑ **Abstract method definitions:** Lastly, the abstract data provider region code was replaced entirely by definitions that support the listed data actions in the beginning of this chapter. All definitions that were created by the template code have been removed from the code and are no longer needed.

Listing 7-3: C# Namespace Change

```
namespace WroxModules.GuestbookCS
```

Listing 7-4: VB Namespace Change

```
Namespace WroxModules.GuestbookVB
```

Listing 7-5: C# Constructor Change

```
static DataProvider()
        {
            instance = (DataProvider)Reflection.CreateObject("data",
                "WroxModules.GuestbookCS", "");
        }
```

Listing 7-6: VB Constructor Change

```
Private Shared Sub CreateProvider()
            objProvider = CType(Framework.Reflection.CreateObject("data",
                "WroxModules.GuestbookVB", ""), DataProvider)
        End Sub
```

Creating the SqlDataProvider (.cs/.vb) File

With the DataProvider class fully defined, it is now possible to define the SqlDataProvider class. As explained in Chapter 6, the SqlDataProvider class is the concrete implementation of the DataProvider, and handles the communication between the application and the database. This file defines the stored procedure names and passes the parameters from the application to the database for processing.

Listing 7-7 (C#) and Listing 7-8 (VB) provide the full text of the SqlDataProvider class. The auto-generated code can be fully replaced with the code in these listings. Elements appearing in bold indicate code that is different from the automatically generated code.

Listing 7-7: C# SqlDataProvider.cs File

```csharp
using System;
using System.Data;
using DotNetNuke.Framework.Providers;
using Microsoft.ApplicationBlocks.Data;

namespace WroxModules.GuestbookCS
{
    public class SqlDataProvider : DataProvider
    {
        #region vars

        private const string providerType = "data";
        private const string moduleQualifier = "DNNModuleProgramming_CS_";

        private ProviderConfiguration providerConfiguration =
            ProviderConfiguration.GetProviderConfiguration(providerType);
        private string connectionString;
        private string providerPath;
        private string objectQualifier;
        private string databaseOwner;

        #endregion

        #region cstor
        /// <summary>
        /// cstor used to create the sqlProvider with required parameters from
        /// the configuration
        /// section of web.config file
        /// </summary>
        public SqlDataProvider()
        {
            Provider provider =
                (Provider)providerConfiguration.Providers
                [providerConfiguration.DefaultProvider];
            connectionString =
                DotNetNuke.Common.Utilities.Config.GetConnectionString();

            if (connectionString == string.Empty)
                connectionString = provider.Attributes["connectionString"];

            providerPath = provider.Attributes["providerPath"];

            objectQualifier = provider.Attributes["objectQualifier"];
            if (objectQualifier != string.Empty &&
                !objectQualifier.EndsWith("_")) objectQualifier += "_";

            databaseOwner = provider.Attributes["databaseOwner"];
            if (databaseOwner != string.Empty && !databaseOwner.EndsWith("."))
                databaseOwner += ".";
        }
```

```
    #endregion

    #region properties
    public string ConnectionString
    {
        get { return connectionString; }
    }
    public string ProviderPath
    {
        get { return providerPath; }
    }
    public string ObjectQualifier
    {
        get { return objectQualifier; }
    }
    public string DatabaseOwner
    {
        get { return databaseOwner; }
    }
    #endregion

    #region private methods
    private string GetFullyQualifiedName(string name)
    {
        return DatabaseOwner + ObjectQualifier + moduleQualifier + name;
    }
    private object GetNull(object field)
    {
        return DotNetNuke.Common.Utilities.Null.GetNull(field, DBNull.Value);
    }
    #endregion

    #region override methods

    public override void InsertGuestbookEntry(int moduleId, string
        submitterName, string submitterWebsite, string submitterComment,
        DateTime submissionDate, bool isApproved)
    {
        SqlHelper.ExecuteNonQuery(connectionString,
            GetFullyQualifiedName("InsertGuestbookEntry"), moduleId,
            submitterName, submitterWebsite, submitterComment,
            submissionDate, isApproved);
    }

    public override void ApproveGuestbookEntry(int moduleId, int entryId)
    {
        SqlHelper.ExecuteNonQuery(connectionString,
            GetFullyQualifiedName("AproveGuestbookEntry"),
            moduleId, entryId);
    }

    public override void DeleteGuestbookEntry(int moduleId, int entryId)
    {
        SqlHelper.ExecuteNonQuery(connectionString,
            GetFullyQualifiedName("DeleteGuestbookEntry"),
```

(continued)

Listing 7-7 *(continued)*

```
            moduleId, entryId);
    }

    public override IDataReader GetApprovedEntries(int moduleId)
    {
        return (IDataReader)SqlHelper.ExecuteReader(connectionString,
            GetFullyQualifiedName("GetApprovedEntries"), moduleId);
    }

    public override IDataReader GetAllEntries(int moduleId)
    {
        return (IDataReader)SqlHelper.ExecuteReader(connectionString,
            GetFullyQualifiedName("GetAllEntries"), moduleId);
    }
    #endregion
    }
}
```

Listing 7-8: VB SqlDataProvider.vb File

```
Imports System
Imports System.Data
Imports System.Data.SqlClient
Imports Microsoft.ApplicationBlocks.Data

Imports DotNetNuke.Common.Utilities
Imports DotNetNuke.Framework.Providers

Namespace WroxModules.GuestbookVB

    ''' -------------------------------------------------------------------------
    ''' <summary>
    ''' SQL Server implementation of the abstract DataProvider class
    ''' </summary>
    ''' <remarks>
    ''' </remarks>
    ''' <history>
    ''' </history>
    ''' -------------------------------------------------------------------------
    Public Class SqlDataProvider

        Inherits DataProvider

#Region "Private Members"

        Private Const ProviderType As String = "data"
        Private Const ModuleQualifier As String = "DNNModuleProgramming_VB_"

        Private _providerConfiguration As ProviderConfiguration =
            ProviderConfiguration.GetProviderConfiguration(ProviderType)
        Private _connectionString As String
```

```vbnet
        Private _providerPath As String
        Private _objectQualifier As String
        Private _databaseOwner As String

#End Region

#Region "Constructors"

        Public Sub New()

            ' Read the configuration specific information for this provider
            Dim objProvider As Provider =
                CType(_providerConfiguration.Providers
                (_providerConfiguration.DefaultProvider),Provider)

            ' Read the attributes for this provider

            'Get Connection string from web.config
            _connectionString = Config.GetConnectionString()

            If _connectionString = "" Then
                ' Use connection string specified in provider
                _connectionString = objProvider.Attributes("connectionString")
            End If

            _providerPath = objProvider.Attributes("providerPath")

            _objectQualifier = objProvider.Attributes("objectQualifier")
            If _objectQualifier <> "" And _objectQualifier.EndsWith("_") = False
                Then
                _objectQualifier += "_"
            End If

            _databaseOwner = objProvider.Attributes("databaseOwner")
            If _databaseOwner <> "" And _databaseOwner.EndsWith(".") = False Then
                _databaseOwner += "."
            End If

        End Sub

#End Region

#Region "Properties"

        Public ReadOnly Property ConnectionString() As String
            Get
                Return _connectionString
            End Get
        End Property

        Public ReadOnly Property ProviderPath() As String
            Get
                Return _providerPath
            End Get
```

(continued)

Listing 7-8 *(continued)*

```
        End Property

        Public ReadOnly Property ObjectQualifier() As String
            Get
                Return _objectQualifier
            End Get
        End Property

        Public ReadOnly Property DatabaseOwner() As String
            Get
                Return _databaseOwner
            End Get
        End Property

#End Region

#Region "Private Methods"

        Private Function GetFullyQualifiedName(ByVal name As String) As String
            Return DatabaseOwner & ObjectQualifier & ModuleQualifier & name
        End Function

        Private Function GetNull(ByVal Field As Object) As Object
            Return DotNetNuke.Common.Utilities.Null.GetNull(Field, DBNull.Value)
        End Function

#End Region

#Region "Public Methods"

        Public Overrides Sub InsertGuestbookEntry(ByVal moduleId As Integer,
            ByVal submitterName As String, ByVal submitterWebsite As String,
            ByVal submitterComment As String, ByVal submissionDate As Date,
            ByVal isApproved As Boolean)
            SqlHelper.ExecuteNonQuery(ConnectionString,
                GetFullyQualifiedName("InsertGuestbookEntry"),
                moduleId, submitterName, submitterWebsite, submitterComment,
                submissionDate, isApproved)
        End Sub

        Public Overrides Sub ApproveGuestbookEntry(ByVal moduleId As Integer,
            ByValentryId As Integer)
            SqlHelper.ExecuteNonQuery(ConnectionString,
                GetFullyQualifiedName("ApproveGuestbookEntry"), moduleId, entryId)
        End Sub

        Public Overrides Sub DeleteGuestbookEntry(ByVal moduleId As Integer,
            ByVal entryId As Integer)
            SqlHelper.ExecuteNonQuery(ConnectionString,
                GetFullyQualifiedName("DeleteGuestbookEntry"), moduleId, entryId)
```

```
        End Sub

        Public Overrides Function GetApprovedEntries(ByVal moduleId As Integer)
                As System.Data.IDataReader
            Return CType(SqlHelper.ExecuteReader(ConnectionString,
                GetFullyQualifiedName("GetApprovedEntries"), moduleId),
                IDataReader)
        End Function

        Public Overrides Function GetAllEntries(ByVal moduleId As Integer) As
                System.Data.IDataReader
            Return CType(SqlHelper.ExecuteReader(ConnectionString,
                GetFullyQualifiedName("GetAllEntries"), moduleId),
                IDataReader)
        End Function
#End Region

    End Class

End Namespace
```

As you can see in the code examples for this file, three distinct elements are modified from the default configuration of the module:

❑   **Namespace definitions:** The namespace declaration has been modified to match the values specified in the project configuration that was completed in Chapter 5. This is a key element, and this change will occur throughout the project to ensure that all pages have the proper namespace references.

❑   **Module qualifier:** The static string value for the `ModuleQualifier` has been changed. This qualifier is appended to *all* database objects used by the module. This enables you to create tables with common names, in a manner that allows you to be confident that you will not conflict with other users. In these examples, the qualifier is `DNNModuleProgramming_VB_` for the VB module, and `DNNModuleProgramming_CS_` for the C# module. This enables you to develop and test both modules on the same DotNetNuke installation.

❑   **Override method definitions:** The override methods section has been updated to include definitions for each of the abstract methods. Each method has been created following the roles outlined in the DAL overview provided in Chapter 6. All existing override methods from the templates were removed because they are no longer valid.

Creating the Information Object Class

Inside a DotNetNuke module, it is very common to take the data from the database, load it into an information object, and use these objects (or collections of objects) to actually facilitate the data-binding actions that typically occur on the front end of an application. The DotNetNuke framework provides a number of helpful classes for the process of actually populating an information object with data. Before you can populate the object, you must define an information object that mimics the database table with which you are working.

When creating the information object class, it is important that each column be represented as a public method that supports both get and set operations, and that it has the exact same name as the column. Later in this book, you will learn about a few alternatives to this limitation.

To meet the needs of the Guestbook module, you must replace the code inside GuestbookCSInfo.cs or GuestbookVBInfo.vb with a class definition that provides storage and access for all data elements. Listing 7-9 (C#) and Listing 7-10 (VB) show this information object.

Listing 7-9: C# GuestbookCSInfo.cs Class

```csharp
using System;
using DotNetNuke.Entities.Portals;
using DotNetNuke.Entities.Users;

namespace WroxModules.GuestbookCS
{
    ///<summary>
    /// This information object holds the information on a single
    /// guestbook entry
    ///</summary>
    public class GuestbookEntryInfo
    {
        #region Private Data Members
        private int _entryId;
        private int _moduleId;
        private string _submitterName;
        private string _submitterWebsite;
        private string _submitterComment;
        private DateTime _submissionDate;
        private bool _isApproved;
        #endregion

        #region Public Constructors
        ///<summary>
        /// Default code constructor
        ///</summary>
        public GuestbookEntryInfo()
        {
            //Initalize any needed values

        }
        #endregion

        #region Public Properties
        /// <summary>
          /// The unique identifier for an entry
          /// </summary>
        public int EntryId
        {
            get { return _entryId; }
            set { _entryId = value; }
        }
        /// <summary>
```

```csharp
        /// The id of the module in which it is located
        /// </summary>
        public int ModuleId
        {
            get { return _moduleId; }
            set { _moduleId = value; }
        }
        /// <summary>
        /// The name of the submitter, as entered via the website
        /// </summary>
        public string SubmitterName
        {
            get { return _submitterName; }
            set { _submitterName = value; }
        }
        /// <summary>
        /// The website of the submitter, as entered via the website
        /// </summary>
        public string SubmitterWebsite
        {
            get { return _submitterWebsite; }
            set { _submitterWebsite = value; }
        }
        /// <summary>
        /// The submitter comments as entered via the website
        /// </summary>
        public string SubmitterComment
        {
            get { return _submitterComment; }
            set { _submitterComment = value; }
        }
        /// <summary>
        /// The date submitted
        /// </summary>
        public DateTime SubmissionDate
        {
            get { return _submissionDate; }
            set { _submissionDate = value; }
        }
        /// <summary>
        /// Is this entry approved?
        /// </summary>
        public bool IsApproved
        {
            get { return _isApproved; }
            set { _isApproved = value; }
        }
        #endregion
    }
}
```

Listing 7-10: VB GuestbookVBInfo.vb Class

```vb
Imports System
Imports System.Configuration
Imports System.Data

Namespace WroxModules.GuestbookVB

    ''' -------------------------------------------------------------------------
    ''' <summary>
    ''' The Info class for GuestbookVB
    ''' </summary>
    ''' <remarks>
    ''' </remarks>
    ''' <history>
    ''' </history>
    ''' -------------------------------------------------------------------------
    Public Class GuestbookEntryInfo

#Region "Private Members"
        Private _entryId As Integer
        Private _moduleId As Integer
        Private _submitterName As String
        Private _submitterWebsite As String
        Private _submitterComment As String
        Private _submissionDate As DateTime
        Private _isApproved As Boolean
#End Region
#Region "Constructor"
        ' initialization
        Public Sub New()
        End Sub
#End Region
#Region "Public Properties"
        Public Property Entryid() As Integer
            Get
                Return _entryId
            End Get
            Set(ByVal value As Integer)
                _entryId = value
            End Set
        End Property
        Public Property ModuleId() As Integer
            Get
                Return _moduleId
            End Get
            Set(ByVal value As Integer)
                _moduleId = value
            End Set
        End Property
        Public Property SubmitterName() As String
            Get
                Return _submitterName
            End Get
```

```
            Set(ByVal value As String)
                _submitterName = value
            End Set
        End Property
        Public Property SubmitterWebsite() As String
            Get
                Return _submitterWebsite
            End Get
            Set(ByVal value As String)
                _submitterWebsite = value
            End Set
        End Property
        Public Property SubmitterComment() As String
            Get
                Return _submitterComment
            End Get
            Set(ByVal value As String)
                _submitterComment = value
            End Set
        End Property
        Public Property SubmissionDate() As DateTime
            Get
                Return _submissionDate
            End Get
            Set(ByVal value As DateTime)
                _submissionDate = value
            End Set
        End Property
        Public Property IsApproved() As Boolean
            Get
                Return _isApproved
            End Get
            Set(ByVal value As Boolean)
                _isApproved = value
            End Set
        End Property
    #End Region
        End Class

    End Namespace
```

The information object classes contained inside these definitions contain nothing specific to DotNetNuke.

Creating the Controller Class

With the underlying code created to facilitate the data access, the final step from a .NET code perspective is to create the Controller class. Following the standard process with DotNetNuke module development, the Controller class serves as a middle tier in an application, providing access to the underlying data methods, and converting the IDataReaders returned into workable objects and object lists that can be use by the module in question.

Listing 7-11 (C#) and Listing 7-12 (VB) provide the full code for the `Controller` class definition. These code listings are vastly different from the code existing in the template, and should be used to replace that code.

Listing 7-11: C# GuestbookCSController.cs

```
using System;
using System.Collections.Generic;
using System.Text;
using System.Xml;
using DotNetNuke;
using DotNetNuke.Common.Utilities;
using DotNetNuke.Entities.Modules;
using DotNetNuke.Services.Search;

namespace WroxModules.GuestbookCS
{
    public class GuestbookCSController
    {
        #region Public Methods
        /// <summary>
        /// This method will insert a guestbook entry to the system
        /// </summary>
        /// <param name="oInfo">The hydrated information object</param>
        public void InsertGuestbookEntry(GuestbookEntryInfo oInfo)
        {
            DataProvider.Instance().InsertGuestbookEntry(oInfo.ModuleId,
                oInfo.SubmitterName, oInfo.SubmitterWebsite,
                oInfo.SubmitterComment,
oInfo.SubmissionDate, oInfo.IsApproved);
        }
        /// <summary>
        /// This method will approve a guestbook entry
        /// </summary>
        /// <param name="moduleId">The id of the module used to modify the
            entries</param>
        /// <param name="entryId">The id of the entry</param>
        public void ApproveGuestbookEntry(int moduleId, int entryId)
        {
            DataProvider.Instance().ApproveGuestbookEntry(moduleId, entryId);
        }
        /// <summary>
        /// This method will delete a guestbook entry
        /// </summary>
        /// <param name="moduleId">The id of the module used to delete the
            entries</param>
        /// <param name="entryId">The id of the entry</param>
        public void DeleteGuestbookEntry(int moduleId, int entryId)
        {
            DataProvider.Instance().DeleteGuestbookEntry(moduleId, entryId);
        }
        /// <summary>
        /// This method will get the listing of all approved entries
        /// </summary>
```

```
/// <param name="moduleId">The instance to get entries for</param>
/// <returns>The hydrated collection of information objects</returns>
public List<GuestbookEntryInfo> GetApprovedEntries(int moduleId)
{
    Return
        CBO.FillCollection<GuestbookEntryInfo>
        (DataProvider.Instance().GetApprovedEntries
        (moduleId));
}
/// <summary>
/// This method will get the listing of all entries
/// </summary>
/// <param name="moduleId">The instance to get entries for</param>
/// <returns>The hydrated collection of information objects</returns>
public List<GuestbookEntryInfo> GetAllEntries(int moduleId)
{
    return
        CBO.FillCollection<GuestbookEntryInfo>
        (DataProvider.Instance().GetAllEntries
        (moduleId));
}
#endregion
    }
}
```

Listing 7-12: VB GuestbookVBController.cs

```vb
Imports System
Imports System.Configuration
Imports System.Data
Imports System.XML
Imports System.Web
Imports System.Collections.Generic

Imports DotNetNuke
Imports DotNetNuke.Common
Imports DotNetNuke.Common.Utilities.XmlUtils
Imports DotNetNuke.Common.Utilities
Imports DotNetNuke.Services.Search

Namespace WroxModules.GuestbookVB

    ''' -------------------------------------------------------------------------
    ''' <summary>
    ''' The Controller class for GuestbookVB
    ''' </summary>
    ''' <remarks>
    ''' </remarks>
    ''' <history>
    ''' </history>
    ''' -------------------------------------------------------------------------
    Public Class GuestbookVBController
```

(continued)

Listing 7-12 *(continued)*

```vb
#Region "Public Methods"
        ''' <summary>
        ''' This method will insert a guestbook entry
        ''' </summary>
        ''' <param name="oInfo">The fully hydrated information object</param>
        ''' <remarks></remarks>
        Public Sub InsertGuestbookEntry(ByVal oInfo As GuestbookEntryInfo)
            DataProvider.Instance().InsertGuestbookEntry(oInfo.ModuleId,
                oInfo.SubmitterName, oInfo.SubmitterWebsite,
                oInfo.SubmitterComment, oInfo.SubmissionDate,
                oInfo.IsApproved)
        End Sub
        ''' <summary>
        ''' This method will approve a guestbook entry
        ''' </summary>
        ''' <param name="moduleId">The id of the module</param>
        ''' <param name="entryId">The id of the entry</param>
        ''' <remarks></remarks>
        Public Sub ApproveGuestbookEntry(ByVal moduleId As Integer,
            ByVal entryId As Integer)
            DataProvider.Instance().ApproveGuestbookEntry(moduleId, entryId)
        End Sub
        ''' <summary>
        ''' This method will delete a guestbook entry
        ''' </summary>
        ''' <param name="moduleId">The id of the module</param>
        ''' <param name="entryId">The id fo the entry</param>
        ''' <remarks></remarks>
        Public Sub DeleteGuestbookEntry(ByVal moduleId As Integer,
            ByVal entryId As Integer)
            DataProvider.Instance().DeleteGuestbookEntry(moduleId, entryId)
        End Sub
        ''' <summary>
        ''' This method will get all approved entries
        ''' </summary>
        ''' <param name="moduleId">The module id to look for</param>
        ''' <returns>The hydrated collection of entries</returns>
        ''' <remarks></remarks>
        Public Function GetApprovedEntries(ByVal moduleId As Integer)
            As List(Of GuestbookEntryInfo)
            Return CBO.FillCollection(Of GuestbookEntryInfo)
                (DataProvider.Instance().GetApprovedEntries(moduleId))
        End Function
        ''' <summary>
        ''' THis method will get all entries
        ''' </summary>
        ''' <param name="moduleId">The module id to look for</param>
        ''' <returns>The hydrated collection of entries</returns>
        ''' <remarks></remarks>
```

```
        Public Function GetAllEntries(ByVal moduleId As Integer)
            As List(Of GuestbookEntryInfo)
            Return CBO.FillCollection(Of GuestbookEntryInfo)
                (DataProvider.Instance().GetAllEntries(moduleId))
        End Function
#End Region


    End Class
End Namespace
```

Note the use of generic collections here to return the listing of guestbook entries to the presentation tier. This process of converting the data readers to a list of objects is added by the Common Business Object (CBO) object provided by the DotNetNuke framework. CBO includes various hydration methods for loading single objects and collections of objects. DNN 4.x provides support for generics in the return, allowing for the strongly typed returns as indicated in the code samples provided previously.

This process is very simple and in most cases it works very well. However, it is important to note that CBO accomplishes its goal by using reflection to determine the properties of the targeted data object. In Chapter 10, you will learn about the IHydratable interface, which allows for the use of CBO, without the performance penalty of using reflection.

Creating the 01.00.00.SqlDataProvider Script

With the .NET portion of the data code complete, there is only one last file to prepare — the .SqlDataProvider script that will actually create and install the database objects that support the Guestbook module. Chapter 6 introduced the different techniques needed to actually create tables, as well as stored procedures.

Listing 7-13 (C#) and Listing 7-14 (VB) show the scripts needed to create the database structure for the module. The examples in this book incorporate a naming convention for all database objects that enables both the C# and VB.NET versions of the module to be installed on the same DotNetNuke installation. If you are working with a specific language, you should remove the language identifier from object names.

Listing 7-13: 01.00.00.SqlDataProvider for a C# Project

```
/**********************************************************/
/*****                 SqlDataProvider              *****/
/*****                                              *****/
/*****                                              *****/
/***** Note: To manually execute this script you must  *****/
/*****       perform a search and replace operation    *****/
/*****       for {databaseOwner} and {objectQualifier} *****/
/*****                                              *****/
/**********************************************************/

/** Create Table **/
```

(continued)

Listing 7-13 *(continued)*

```
if not exists (select * from dbo.sysobjects where id =
        object_id(N'{databaseOwner}[{objectQualifier}
        DNNModuleProgramming_CS_Guestbook]')
        and OBJECTPROPERTY(id, N'IsTable') = 1)
    BEGIN
        CREATE TABLE {databaseOwner}
            [{objectQualifier}DNNModuleProgramming_CS_Guestbook]
        (
            [ModuleId] [int] NOT NULL,
            [EntryId] [int] NOT NULL IDENTITY(1, 1),
            [SubmitterName] nvarchar(255) NOT NULL,
            [SubmitterWebsite] nvarchar(255),
            [SubmitterComment] ntext,
            [SubmissionDate] DateTime NOT NULL,
            [IsApproved] BIT NOT NULL
        )

        ALTER TABLE {databaseOwner}
            [{objectQualifier}DNNModuleProgramming_CS_Guestbook]
            ADD CONSTRAINT [PK_{objectQualifier}
            DNNModuleProgramming_CS_Guestbook]
                PRIMARY KEY CLUSTERED  ([EntryId])
        CREATE NONCLUSTERED INDEX
            [IX_{objectQualifier}
            DNNModuleProgramming_CS_Guestbook]
            ON {databaseOwner}
                [{objectQualifier}DNNModuleProgramming_CS_Guestbook]
                ([ModuleID])

        ALTER TABLE {databaseOwner}
            [{objectQualifier}DNNModuleProgramming_CS_Guestbook]
                WITH NOCHECK
            ADD CONSTRAINT [FK_{objectQualifier}
                DNNModuleProgramming_CS_Guestbook_{objectQualifier}
                Modules]
                FOREIGN KEY ([ModuleID])
                    REFERENCES {databaseOwner}[{objectQualifier}Modules]
                        ([ModuleID]) ON DELETE CASCADE NOT FOR REPLICATION
    END
GO


/** Drop Existing Stored Procedures **/

if exists (select * from dbo.sysobjects where id =
        object_id(N'{databaseOwner}
        [{objectQualifier}DNNModuleProgramming_CS_InsertGuestbookEntry]')
        and OBJECTPROPERTY(id, N'IsProcedure') = 1)
    drop procedure {databaseOwner}
        [{objectQualifier}DNNModuleProgramming_CS_InsertGuestbookEntry]
GO
if exists (select * from dbo.sysobjects where id =
```

```
                  object_id(N'{databaseOwner}
                  [{objectQualifier}DNNModuleProgramming_CS_ApproveGuestbo
                  okEntry]') and OBJECTPROPERTY(id, N'IsProcedure') = 1)
            drop procedure
                  {databaseOwner}[{objectQualifier}
                  DNNModuleProgramming_CS_ApproveGuestbookEntry]
GO
if exists (select * from dbo.sysobjects where id =
            object_id(N'{databaseOwner}[{objectQualifier}
            DNNModuleProgramming_CS_DeleteGuestbookEntry]')
            and OBJECTPROPERTY(id, N'IsProcedure') = 1)
            drop procedure
                  {databaseOwner}[{objectQualifier}
                  DNNModuleProgramming_CS_DeleteGuestbookEntry]
GO
if exists (select * from dbo.sysobjects where id =
            object_id(N'{databaseOwner}[{objectQualifier}
            DNNModuleProgramming_CS_GetApprovedEntries]')
            and OBJECTPROPERTY(id, N'IsProcedure') = 1)
            drop procedure
                  {databaseOwner}[{objectQualifier}
                  DNNModuleProgramming_CS_GetApprovedEntries]
GO
if exists (select * from dbo.sysobjects where id =
            object_id(N'{databaseOwner}[{objectQualifier}
            DNNModuleProgramming_CS_GetAllEntries]')
            and OBJECTPROPERTY(id, N'IsProcedure') = 1)
            drop procedure
                  {databaseOwner}[{objectQualifier}
                  DNNModuleProgramming_CS_GetAllEntries]
GO


/** Create Stored Procedures **/
CREATE PROCEDURE
            {databaseOwner}
            [{objectQualifier}DNNModuleProgramming_CS_InsertGuestbookEntry]
      @ModuleId INT,
      @SubmitterName NVARCHAR(255),
      @SubmitterWebsite NVARCHAR(255),
      @SubmitterComment NTEXT,
      @SubmissionDate DATETIME,
      @IsApproved BIT
AS
INSERT INTO {databaseOwner}[{objectQualifier}DNNModuleProgramming_CS_Guestbook]
      (ModuleId, SubmitterName, SubmitterWebsite, SubmitterComment,
            SubmissionDate, IsApproved)
      VALUES
      (@ModuleId, @SubmitterName, @SubmitterWebsite, @SubmitterComment,
            @SubmissionDate, @IsApproved)

GO

CREATE PROCEDURE
            {databaseOwner}[{objectQualifier}
```

(continued)

Listing 7-13 *(continued)*

```
      DNNModuleProgramming_CS_ApproveGuestbookEntry]
    @ModuleId INT,
    @EntryId INT
AS
UPDATE {databaseOwner}[{objectQualifier}DNNModuleProgramming_CS_Guestbook]
SET IsApproved = 1
WHERE ModuleId = @ModuleId
    AND EntryId = @EntryId

GO

CREATE PROCEDURE
      {databaseOwner}[{objectQualifier}
      DNNModuleProgramming_CS_DeleteGuestbookEntry]
    @ModuleId INT,
    @EntryId INT
AS
DELETE FROM {databaseOwner}[{objectQualifier}
         DNNModuleProgramming_CS_Guestbook]
WHERE ModuleId = @ModuleId
    AND EntryId = @EntryId

GO

CREATE PROCEDURE
      {databaseOwner}[{objectQualifier}
      DNNModuleProgramming_CS_GetApprovedEntries]
    @ModuleId INT
AS
SELECT
    ModuleId,
    EntryId,
    SubmitterName,
    SubmitterWebsite,
    SubmitterComment,
    SubmissionDate,
    IsApproved
FROM {databaseOwner}[{objectQualifier}DNNModuleProgramming_CS_Guestbook]
WHERE ModuleId = @ModuleId
    AND IsApproved = 1
ORDER BY SubmissionDate DESC

GO

CREATE PROCEDURE
      {databaseOwner}[{objectQualifier}
      DNNModuleProgramming_CS_GetAllEntries]
    @ModuleId INT
```

```
AS
SELECT
     ModuleId,
     EntryId,
     SubmitterName,
     SubmitterWebsite,
     SubmitterComment,
     SubmissionDate,
     IsApproved
FROM {databaseOwner}[{objectQualifier}DNNModuleProgramming_CS_Guestbook]
WHERE ModuleId = @ModuleId
ORDER BY SubmissionDate DESC

GO


/****************************************************************/
/*****              SqlDataProvider                    *****/
/****************************************************************/
```

Listing 7-14: 01.00.00.SqlDataProvider for a VB.NET Project

```
/****************************************************************/
/*****              SqlDataProvider                    *****/
/*****                                                 *****/
/*****                                                 *****/
/***** Note: To manually execute this script you must  *****/
/*****       perform a search and replace operation    *****/
/*****       for {databaseOwner} and {objectQualifier} *****/
/*****                                                 *****/
/****************************************************************/


/** Create Table **/

if not exists (select * from dbo.sysobjects where id = object_id
        (N'{databaseOwner}[{objectQualifier}
        DNNModuleProgramming_VB_Guestbook]') and
        OBJECTPROPERTY(id, N'IsTable') = 1)
    BEGIN
        CREATE TABLE
            {databaseOwner}
            [{objectQualifier}DNNModuleProgramming_VB_Guestbook]
        (
            [ModuleId] [int] NOT NULL,
            [EntryId] [int] NOT NULL IDENTITY(1, 1),
            [SubmitterName] nvarchar(255) NOT NULL,
            [SubmitterWebsite] nvarchar(255),
            [SubmitterComment] ntext,
            [SubmissionDate] DateTime NOT NULL,
            [IsApproved] BIT NOT NULL
        )

        ALTER TABLE
          {databaseOwner}
```

(continued)

Listing 7-14 *(continued)*

```
                [{objectQualifier}DNNModuleProgramming_VB_Guestbook]
                    ADD CONSTRAINT [PK_{objectQualifier}
                        DNNModuleProgramming_VB_Guestbook]
                            PRIMARY KEY CLUSTERED  ([EntryId])
            CREATE NONCLUSTERED INDEX
                        [IX_{objectQualifier}DNNModuleProgramming_VB_Guestbook]
                    ON {databaseOwner}
                        [{objectQualifier}DNNModuleProgramming_VB_Guestbook]
                        ([ModuleID])

            ALTER TABLE
                {databaseOwner}
                [{objectQualifier}DNNModuleProgramming_VB_Guestbook]
                WITH NOCHECK
                    ADD CONSTRAINT
                            [FK_{objectQualifier}
                            DNNModuleProgramming_VB_Guestbook_{objectQualifier}
                            Modules]
                        FOREIGN KEY ([ModuleID])
                            REFERENCES {databaseOwner}[{objectQualifier}Modules]
                                ([ModuleID]) ON DELETE CASCADE NOT FOR REPLICATION
        END
GO


/** Drop Existing Stored Procedures **/

if exists (select * from dbo.sysobjects where id =
            object_id(N'{databaseOwner}
            [{objectQualifier}DNNModuleProgramming_VB_InsertGuestbookEntry]')
            and OBJECTPROPERTY(id, N'IsProcedure') = 1)
        drop procedure
            {databaseOwner}
            [{objectQualifier}DNNModuleProgramming_VB_InsertGuestbookEntry]
GO
if exists (select * from dbo.sysobjects where id =
            object_id(N'{databaseOwner}
            [{objectQualifier}DNNModuleProgramming_VB_ApproveGuestbookEntry]')
            and OBJECTPROPERTY(id, N'IsProcedure') = 1)
        drop procedure
            {databaseOwner}
            [{objectQualifier}DNNModuleProgramming_VB_ApproveGuestbookEntry]
GO
if exists (select * from dbo.sysobjects where id =
            object_id(N'{databaseOwner}
            [{objectQualifier}DNNModuleProgramming_VB_DeleteGuestbookEntry]')
            and OBJECTPROPERTY(id, N'IsProcedure') = 1)
        drop procedure
            {databaseOwner}
            [{objectQualifier}DNNModuleProgramming_VB_DeleteGuestbookEntry]
```

```
GO
if exists (select * from dbo.sysobjects where id =
        object_id(N'{databaseOwner}
        [{objectQualifier}DNNModuleProgramming_VB_GetApprovedEntries]')
        and OBJECTPROPERTY(id, N'IsProcedure') = 1)
    drop procedure
        {databaseOwner}
        [{objectQualifier}DNNModuleProgramming_VB_GetApprovedEntries]
GO
if exists (select * from dbo.sysobjects where id =
        object_id(N'{databaseOwner}[{objectQualifier}
        DNNModuleProgramming_VB_GetAllEntries]')
        and OBJECTPROPERTY(id, N'IsProcedure') = 1)
    drop procedure
        {databaseOwner}[{objectQualifier}DNNModuleProgramming_VB_GetAllEntries]
GO


/** Create Stored Procedures **/
CREATE PROCEDURE
        {databaseOwner}
        [{objectQualifier}DNNModuleProgramming_VB_InsertGuestbookEntry]
    @ModuleId INT,
    @SubmitterName NVARCHAR(255),
    @SubmitterWebsite NVARCHAR(255),
    @SubmitterComment NTEXT,
    @SubmissionDate DATETIME,
    @IsApproved BIT
AS
INSERT INTO {databaseOwner}[{objectQualifier}DNNModuleProgramming_VB_Guestbook]
    (ModuleId, SubmitterName, SubmitterWebsite, SubmitterComment,
        SubmissionDate, IsApproved)
    VALUES
    (@ModuleId, @SubmitterName, @SubmitterWebsite, @SubmitterComment,
        @SubmissionDate, @IsApproved)

GO

CREATE PROCEDURE
        {databaseOwner}[{objectQualifier}
        DNNModuleProgramming_VB_ApproveGuestbookEntry]
    @ModuleId INT,
    @EntryId INT
AS
UPDATE {databaseOwner}[{objectQualifier}DNNModuleProgramming_VB_Guestbook]
SET IsApproved = 1
WHERE ModuleId = @ModuleId
    AND EntryId = @EntryId

GO

CREATE PROCEDURE
        {databaseOwner}[{objectQualifier}
        DNNModuleProgramming_VB_DeleteGuestbookEntry]
```

(continued)

Listing 7-14 *(continued)*

```
        @ModuleId INT,
        @EntryId INT
AS
DELETE FROM {databaseOwner}[{objectQualifier}DNNModuleProgramming_VB_Guestbook]
WHERE ModuleId = @ModuleId
        AND EntryId = @EntryId

GO

CREATE PROCEDURE
        {databaseOwner}[{objectQualifier}
        DNNModuleProgramming_VB_GetApprovedEntries]
        @ModuleId INT
AS
SELECT
        ModuleId,
        EntryId,
        SubmitterName,
        SubmitterWebsite,
        SubmitterComment,
        SubmissionDate,
        IsApproved
FROM {databaseOwner}[{objectQualifier}DNNModuleProgramming_VB_Guestbook]
WHERE ModuleId = @ModuleId
        AND IsApproved = 1
ORDER BY SubmissionDate DESC

GO

CREATE PROCEDURE
        {databaseOwner}[{objectQualifier}DNNModuleProgramming_VB_GetAllEntries]
        @ModuleId INT
AS
SELECT
        ModuleId,
        EntryId,
        SubmitterName,
        SubmitterWebsite,
        SubmitterComment,
        SubmissionDate,
        IsApproved
FROM {databaseOwner}[{objectQualifier}DNNModuleProgramming_VB_Guestbook]
WHERE ModuleId = @ModuleId
ORDER BY SubmissionDate DESC

GO

/************************************************************/
/*****                  SqlDataProvider              *****/
/************************************************************/
```

The code provided here is a direct replacement for the template code. In each of the examples, scripts are used to first create the needed database table, with a foreign key that ties the entries to the modules. This ensures that if the module is uninstalled from the system, then all remnants of the data are cleaned up. When tying into the core DotNetNuke tables in this manner, you should use the ON DELETE CASCADE command to ensure that you do not break existing DotNetNuke functionality.

After installing the table, scripts are executed to remove the stored procedures, should they happen to exist in the database already. Lastly, the script creates all needed stored procedures that actually process the information. The methods and items created through this process mirror the logic created in previous steps of this process.

For this file, the only difference between the C# and VB versions are the qualifiers appended to each of the object names. There is no syntax difference between languages when it comes to these files.

Creating the Uninstall.SqlDataProvider File

From a data perspective, you must take one last action to ensure that when modules are uninstalled by the site administrator, they are removed. This step is to create an uninstall.sqldataprovider file. This file simply includes SQL statements, with the same syntax as the xx.xx.xx.sqldataprovider files that will remove all created objects from the database.

Listing 7-15 (C#) and Listing 7-16 (VB) show the code for the uninstall files. Because these files are used when an individual is requesting to remove the module, it is very important that these scripts accurately remove the data objects. This includes following any needed order to remove constraints, indexes, and/ or stored procedures.

Listing 7-15: C# Uninstall.SqlDataProvider File

```
/**************************************************************/
/*****               SqlDataProvider                  *****/
/*****                                                *****/
/*****                                                *****/
/***** Note: To manually execute this script you must *****/
/*****       perform a search and replace operation   *****/
/*****       for {databaseOwner} and {objectQualifier} *****/
/*****                                                *****/
/**************************************************************/

/** Drop Table Items **/

ALTER TABLE {databaseOwner}[{objectQualifier}DNNModuleProgramming_CS_Guestbook]
    WITH NOCHECK
      DROP CONSTRAINT
          [FK_{objectQualifier}DNNModuleProgramming_CS_Guestbook_
          {objectQualifier}Modules]
GO

ALTER TABLE {databaseOwner}[{objectQualifier}DNNModuleProgramming_CS_Guestbook]
    DROP CONSTRAINT [PK_{objectQualifier}DNNModuleProgramming_CS_Guestbook]
```

(continued)

Listing 7-15 *(continued)*

```sql
GO

DROP INDEX
 {databaseOwner}
        [{objectQualifier}DNNModuleProgramming_CS_Guestbook].[IX_{objectQualifier}
        DNNModuleProgramming_CS_Guestbook]
GO

DROP TABLE {databaseOwner}[{objectQualifier}DNNModuleProgramming_CS_Guestbook]
GO

/** Drop Stored Procedures **/

if exists (select * from dbo.sysobjects where id =
    object_id(N'{databaseOwner}[{objectQualifier}
    DNNModuleProgramming_CS_InsertGuestbookEntry]')
    and OBJECTPROPERTY(id, N'IsProcedure') = 1)
      drop procedure
          {databaseOwner}
          [{objectQualifier}DNNModuleProgramming_CS_InsertGuestbookEntry]
GO
if exists (select * from dbo.sysobjects where id =
    object_id(N'{databaseOwner}
    [{objectQualifier}DNNModuleProgramming_CS_ApproveGuestbookEntry]')
    and OBJECTPROPERTY(id, N'IsProcedure') = 1)
      drop procedure
          {databaseOwner}
          [{objectQualifier}DNNModuleProgramming_CS_ApproveGuestbookEntry]
GO
if exists (select * from dbo.sysobjects where id =
    object_id(N'{databaseOwner}
    [{objectQualifier}DNNModuleProgramming_CS_DeleteGuestbookEntry]')
    and OBJECTPROPERTY(id, N'IsProcedure') = 1)
      drop procedure
          {databaseOwner}
          [{objectQualifier}DNNModuleProgramming_CS_DeleteGuestbookEntry]
GO
if exists (select * from dbo.sysobjects where id =
    object_id(N'{databaseOwner}
    [{objectQualifier}DNNModuleProgramming_CS_GetApprovedEntries]')
    and OBJECTPROPERTY(id, N'IsProcedure') = 1)
      drop procedure
          {databaseOwner}
          [{objectQualifier}DNNModuleProgramming_CS_GetApprovedEntries]
GO
if exists (select * from dbo.sysobjects where id =
    object_id(N'{databaseOwner}
    [{objectQualifier}DNNModuleProgramming_CS_GetAllEntries]')
    and OBJECTPROPERTY(id, N'IsProcedure') = 1)
```

```
          drop procedure
                {databaseOwner}
                [{objectQualifier}DNNModuleProgramming_CS_GetAllEntries]
GO


/*************************************************************/
/*****              SqlDataProvider              *****/
/*************************************************************/
```

Listing 7-16: VB Uninstall.SqlDataProvider File

```
/*************************************************************/
/*****              SqlDataProvider              *****/
/*****                                           *****/
/*****                                           *****/
/***** Note: To manually execute this script you must    *****/
/*****        perform a search and replace operation    *****/
/*****        for {databaseOwner} and {objectQualifier}  *****/
/*****                                           *****/
/*************************************************************/


/** Drop Table Items **/

ALTER TABLE {databaseOwner}[{objectQualifier}DNNModuleProgramming_VB_Guestbook]
    WITH NOCHECK
        DROP CONSTRAINT
            [FK_{objectQualifier}
            DNNModuleProgramming_VB_Guestbook_{objectQualifier}Modules]
GO

ALTER TABLE {databaseOwner}[{objectQualifier}DNNModuleProgramming_VB_Guestbook]
    DROP CONSTRAINT [PK_{objectQualifier}DNNModuleProgramming_VB_Guestbook]
GO

DROP INDEX
    {databaseOwner}
    [{objectQualifier}DNNModuleProgramming_VB_Guestbook].[IX_{objectQualifier}
    DNNModuleProgramming_VB_Guestbook]
GO

DROP TABLE {databaseOwner}[{objectQualifier}DNNModuleProgramming_VB_Guestbook]
GO

/** Drop Stored Procedures **/

if exists (select * from dbo.sysobjects where id =
    object_id(N'{databaseOwner}
    [{objectQualifier}DNNModuleProgramming_VB_InsertGuestbookEntry]')
    and OBJECTPROPERTY(id, N'IsProcedure') = 1)
        drop procedure
            {databaseOwner}
            [{objectQualifier}DNNModuleProgramming_VB_InsertGuestbookEntry]
```

(continued)

Listing 7-16 *(continued)*

```
GO
if exists (select * from dbo.sysobjects where id =
    object_id(N'{databaseOwner}
    [{objectQualifier}DNNModuleProgramming_VB_ApproveGuestbookEntry]')
    and OBJECTPROPERTY(id, N'IsProcedure') = 1)
      drop procedure
          {databaseOwner}
          [{objectQualifier}DNNModuleProgramming_VB_ApproveGuestbookEntry]
GO
if exists (select * from dbo.sysobjects where id =
    object_id(N'{databaseOwner}
    [{objectQualifier}DNNModuleProgramming_VB_DeleteGuestbookEntry]')
    and OBJECTPROPERTY(id, N'IsProcedure') = 1)
      drop procedure
          {databaseOwner}
          [{objectQualifier}DNNModuleProgramming_VB_DeleteGuestbookEntry]
GO
if exists (select * from dbo.sysobjects where id =
    object_id(N'{databaseOwner}
    [{objectQualifier}DNNModuleProgramming_VB_GetApprovedEntries]')
    and OBJECTPROPERTY(id, N'IsProcedure') = 1)
      drop procedure
          {databaseOwner}[{objectQualifier}
          DNNModuleProgramming_VB_GetApprovedEntries]
GO
if exists (select * from dbo.sysobjects where id =
    object_id(N'{databaseOwner}
    [{objectQualifier}DNNModuleProgramming_VB_GetAllEntries]')
    and OBJECTPROPERTY(id, N'IsProcedure') = 1)
      drop procedure
          {databaseOwner}
              [{objectQualifier}DNNModuleProgramming_VB_GetAllEntries]
GO


/*************************************************************/
/*****                SqlDataProvider                  *****/
/*************************************************************/
```

These listings should be used to replace the entire contents of the automatically generated files. The listings first remove the table constraint, then the index, and lastly the table and stored procedures.

Summary

This chapter walked you through the creation of the module back end using the standard DotNetNuke DAL method. First, you created the abstract `DataProvider`, and then the concrete `SqlDataProvider`. These two components together formed the .NET data input and output methods that will be used across the module.

Next, you created the information object class that is used to store and transfer the guestbook entry information from the module front end to the back-end systems. The .NET code was wrapped up with the creation of the `Controller` class that provided the front-end code access to the DAL methods.

Finally, you created the .`SqlDataProvider` files that are used to add and remove data objects to the target installation database. This completes the first major portion of coding, and sets the stage for Chapter 8, where you will create the user-facing front end of the application. Chapter 8 introduces the DotNetNuke localization process, and demonstrates how to create the front end of the application, which will complete the first round of development for the module.

Creating the Localized Module Interface

So far, you have taken steps to create the DotNetNuke module project and back-end framework that is needed to support the module functionality. Now it is time to actually create the front-end user interface that will be used to display information to the users. This chapter focuses on the DotNetNuke implementation specifics, and provides basic coverage of the standard ASP.NET and HTML items necessary to complete the front-end interface. Therefore, for simplicity, HTML tables are used for alignment to avoid lengthy discussions regarding Cascading Stylesheets (CSS) and browser differences.

This chapter begins by introducing DotNetNuke localization, including the DotNetNuke `Label` control and the `App_LocalResources` folder, along with its included `.resx` files. After you are familiar with the elements needed for a localized interface, you will create each of the needed interfaces. This chapter wraps up with a brief discussion about DotNetNuke CSS classes, and incorporation of custom module CSS elements. This will lay the foundation for testing and working with the module inside of DotNetNuke in Chapter 9.

DotNetNuke Localization

The DotNetNuke framework includes methods that support static text localization, enabling module developers to create modules that can easily be used for multiple languages. As of this writing, the framework does not provide any support for dynamic content localization, but that is an item on the agenda for future versions of the Cambrian series of releases.

When you are embarking on the creation of a localized DotNetNuke interface, two fundamental elements are typically in play:

❑ **DotNetNuke resource files:** These store the localized text.

❑ **DotNetNuke localization classes and localizable controls:** These provide basic components.

DotNetNuke Resource Files

When you used the templates to create the Guestbook modules in Chapter 5, you created a folder with the name `App_LocalResources`. This folder contained multiple files that ended with a `.resx` file extension, and shared the first part of the name with one of the `.ascx` user controls. For example, there is a file called `Settings.ascx.resx`, which is the resource file for the `Settings` control within the Guestbook module.

These files are standard ASP.NET resource files, and they store text elements in a key/value pair combination. Figure 8-1 shows the default view of the `Settings.ascx.resx` file created by the module templates.

Name	Value	Comment
ControlTitle_settings.Text	Guestbook Settings	This localizes the title of the control, using the key from the .dnn file as part of the key
lblAllowAnon.Help	If selected ANY user can post an entry to the guestbook, if not selected only authenticated users can post	The help text display for the lblAllowAnon control
lblAllowAnon.Text	Allow Anon. Posts	The display for the lblAllowAnon control
lblEnableCaptcha.Help	If selected the user must successfully copy the text from the CAPTCHA image before their post can be inserted	The help text display for the lblEnableCaptcha control
lblEnableCaptcha.Text	Enable Captcha	The display for the lblEnableCaptcha control
lblModerateEntries.Help	If selected all posts must be approved by a user with edit permissions to the module	The help text display for the lblModerateEntries control
lblModerateEntries.Text	Moderate Posts	The display for the lblModerateEntries control
ModuleHelp.Text	Module Specific Help to Go Here	This is an optional localization key that can be used to store help information on the module

Figure 8-1

When working with static text localization, the key values are typically formed in two parts separated with a period. The first part is the unique identifier for the text element. The second part is typically the word `Text`. However, certain localization elements will have different suffixes. For example, grid headers will have `Header`, rather than `Text`. The specifics of these differences are discussed in detail as code for the module progresses in later chapters.

Localized Controls and Classes

The DotNetNuke framework contains multiple controls that can be used to provide a consistent user interface. These controls include the DotNetNuke `Label` control (the standard control with label text and a help icon), as well as section headers, CAPTCHA controls, and more. Implementations of the individual controls are addressed in upcoming chapters.

In addition to the localized controls, DotNetNuke provides a series of static localization methods available in the `DotNetNuke.Services.Localization` namespace. These very helpful methods will be used throughout this book to handle static text localization. Table 8-1 shows some helpful localization methods and properties that are used to localize static text content.

Table 8-1

Method/Property	Usage
GetString(string, string)	This method is used to get a localized text element. The first parameter is the key to find; the second parameter is the path to the localization file. You can use the LocalResourceFile property to obtain this value.
LocalResourceFile	This is a property available on all controls that inherit from PortalModuleBase or PortalSettingsBase, and represents the path to the individual localization file for the control. It is used as a parameter for most localization methods.
LocalizeDataGrid(ref DataGrid, string)	This method will localize the headers in the passed DataGrid control using the resource file location provided in the second parameter. Resource keys must match the HeaderText of the column, and the key must end in .Header, rather than .Text.

In addition to the localization methods that enable explicit localization of text elements inside the C# and Visual Basic (VB) code, any control that inherits from the base DotNetNuke classes will also have controls implicitly localized. This implicit localization is completed on DotNetNuke controls, as well as specific ASP.NET controls that have an added ResourceKey attribute.

This book will continue to introduce content localization topics as the module interface is built. Full documentation on localization strategies is available from DotNetNuke Corporation at www .dotnetnuke.com/Resources/Documentation/DownloadableFiles/tabid/478/Default.aspx. To provide the best application of these concepts, the following sections introduce each of the localization schemes as needed while creating the module interfaces.

Creating Settings.ascx

Chapter 4 introduced the specifications for each of the controls. Because the Settings control is the first control that will be used by administrative users of the module, it is the most logical point to start with as you create the interface. Per the specifications, this control should provide an administrative user with three options:

❑ Allow anonymous user postings

❑ Enable CAPTCHA

❑ Moderate entries

Three distinct components are required in order to implement this control:

❑ The `settings.ascx` markup

❑ The `settings.ascx.cs/.vb` code

❑ The `settings.ascx.resx` localization content

The following sections take a closer look at each of these in a bit more detail.

User Control Markup

The `settings.ascx` file contains the HTML markup and ASP.NET server controls needed to present the user interface. To provide the settings interface, a simple HTML table is used for layout, as well as individual checkboxes for the various controls. Listing 8-1 (C#) and Listing 8-2 (VB.NET) show the code samples for the interface.

Listing 8-1: C# Settings.ascx Markup

```
<%@ Control Language="C#" AutoEventWireup="true"
      CodeBehind="Settings.ascx.cs"
    Inherits="WroxModules.GuestbookCS.Settings" %>
<%@ Register TagPrefix="dnn" TagName="Label"
      Src="~/controls/LabelControl.ascx" %>

<table cellspacing="0" cellpadding="2" border="0" summary=
      "Guestbook CS Design Table">
    <tr>
        <td class="SubHead" width="150">
            <dnn:label id="lblAllowAnon" runat="server"
                controlname="chkAllowAnon" suffix=":" />
        </td>
        <td>
            <asp:CheckBox ID="chkAllowAnon" runat="server" />
        </td>
    </tr>
    <tr>
        <td class="SubHead">
            <dnn:Label ID="lblEnableCaptcha" runat="server"
                ControlName="chkEnableCaptcha" Suffix=":" />
        </td>
        <td>
            <asp:CheckBox ID="chkEnableCaptcha" runat="server" />
        </td>
    </tr>
    <tr>
        <td class="SubHead">
            <dnn:Label ID="lblModerateEntries" runat="server"
                ControlName="chkModerateEntries" Suffix=":" />
        </td>
        <td>
            <asp:CheckBox ID="chkModerateEntries" runat="server" />
        </td>
    </tr>
</table>
```

Listing 8-2: VB.NET Settings.ascx Markup

```
<%@ Control Language="vb" AutoEventWireup="false"
    Inherits="WroxModules.GuestbookVB.Settings"
    Codebehind="Settings.ascx.vb" %>
<%@ Register TagPrefix="dnn" TagName="Label"
    Src="~/controls/LabelControl.ascx" %>

<table cellspacing="0" cellpadding="2" border="0" summary=
    "Guestbook CS Design Table">
    <tr>
        <td class="SubHead" width="150">
            <dnn:label id="lblAllowAnon" runat="server" controlname=
                "chkAllowAnon" suffix=":" />
        </td>
        <td>
            <asp:CheckBox ID="chkAllowAnon" runat="server" />
        </td>
    </tr>
    <tr>
        <td class="SubHead">
            <dnn:Label ID="lblEnableCaptcha" runat=
                "server" ControlName="chkEnableCaptcha" Suffix=":" />
        </td>
        <td>
            <asp:CheckBox ID="chkEnableCaptcha" runat="server" />
        </td>
    </tr>
    <tr>
        <td class="SubHead">
            <dnn:Label ID="lblModerateEntries" runat=
                "server" ControlName="chkModerateEntries" Suffix=":" />
        </td>
        <td>
            <asp:CheckBox ID="chkModerateEntries" runat="server" />
        </td>
    </tr>
</table>
```

This code is very basic ASP.NET markup, with a few DotNetNuke-specific elements that are worth noting. First, note the registering of a user control in the second line of the example. This registers a control with a tag prefix of dnn and a tag name of Label. The source of the control points to an application root relative path of ~/controls/LabelControl.ascx. This is where the default Label control is stored.

As this code is entered into Visual Studio, an error will likely appear stating that the control cannot be found. This is *not* an issue, and is one item that must be dealt with when working with WAP module development. The good news is that Visual Studio 2008 resolves the issues surrounding "not found" errors, and provides full design-time support for the Label control.

The remainder of the code in this example creates a simple two-column HTML table. The first column includes the DotNetNuke `Label` control, and the second column includes a checkbox for each setting. Each implementation of the DotNetNuke `Label` control contains four property definitions. These properties are the most commonly set, and are defined in Table 8-2.

Table 8-2

Property Name	Purpose	Example
Id	Unique identifier for the control that serves the same purpose as the ID for any other control	lblAllowAnon
Runat	Identifier to designate as a server control (standard ASP.NET property)	Server
ControlName	The ID of the control that is the label. Used to provide linking, for accessibility purposes, between the label and the control it is labeling.	chkAllowAnon
Suffix	The suffix to add after the text of the control. Used to provide uniformity among input labels.	:
Text	The actual text of the element, typically *not* specified in the .ascx markup	
Help	The text for the help portion of the display, typically *not* specified in the .ascx markup	

Note that the `Text` and `HelpText` properties of the `Label` control are automatically localized by the DotNetNuke framework using the implicit localization. Therefore, it is standard practice to omit these values from the .ascx definition, and to rely on the localization framework to specify the proper values.

Code Behind

With the markup now defined, it's time to create the back-end .cs or .vb file needed for the `Settings` control. Listing 8-3 (C#) and Listing 8-4 (VB.NET) show the markup needed to create the back-end process. Note that *all* text from the template should be replaced to resemble the code in these listings, because namespace references have been modified to work properly with the code created previously.

Listing 8-3: C# Settings.ascx.cs Code

```
using System;
using DotNetNuke.Entities.Modules;
using DotNetNuke.Services.Exceptions;

namespace WroxModules.GuestbookCS
{
    public partial class Settings : ModuleSettingsBase
    {
        public override void LoadSettings()
```

```
        {
            try
            {
                if (!IsPostBack)
                {
                    object allowAnon = ModuleSettings
                        ["WROX_Guestbook_AllowAnon"];
                    object enableCaptcha = ModuleSettings
                        ["WROX_Guestbook_EnableCaptcha"];
                    object moderateEntries = ModuleSettings
                        ["WROX_Guestbook_ModerateEntries"];

                    //if it exists, load the setting
                    if (allowAnon != null)
                        chkAllowAnon.Checked =
                            bool.Parse(allowAnon.ToString());

                    if (enableCaptcha != null)
                        chkEnableCaptcha.Checked =
                            bool.Parse(enableCaptcha.ToString());

                    if (moderateEntries != null)
                        chkModerateEntries.Checked =
                            bool.Parse(moderateEntries.ToString());
                }
            }
            catch (Exception ex)
            {
                Exceptions.ProcessModuleLoadException(this, ex);
            }
        }
        public override void UpdateSettings()
        {
            try
            {
                ModuleController controller = new ModuleController();
                controller.UpdateModuleSetting(this.ModuleId,
     "WROX_Guestbook_AllowAnon", chkAllowAnon.Checked.ToString());
                controller.UpdateModuleSetting(this.ModuleId,
     "WROX_Guestbook_EnableCaptcha",
                    chkEnableCaptcha.Checked.ToString());
                controller.UpdateModuleSetting(this.ModuleId,
     "WROX_Guestbook_ModerateEntries",
                    chkModerateEntries.Checked.ToString());
            }
            catch (Exception ex)
            {
                Exceptions.ProcessModuleLoadException(this, ex);
            }
        }
    }
}
```

Listing 8-4: VB.NET Settings.ascx.vb Code

```
Imports System.Web.UI
Imports DotNetNuke
Imports DotNetNuke.Services.Exceptions

Namespace WroxModules.GuestbookVB
    Partial Class Settings
        Inherits Entities.Modules.ModuleSettingsBase

        Public Overrides Sub LoadSettings()
            Try
                If (Page.IsPostBack = False) Then
                    If CType(ModuleSettings("WROX_Guestbook_AllowAnon"), String)
                        <> "" Then
                        chkAllowAnon.Checked =
                            Boolean.Parse(ModuleSettings
                            ("WROX_Guestbook_AllowAnon").ToString())
                    End If
                    If CType(ModuleSettings
                        ("WROX_Guestbook_EnableCaptcha"),
                        String) <> "" Then
                        chkEnableCaptcha.Checked =
                            Boolean.Parse(ModuleSettings
                            ("WROX_Guestbook_EnableCaptcha").ToString())
                    End If
                    If CType(ModuleSettings
                        ("WROX_Guestbook_ModerateEntries"),
                        String) <> "" Then
                        chkAllowAnon.Checked =
                            Boolean.Parse(ModuleSettings
                            ("WROX_Guestbook_ModerateEntries").ToString())
                    End If
                End If
            Catch exc As Exception 'Module failed to load
                ProcessModuleLoadException(Me, exc)
            End Try
        End Sub
        Public Overrides Sub UpdateSettings()
            Dim oController As New Entities.Modules.ModuleController
            oController.UpdateModuleSetting(Me.ModuleId,
        "WROX_Guestbook_AllowAnon", chkAllowAnon.Checked.ToString())
            oController.UpdateModuleSetting(Me.ModuleId,
        "WROX_Guestbook_EnableCaptcha",
            chkEnableCaptcha.Checked.ToString())
            oController.UpdateModuleSetting(Me.ModuleId,
        "WROX_Guestbook_ModerateEntries",
            chkModerateEntries.Checked.ToString())
        End Sub
    End Class
End Namespace
```

Internal DotNetNuke module settings options were used to persist the settings for the module. This makes the storage and retrieval process very simple. Because this control inherits from the SettingsModuleBase class discussed in previous chapters, LoadSettings and UpdateSettings methods were provided to enable the proper storage and retrieval of settings based on the user's actions. This is an important integration point, as the `Settings` control is embedded on a page where the Update button is controlled by DotNetNuke.

Using the `ModuleSettings` functionality provided by DotNetNuke enables settings to be stored via a key/value pair. Therefore, when retrieving settings, a simple check is needed to determine whether the key was found. This is done to ensure that `null` references are not encountered. After the settings have been verified, the checkboxes are updated if necessary.

The save process is similar using the `ModuleController` provided by the DotNetNuke framework. The `UpdateModuleSetting` method simply takes three parameters: module ID, setting key, and setting value. The update method will handle both inserts and updates to the settings collection.

Localization File

The final step in creating the `Settings` control is to properly define the localization values for the static text elements, including the control's title property. Table 8-3 provides a list of all the values that should be added to the `Settings.ascx.resx` file inside the project. These values are the same for both the C# and VB versions of the Guestbook module. The "Comment" column describes the purpose of the setting. It is *not* necessary to copy this value into the actual `resx` file, although it is allowed.

Table 8-3

Name	Value	Comment
ControlTitle_settings.Text	Guestbook settings	This localizes the title of the control, using the key from the .dnn file as part of the key.
ModuleHelp.Text	Module-specific help to go here	This is an optional localization key that can be used to store help information about the module.
lblAllowAnon.Text	Allow anonymous posts	This is the display for the lblAllowAnon control.
lblAllowAnon.Help	If selected, then *any* user can post an entry to the guestbook. If not selected, then only authenticated users can post.	This is the help text display for the lblAllowAnon control.
lblEnableCaptcha.Text	Enable CAPTCHA	This is the display for the lblEnableCaptcha control.
lblEnableCaptcha.Help	If selected, then the user must successfully copy the text from the CAPTCHA image before the user's post can be inserted.	This is the help text display for the lblEnableCaptcha control.

(continued)

Table 8-3 (continued)

Name	Value	Comment
lblModerateEntries.Text	Moderate posts	This is the display for the lblModerateEntries control.
lblModerateEntries.Help	If selected, then all posts must be approved by a user with edit permissions to the module.	This is the help text display for the lblModerateEntries control.

Creating ViewSettings.ascx

In addition to the standard settings control implemented previously in this chapter for guestbook signing permissions, it is necessary to create the view settings control. You might recall from Chapter 4 that this was described as the control to associate the View control to the Sign control. The final sections of this chapter will actually walk you through the steps necessary to link up the various controls inside the manifest. This control is created in a manner very similar to that of the Settings.ascx control. However, it is not yet an object in the project.

You can create the control by right-clicking on the project and selecting Add ⇨ New Item. From this list, select Web User Control and provide the name **ViewSettings.ascx**. Click OK to finish. The auto-generated code will be replaced with the code examples in the following discussions.

User Control Markup

The purpose of this control is very simple. It is designed to allow users to select the module instance on the current tab that contains the Sign Guestbook module. Therefore, a single configuration option is needed to enable users to select the module instance. Listing 8-5 (C#) and Listing 8-6 (VB) show the markup needed.

Listing 8-5: C# ViewSettings.ascx Markup

```
<%@ Control Language="C#" AutoEventWireup="true"
    CodeBehind="ViewSettings.ascx.cs"
    Inherits="WroxModules.GuestbookCS.ViewSettings" %>
<%@ Register TagPrefix="dnn" TagName="Label"
    Src="~/controls/LabelControl.ascx" %>

<table>
    <tr>
        <td class="SubHead" width="100px">
            <dnn:Label ID="lblSignModule" runat="server"
                ControlName="ddlSignModule" Suffix=":" />
        </td>
        <td class="Normal">
            <asp:DropDownList ID="ddlSignModule" runat="server"
                CssClass="NormalTextbox" />
        </td>
    </tr>
</table>
```

Listing 8-6: VB.NET ViewSettings.ascx Markup

```
<%@ Control Language="vb" AutoEventWireup="false"
    CodeBehind="ViewSettings.ascx.vb"
    Inherits="WroxModules.GuestbookVB.ViewSettings" %>
<%@ Register TagPrefix="dnn" TagName="Label"
    Src="~/controls/LabelControl.ascx" %>

<table>
    <tr>
        <td class="SubHead" width="100px">
            <dnn:Label ID="lblSignModule" runat="server"
                ControlName="ddlSignModule" Suffix=":" />
        </td>
        <td class="Normal">
            <asp:DropDownList ID="ddlSignModule" runat="server"
                CssClass="NormalTextbox" />
        </td>
    </tr>
</table>
```

As you can see, a single HTML table is used for layout, a DotNetNuke Label control is used for input labels, and a DropDownList is used for the module listing.

Code Behind

The required code-behind file for this control is equally simple. It uses many of the key features investigated for the Settings control, including the use of the module controller to save settings. Listing 8-7 (C#) and Listing 8-8 (VB) show the code-behind files.

Listing 8-7: C# ViewSettings.ascx.cs Code

```
using System;
using System.Collections.Generic;
using DotNetNuke.Entities.Modules;
using DotNetNuke.Services.Exceptions;

namespace WroxModules.GuestbookCS
{
    public partial class ViewSettings : ModuleSettingsBase
    {
        public override void LoadSettings()
        {
            //Get module listing
            ModuleController oController = new ModuleController();
            Dictionary<int, ModuleInfo> oModules =
                oController.GetTabModules(this.TabId);
            ddlSignModule.DataSource = oModules.Values;
            ddlSignModule.DataTextField = "ModuleTitle";
            ddlSignModule.DataValueField = "ModuleID";
            ddlSignModule.DataBind();
```

(continued)

Listing 8-7 *(continued)*

```
            //Load setting if available
            object signModuleSetting =
                ModuleSettings["WroxModules_Guestbook_SignModule"];
            if (signModuleSetting != null)
                ddlSignModule.SelectedValue =
                signModuleSetting.ToString();
        }

        public override void UpdateSettings()
        {
            ModuleController oController = new ModuleController();
            oController.UpdateModuleSetting(this.ModuleId,
                "WroxModules_Guestbook_SignModule", ddlSignModule.SelectedValue);
        }
    }
}
```

Listing 8-8: VB.NET ViewSettings.ascx.vb Code

```
Imports System.Web.UI
Imports DotNetNuke
Imports DotNetNuke.Entities.Modules

Namespace WroxModules.GuestbookVB
    Partial Public Class ViewSettings
        Inherits ModuleSettingsBase

        Public Overrides Sub LoadSettings()
            Dim oController As New ModuleController
            Dim oModules As Dictionary(Of Integer, ModuleInfo) =
                    oController.GetTabModules(Me.TabId)
            ddlSignModule.DataSource = oModules.Values
            ddlSignModule.DataTextField = "ModuleTitle"
            ddlSignModule.DataValueField = "ModuleID"
            ddlSignModule.DataBind()

            If CType(ModuleSettings
                    ("WroxModules_Guestbook_SignModule"), String)
                <> "" Then
                ddlSignModule.SelectedValue = CType(ModuleSettings
                    ("WroxModules_Guestbook_SignModule"), String)
            End If
        End Sub
        Public Overrides Sub UpdateSettings()
            Dim oController As New ModuleController
            oController.UpdateModuleSetting(Me.ModuleId,
                "WroxModules_Guestbook_SignModule",
                ddlSignModule.SelectedValue)
        End Sub
    End Class
End Namespace
```

The most important item to note in these code samples is the introduction of the new `GetTabModules` call from the module controller. This call simply grabs all modules that are defined on a specific tab. Appendix E provides a helpful listing of common integration points for users, modules, and tabs within custom modules.

> **A good learning exercise with this code sample would be to extend the module functionality to reference sign modules located on different tabs within the portal.**

Localization File

The final step is to create the localization file with the needed values to properly display the code for the module. Table 8-4 provides the required values that can be entered into the `ViewSettings.ascx.resx` file. This file must be added to the project. You can do this by right-clicking on the `App_LocalResources` folder and selecting Add ⇨ New Item from the menu.

Table 8-4

Name	Value	Comment
lblSignModules.Text	Sign Guestbook module	This is the label text for the `DropDownList`.
lblSignModule.Help	The Sign Guestbook module to use for input	This is the help text provided to the user.

Creating ViewGuestbook(CS/VB).ascx

With the `Settings` control fully created and ready to handle the configuration of the module, it's time to start creating the view interface for the Guestbook module. This control is simply responsible for the creation of the display interface for the guestbook entries. Per the module specifications defined in Chapter 4, a template design must be created, which provides site administrators with the capability to quickly modify the layout of the module. Paging is an additional requirement that will be added in later chapters when other DotNetNuke controls are introduced.

You will use an ASP.NET repeater control to achieve the template-driven display of this module. This will allow full customization of the header, footer, and item templates. To support localization, all templates will be stored in the `.resx` file for the module. Alternative options are available, but this option allows for the best implementation without needing custom code to handle header localization at the module level. A limitation to this template system is that the module display can only be customized at the portal level, and not the module instance level.

User Control Markup

The user control markup for this control is very straightforward. Only two controls are needed to handle the interface. The first is a repeater control that will handle the display of the actual entries. The second is a "no entries" label that will be displayed if no guestbook entries are found. This results in a simple interface, with minimal markup. Listing 8-9 shows the C# code and Listing 8-10 shows the VB.NET version of the module.

Listing 8-9: C# Markup for ViewGuestbookCS.ascx

```
<%@ Control Language="C#" AutoEventWireup="true"
    CodeBehind="ViewGuestbookCS.ascx.cs"
    Inherits="WroxModules.GuestbookCS.ViewGuestbookCS" %>

<asp:Repeater ID="rptEntries" runat="server"
    onitemdatabound="rptEntries_ItemDataBound">
    <HeaderTemplate>
        <asp:Literal ID="litHeader" runat="server" />
    </HeaderTemplate>
    <ItemTemplate>
        <asp:Literal ID="litItem" runat="server" />
    </ItemTemplate>
    <AlternatingItemTemplate>
        <asp:Literal ID="litAlternateItem" runat="server" />
    </AlternatingItemTemplate>
    <FooterTemplate>
        <asp:Literal ID="litFooter" runat="server" />
    </FooterTemplate>
</asp:Repeater>

<asp:Label ID="lblNoEntries" runat="server" CssClass="Normal"
    resourcekey="lblNoEntries" />
```

Listing 8-10: VB Markup for ViewGuestbookVB.ascx

```
<%@ Control language="vb" Inherits=
    "WroxModules.GuestbookVB.ViewGuestbookVB"
    AutoEventWireup="false" Explicit="True" Codebehind="ViewGuestbookVB.ascx.vb" %>

<asp:Repeater ID="rptEntries" runat="server"
    onitemdatabound="rptEntries_ItemDataBound">
    <HeaderTemplate>
        <asp:Literal ID="litHeader" runat="server" />
    </HeaderTemplate>
    <ItemTemplate>
        <asp:Literal ID="litItem" runat="server" />
    </ItemTemplate>
    <AlternatingItemTemplate>
        <asp:Literal ID="litAlternateItem" runat="server" />
    </AlternatingItemTemplate>
    <FooterTemplate>
        <asp:Literal ID="litFooter" runat="server" />
    </FooterTemplate>
</asp:Repeater>

<asp:Label ID="lblNoEntries" runat="server" CssClass="Normal"
    resourcekey="lblNoEntries" />
```

These definitions are very basic .NET controls. The important element to note is that the `lblNoEntries` control does *not* have the text property set, but has the `resourcekey` attribute added. This will tie into the DotNetNuke localization system, and the text will be dynamically loaded for the user.

> Note that the addition of `resourcekey` in Visual Studio 2005 will most likely result in a validation warning. The warning message can be ignored, and this behavior is not present in Visual Studio 2008.

Code Behind

With the front-end code created, let's now define the code behind for the `View` control. This code must handle two distinct actions: the loading of the page and the binding of repeater elements. Listing 8-11 (C#) and Listing 8-12 (VB) provide the code necessary to complete the code-behind files.

Listing 8-11: C# Code Behind for ViewGuestbookCS.ascx.cs

```
using System;
using System.Collections;
using System.Collections.Generic;
using System.Reflection;
using System.Web.UI;
using System.Web.UI.WebControls;
using DotNetNuke.Common.Utilities;
using DotNetNuke.Entities.Modules;
using DotNetNuke.Entities.Modules.Actions;
using DotNetNuke.Services.Exceptions;
using DotNetNuke.Services.Localization;

namespace WroxModules.GuestbookCS
{
    public partial class ViewGuestbookCS : PortalModuleBase
    {
        protected void Page_Load(object sender, EventArgs e)
        {
            try
            {
                if (!IsPostBack)
                {
                    //See if configured, if the setting is null,
                      it is not
                    object signModuleSetting = Settings
                        ["WroxModules_Guestbook_SignModule"];
                    if (signModuleSetting != null)
                    {
                        GuestbookCSController oController = new
                        GuestbookCSController();
                        List<GuestbookEntryInfo> oEntries;
                        int signModuleId = int.parse
```

(continued)

Listing 8-11 *(continued)*

```
                        (signModuleSetting.toString());
                    if (IsEditable)
                        oEntries = oController.GetAllEntries
                            (signModuleId);
                    else
                        oEntries =
                            oController.GetApprovedEntries
                                (signModuleId);

                    if (oEntries != null && oEntries.Count > 0)
                    {
                        rptEntries.DataSource = oEntries;
                        rptEntries.DataBind();

                        lblNoEntries.Visible = false;
                    }
                    else
                        rptEntries.Visible = false;
                }
                else
                {
                    rptEntries.Visible = false;
                    string message = Localization.GetString
                        ("NotConfigured", this.LocalResourceFile);
                    DotNetNuke.UI.Skins.Skin.AddModuleMessage
                        (this, message,
                        DotNetNuke.UI.Skins.Controls.
                        ModuleMessage.ModuleMessageType.
                        YellowWarning);
                }
            }
        }
        catch (Exception ex)
        {
            Exceptions.ProcessModuleLoadException(this, ex);
        }        }


    protected void rptEntries_ItemDataBound(object sender,
                                RepeaterItemEventArgs e)
{
        if (e.Item.ItemType == ListItemType.Header)
        {
            Literal litHeader =
                (Literal)e.Item.FindControl("litHeader");
            litHeader.Text =
                Localization.GetString("HeaderTemplate",
                this.LocalResourceFile);
        }
        else if (e.Item.ItemType == ListItemType.Footer)
```

```
        {
            Literal litFooter =
                (Literal)e.Item.FindControl("litFooter");
            litFooter.Text =
                Localization.GetString("FooterTemplate",
                this.LocalResourceFile);
        }
        else if (e.Item.ItemType == ListItemType.Item)
        {
            Literal litItem = (Literal)e.Item.FindControl("litItem");
            GuestbookEntryInfo oDataItem =
                (GuestbookEntryInfo)e.Item.DataItem;
            string template =
                Localization.GetString("ItemTemplate",
                this.LocalResourceFile);

            LoadEntryInfo(litItem, oDataItem, template);
        }
        else if (e.Item.ItemType == ListItemType.AlternatingItem)
        {
            Literal litItem = (Literal)e.Item.FindControl("litAlternateItem");
            GuestbookEntryInfo oDataItem =
                (GuestbookEntryInfo)e.Item.DataItem;
            string template =
                Localization.GetString("AlternateItemTemplate",
                this.LocalResourceFile);

            LoadEntryInfo(litItem, oDataItem, template);
        }
}
private void LoadEntryInfo(Literal litItem,
    GuestbookEntryInfo oInfo, string template)
{
    System.Text.StringBuilder oDisplay = new
        System.Text.StringBuilder(template);
    oDisplay.Replace("[NAME]", oInfo.SubmitterName);
    oDisplay.Replace("[WEBSITE]", oInfo.SubmitterWebsite);
    oDisplay.Replace("[COMMENT]", oInfo.SubmitterComment);
    oDisplay.Replace("[DATE]",
        oInfo.SubmissionDate.ToString());

    if (IsEditable)
    {
        string deleteUrl = string.Format
            ("<a href='{0}'>Delete</a>",
        EditUrl("EntryId", oInfo.EntryId.ToString(),
            "Edit", "delete=1"));
        oDisplay.Replace("[DELETE]", deleteUrl);

        string approveUrl = "";
        if (!oInfo.IsApproved)
```

(continued)

Listing 8-11 *(continued)*

```
                    {
                        approveUrl = string.Format
                            ("<a href='{0}'>Approve</a>",
                    EditUrl("EntryId", oInfo.EntryId.ToString(),
                        "Edit", "approve=1"));
                    }
                    oDisplay.Replace("[APPROVE]", approveUrl);
                }
                else
                {
                    oDisplay.Replace("[DELETE]", "");
                    oDisplay.Replace("[APPROVE]", "");
                }

                litItem.Text = oDisplay.ToString();
            }
        }
}
```

Listing 8-12: VB Code Behind for ViewGuestbookVB.ascx.vb

```vb
Imports System.Web.UI
Imports System.Collections.Generic
Imports System.Reflection

Imports DotNetNuke
Imports DotNetNuke.Services.Exceptions
Imports DotNetNuke.Services.Localization

Namespace WroxModules.GuestbookVB
    Partial Class ViewGuestbookVB
        Inherits Entities.Modules.PortalModuleBase

        Private Sub Page_Load(ByVal sender As System.Object, _
            ByVal e As System.EventArgs) Handles MyBase.Load
            Try
                If Not IsPostBack Then
                    'See if the user has specified the setting from
                     the settings control
                    If CType(Settings _
                        ("WroxModules_Guestbook_SignModule"), String) _
                            <> "" Then
                        Dim oController As New GuestbookVBController()
                        Dim oEntries As List(Of GuestbookEntryInfo)
                        Dim oSignModuleId As Integer = _
                            Integer.Parse(Settings _
                            ("WroxModules_Guestbook_SignModule"))

                        If IsEditable Then
                            oEntries = oController.GetAllEntries _
                                (oSignModuleId)
```

```vb
            Else
                oEntries =
                    oController.GetApprovedEntries
                    (oSignModuleId)
            End If

            If oEntries.Count > 0 Then
                rptEntries.DataSource = oEntries
                rptEntries.DataBind()
                lblNoEntries.Visible = False
            Else
                rptEntries.Visible = False
            End If
        Else
            rptEntries.Visible = False
            Dim omessage As String =
                Localization.GetString
                ("NotConfigured", Me.LocalResourceFile)
            DotNetNuke.UI.Skins.Skin.
                AddModuleMessage(Me, omessage,
                Skins.Controls.ModuleMessage.
                ModuleMessageType.YellowWarning)
        End If
    End If
    Catch exc As Exception 'Module failed to load
        ProcessModuleLoadException(Me, exc)
    End Try
End Sub


Protected Sub rptEntries_ItemDataBound
    (ByVal sender As Object, ByVal e As
        System.Web.UI.WebControls.RepeaterItemEventArgs)
        Handles rptEntries.ItemDataBound
    If e.Item.ItemType = ListItemType.Header Then
        Dim litHeader As Literal =
            CType(e.Item.FindControl("litHeader"),Literal)
        litHeader.Text =
            Localization.GetString("HeaderTemplate",
            Me.LocalResourceFile)
    ElseIf e.Item.ItemType = ListItemType.Footer Then
        Dim litFooter As Literal =
            CType(e.Item.FindControl("litFooter"),Literal)
        litFooter.Text =
            Localization.GetString("FooterTemplate",
            Me.LocalResourceFile)
    ElseIf e.Item.ItemType = ListItemType.Item Then
        Dim litItem As Literal =
            CType(e.Item.FindControl("litItem"),Literal)
        Dim oDataItem As GuestbookEntryInfo =
            CType(e.Item.DataItem,GuestbookEntryInfo)
        Dim oTemplate As String =
            Localization.GetString("ItemTemplate",
            Me.LocalResourceFile)
```

(continued)

Listing 8-12 *(continued)*

```vbnet
                LoadEntryInfo(litItem, oDataItem, oTemplate)
        ElseIf e.Item.ItemType = ListItemType.AlternatingItem Then
            Dim litItem As Literal =
                CType(e.Item.FindControl("litAlternateItem"),
                    Literal)
            Dim oDataItem As GuestbookEntryInfo =
                CType(e.Item.DataItem,GuestbookEntryInfo)
            Dim oTemplate As String =
                Localization.GetString("AlternateItemTemplate",
                Me.LocalResourceFile)
            LoadEntryInfo(litItem, oDataItem, oTemplate)
        End If
    End Sub

    Private Sub LoadEntryInfo(ByVal litItem As Literal,
            ByVal oInfo As GuestbookEntryInfo, ByVal
            template As String)
        Dim oDisplay As New StringBuilder(template)
        oDisplay.Replace("[NAME]", oInfo.SubmitterName)
        oDisplay.Replace("[WEBSITE]", oInfo.SubmitterWebsite)
        oDisplay.Replace("[COMMENT]", oInfo.SubmitterComment)
        oDisplay.Replace("[DATE]", oInfo.SubmissionDate.ToString())

        If IsEditable Then
            Dim deleteUrl As String = String.Format
                ("<a href='{0}'>Delete</a>", EditUrl("EntryId",
                oInfo.Entryid.ToString(), "Edit", "delete=1"))
            oDisplay.Replace("[DELETE]", deleteUrl)

            Dim approveUrl As String = ""
            If Not oInfo.IsApproved Then
                approveUrl = String.Format
                ("<a href='{0}'>Approve</a>", EditUrl("EntryId",
                oInfo.Entryid.ToString(), "Edit", "approve=1"))
            End If
            oDisplay.Replace("[APPROVE]", approveUrl)
        Else
            oDisplay.Replace("[DELETE]", "")
            oDisplay.Replace("[APPROVE]", "")
        End If

        litItem.Text = oDisplay.ToString()
    End Sub
End Class

End Namespace
```

The code presented for this process is fairly simple. In the page load event, a check is completed to determine whether it is a postback. If it isn't, the data is bound to the grid for display. The IsEditable property of PortalModuleBase is checked to determine whether it is necessary to load *all* entries, including the ones awaiting approval.

In addition to this, a simple check for module configuration is completed. If the module is not configured, then the `AddModuleMessage` method is used to display a module-level message notifying the user that the module is not ready for public display. The localization object's `GetString` method is used to obtain the localized text for `"NotConfigured"`. Additional enumeration values can be passed to the `AddModuleMessage` method to show a `GreenSuccess` image or a `RedError` message. This enables the module to display messages in a manner that is familiar to all DotNetNuke users.

The additional elements of the control are used to handle the `ItemDataBound` event of the repeater control, conditionally loading the header, the footer, and items. In the case of a guestbook item, a helper function is called that will perform the static text replacement. From this, you can tell that the module contains various tokens that users can use to place the user input. Table 8-5 describes all supported tokens and their actions.

Table 8-5

Token	Purpose
[NAME]	To provide the full name of the user submitting the guestbook entry
[WEBSITE]	To provide the website address added by the user
[COMMENT]	To provide the comment left by the user
[DATE]	To provide the date and time the entry was created
[APPROVE]	To render an approve link *if and only if* a user is an administrative user *and* the post is not approved
[DELETE]	To render a delete link *if and only if* a user is an administrative user

Using this systematic approach to layout, site administrators have a variety of flexible options to configure the module for display.

Note the use of the `EditUrl` function inside the code. This function has multiple overloads, and can redirect users to other controls inside a specific module. In the code for this control, an overload was used for the first two parameters to provide a key and value for editing (in this case, a key of `EntryId` and a value that represents the ID of the individual entry that is to be approved).

The next parameter is the `"Key"` for the control. When the `.dnn` file was created in Chapter 6, the `"Key"` was defined for the `Edit` control to be `"Edit"`. This tells DotNetNuke which control should be loaded. The last parameter enables a collection of additional query string parameters to be passed. The module code uses this to define an action.

Localization File

The final step in creating the `View` control is to properly define the localization values for the static text elements, including the display templates. Table 8-6 describes all the values that should be added to the `ViewGuestbook(CS/VB).ascx.resx` file inside the project. These values are the same for both the C# and VB versions of the Guestbook module. The Comment column describes the purpose of the setting. It is *not* necessary to copy this value into the actual `resx` file, although it is allowed.

Table 8-6

Name	Value	Comment
NotConfigured.Text	`<p>This module has not yet been configured. Please check back later.</p>`	Message displayed to users if the settings page has not been configured for the module instance
lblNoEntries.Text	`<p>At this time there are no guestbook entries to report. Please check back later, or use the "Sign Guestbook" module to leave a message.</p>`	Message displayed to users if the module is properly configured and no guestbook entries exist

HeaderTemplate.Text	`<table>`
	
	`<tr>`
	`<td class="SubHead">Name</td>`
	`<td class="SubHead">Website</td>`
	`<td class="SubHead">Comment</td>`
	`<td class="SubHead">Date</td>`
	`</tr>`
		The template used to render the header of the guestbook display

FooterTemplate.Text	`</table>`	The template used to render the footer of the guestbook display

ItemTemplate.Text	`<tr>`
	
	`<td class="Normal">[APPROVE] [DELETE] [NAME]</td>`
	`<td class="Normal">[WEBSITE]</td>`
	`<td class="Normal">[COMMENT]</td>`
	`<td class="Normal">[DATE]</td></tr>`
		The template used to display individual standard rows of the guestbook

AlternateItemTemplate .Text	`<tr style="background-color:#eeeeee;">`
	
	`<td class="Normal">[APPROVE] [DELETE] [NAME]</td>`
	`<td class="Normal">[WEBSITE]</td>`
	`<td class="Normal">[COMMENT]</td>`
	`<td class="Normal">[DATE]</td>`
	`</tr>`
		The template used to display individual alternating rows of the guestbook

Creating EditGuestbook(CS/VB).ascx

The `View` control you just created was designed to be a minimal-effort control that enables DotNetNuke caching methods to be used. Therefore, the `EditGuestbook` control should be used to process entry approvals and deletions. This control is unique because it does not have a user interface. However, it will do processing on the load of the page and if everything checks out, it will approve or delete the entry, update the module cache, and return the user to the guestbook view.

User Control Markup

Even though no actual user interface elements will exist for this control, it is important that the control definition be updated to reflect the proper project namespaces. Therefore, for the `EditGuestbookCS` `.ascx` file, the following lines are needed:

```
<%@ Control Language="C#" AutoEventWireup="true"
    CodeBehind="EditGuestbookCS.ascx.cs"
    Inherits="WroxModules.GuestbookCS.EditGuestbookCS" %>
```

The `EditGuestbookVB.ascx` file should contain the following:

```
<%@ Control language="vb" Inherits="WroxModules.GuestbookVB.EditGuestbookVB"
    AutoEventWireup="false" Explicit="True" Codebehind="EditGuestbookVB.ascx.vb" %>
```

These lines of code ensure that all namespaces are properly referenced for the user control and associated code files.

Code Behind

The code behind for this control is fairly straightforward. On the load of the page, the query string will be examined to obtain the entry ID and action that is to be performed. After this has been identified, the proper controller method will be called to complete the action. The module is then updated, and the user is redirected back to the page. If, at any time, an exception is encountered (such as an invalid entry ID or another error), then the user is simply returned to the page. Listing 8-13 (C#) and Listing 8-14 (VB) provide the code-behind information.

Listing 8-13: C# EditGuestbookCS.ascx.cs Code

```csharp
using System;
using DotNetNuke.Common;
using DotNetNuke.Common.Utilities;
using DotNetNuke.Entities.Modules;
using DotNetNuke.Services.Exceptions;
using DotNetNuke.Services.Localization;

namespace WroxModules.GuestbookCS
{
    public partial class EditGuestbookCS : PortalModuleBase
    {
        int entryId = Null.NullInteger;

        protected void Page_Load(object sender, EventArgs e)
        {
            try
            {
                if (!IsPostBack)
                {
                    if (Request.QueryString["EntryId"] != null)
                    {
                        entryId = Int32.Parse
                            (Request.QueryString["EntryId"]);
                        bool isApprove = false;

                        if (Request.QueryString["approve"] != null)
                            isApprove = true;

                        GuestbookCSController oController =
                            new GuestbookCSController();
                        if (isApprove)
                            oController.ApproveGuestbookEntry
                            (this.ModuleId,entryId);
                        else
                            oController.DeleteGuestbookEntry
                            (this.ModuleId,entryId);

                        ModuleController.SynchronizeModule
                            (this.ModuleId);
                    }
                    Response.Redirect(Globals.NavigateURL(this.TabId));
                }
            }
            catch (Exception ex)
            {
                Exceptions.ProcessModuleLoadException(this, ex);
                Response.Redirect(Globals.NavigateURL(this.TabId));
            }
        }
    }
}
```

Listing 8-14: VB EditGuestbookVB.ascx.vb Code

```vb
Imports DotNetNuke
Imports DotNetNuke.Common
Imports DotNetNuke.Entities.Modules;
Imports DotNetNuke.Services.Exceptions
Imports DotNetNuke.Services.Localization

Namespace WroxModules.GuestbookVB
    Partial Class EditGuestbookVB
        Inherits Entities.Modules.PortalModuleBase

        Private entryId As Integer

        Private Sub Page_Load(ByVal sender As System.Object,
            ByVal e As System.EventArgs) Handles MyBase.Load
        Try
            If Page.IsPostBack = False Then
                If Not (Request.QueryString
                    ("EntryId") Is Nothing) Then
                    entryId =
                        Int32.Parse(Request.QueryString
                        ("EntryId"))
                    Dim isApprove As Boolean = False

                If Not (Request.QueryString("approve")
                    Is Nothing) Then
                        isApprove = True
                    End If

                    Dim oController As New GuestbookVBController

                    If (isApprove) Then
                        oController.ApproveGuestbookEntry
                        (Me.ModuleId, entryId)
                    Else
                        oController.DeleteGuestbookEntry
                        (Me.ModuleId, entryId)
                    End If

                    ModuleController.SynchronizeModule(Me.ModuleId)
                End If

                Response.Redirect(NavigateURL(Me.TabId))
            End If
        Catch exc As Exception     'Module failed to load
            ProcessModuleLoadException(Me, exc)
            Response.Redirect(NavigateURL(Me.TabId))
        End Try
        End Sub
    End Class
End Namespace
```

> Note that this security model is not 100 percent accurate. The `moduleId` is used as a secondary modification key to prevent users from manipulating the query string. Additionally, in order for this page to load, the user must have edit permissions. When you are working on approval and deletion methods types, it is very important to consider all aspects of application security.

In addition to the business rules identified in Listing 8-13 and Listing 8-14, there are two important code items to obtain from the preceding example:

❑ The first is the use of the `ModuleController.SyncronizeModule` method. This method notifies DotNetNuke that a change has occurred in the module that has invalidated the cache version, forcing it to refresh the cache prior to the expiration of the cache time specified.

❑ The second is the use of `NavigateUrl` to generate the redirection URL back to the current page. `NavigateUrl` has many overloads, which are discussed at various times later in this book. The key override, though, is the one accepting a `TabId` for redirection.

Localization File

Given that this module has no visible user interface at this time, it is not necessary to identify any localization elements. The file is still included in the solution to allow for future development of the module.

Creating SignGuestbook.ascx

Now that you have created the interfaces to configure, view, and administer the Guestbook module, you have one final control to create, and that is the one enabling users to sign the guestbook. For the initial development of this module, we'll create a simple interface for input. In later chapters you will actually implement the CAPTCHA control functionality.

To start the process, you will add the `SignGuestbook.ascx` control to the project:

1. Right-click on the project and select Add New Item.
2. Select Web User Control from the list and name it **SignGuestbook.ascx**.
3. Click OK to create the control.

You will update the auto-generated code with the proper code as you follow along in the next few sections.

User Control Markup

The user interface needed for user input is very simple. This example will use two panels. One will be used if signing is allowed. This panel will contain the input form for the module. The second panel will contain a label notifying the user that he or she must log in to sign the guestbook. This interface design enables all business functions to be carried out. As with the Settings control, the created module interface is very simple, relying on an HTML table for layout. This is done in order to keep the example as simple as possible. Listing 8-15 (C#) and Listing 8-16 (VB) show the markup needed for the SignGuestbook control.

Listing 8-15: C# SignGuestbook.ascx Markup

```
<%@ Control Language="C#" AutoEventWireup="true"
    CodeBehind="SignGuestbook.ascx.cs"
    Inherits="WroxModules.GuestbookCS.SignGuestbook" %>
<%@ Register TagPrefix="dnn" TagName="Label"
    Src="~/controls/LabelControl.ascx" %>

<asp:Panel ID="pnlSignGuestbook" runat="server">
    <table>
        <tr>
            <td class="SubHead" width="200">
                <dnn:Label id="lblName" runat="server"
                    ControlName="txtName"
                    Suffix=":" />
            </td>
            <td>
                <asp:TextBox ID="txtName" runat="server"
                    MaxLength="255"
                    CssClass="NormalTextbox" ValidationGroup=
                    "Guestbook" />
                <asp:RequiredFieldValidator ID=
                    "NameRequired" runat="server"
                    CssClass="NormalRed" Display="Dynamic"
                    ControlToValidate="txtName"
                    resourcekey="NameRequired"
                    ValidationGroup="Guestbook" />
            </td>
        </tr>
        <tr>
            <td class="SubHead">
                <dnn:Label ID="lblWebsite" runat="server"
                    ControlName="txtWebsite"
                    Suffix=":" />
            </td>
            <td>
                <asp:TextBox ID="txtWebsite" runat=
                    "server" MaxLength="255"
                    CssClass="NormalTextbox" ValidationGroup=
                    "Guestbook" />
                <asp:RegularExpressionValidator ID=
                    "WebsiteFormat" runat="server"
```

(continued)

Listing 8-15 *(continued)*

```
                        CssClass="NormalRed" Display="Dynamic"
                        ControlToValidate="txtWebsite" resourcekey="WebsiteFormat"
                        ValidationGroup="Guestbook"
                        ValidationExpression="http(s)?:
                            //([\w-]+\.)+[\w-]+(/[\w-
                            ./?%&amp;=]*)?" />
                </td>
            </tr>
            <tr>
                <td class="SubHead">
                    <dnn:Label ID="lblComment" runat=
                        "server" ControlName="txtComment"
                        Suffix=":" />
                </td>
                <td>
                    <asp:TextBox ID="txtComment" runat=
                        "server" TextMode="MultiLine"
                        CssClass="NormalTextbox" ValidationGroup=
                        "Guestbook"
                        width="200px" Height="50px" />
                    <asp:RequiredFieldValidator ID=
                        "CommentRequired" runat="server"
                        CssClass="NormalRed" Display="Dynamic"
                        ControlToValidate=
                        "txtComment" resourcekey="CommentRequired"
                        ValidationGroup="Guestbook" />
                </td>
            </tr>
            <tr>
                <td colspan="2"> </td>
            </tr>
            <tr>
                <td colspan="2">
                    <asp:LinkButton ID="btnSign" runat="server"
                        CssClass="CommandButton"
                        ValidationGroup="Guestbook" resourcekey="btnSign"
                        onclick="btnSign_Click" />
                </td>
            </tr>
        </table>
    </asp:Panel>

<asp:Panel ID="pnlCannotSign" runat="server">
    <asp:Label ID="lblCannotSign" runat="server" CssClass="Normal"
        resourcekey="lblCannotSign" />
</asp:Panel>
```

Listing 8-16: VB SignGuestbook.ascx Markup

```
<%@ Control Language="vb" AutoEventWireup="false"
    CodeBehind="SignGuestbook.ascx.vb"
    Inherits="WroxModules.GuestbookVB.SignGuestbook" %>
<%@ Register TagPrefix="dnn" TagName="Label"
    Src="~/controls/LabelControl.ascx" %>

<asp:Panel ID="pnlSignGuestbook" runat="server">
    <table>
        <tr>
            <td class="SubHead" width="200">
                <dnn:Label id="lblName" runat="server"
                    ControlName="txtName"
                    Suffix=":" />
            </td>
            <td>
                <asp:TextBox ID="txtName" runat=
                    "server" MaxLength="255"
                    CssClass="NormalTextbox"
                    ValidationGroup="Guestbook" />
                <asp:RequiredFieldValidator ID=
                    "NameRequired" runat="server"
                    CssClass="NormalRed" Display="Dynamic"
                    ControlToValidate=
                    "txtName" resourcekey="NameRequired"
                    ValidationGroup="Guestbook" />
            </td>
        </tr>
        <tr>
            <td class="SubHead">
                <dnn:Label ID="lblWebsite" runat=
                    "server" ControlName="txtWebsite"
                    Suffix=":" />
            </td>
            <td>
                <asp:TextBox ID="txtWebsite" runat=
                    "server" MaxLength="255"
                    CssClass="NormalTextbox"
                    ValidationGroup="Guestbook" />
                <asp:RegularExpressionValidator ID=
                    "WebsiteFormat" runat="server"
                    CssClass="NormalRed" Display="Dynamic"
                    ControlToValidate=
                    "txtWebsite" resourcekey="WebsiteFormat"
                    ValidationGroup="Guestbook"
                    ValidationExpression="http(s)?:
                        //([\w-]+\.)+[\w-]+(/[\w-
                        ./?%&amp;=]*)?" />
            </td>
        </tr>
```

(continued)

Listing 8-16 *(continued)*

```
        <tr>
            <td class="SubHead">
                <dnn:Label ID="lblComment" runat=
                    "server" ControlName="txtComment"
                    Suffix=":" />
            </td>
            <td>
                <asp:TextBox ID="txtComment" runat=
                    "server" TextMode="MultiLine"
                        CssClass="NormalTextbox"
                        ValidationGroup="Guestbook" width="200px" Height="50px" />
                <asp:RequiredFieldValidator ID="CommentRequired"
                    runat="server"
                        CssClass="NormalRed" Display="Dynamic"
                        ControlToValidate="txtComment" resourcekey="CommentRequired"
                        ValidationGroup="Guestbook" />
            </td>
        </tr>
        <tr>
            <td colspan="2"> </td>
        </tr>
        <tr>
            <td colspan="2">
                <asp:LinkButton ID="btnSign" runat="server"
                    CssClass="CommandButton" ValidationGroup="Guestbook"
                    resourcekey="btnSign" onclick="btnSign_Click"  />
            </td>
        </tr>
    </table>
</asp:Panel>

<asp:Panel ID="pnlCannotSign" runat="server">
    <asp:Label ID="lblCannotSign" runat="server" CssClass="Normal"
        resourcekey="lblCannotSign" />
</asp:Panel>
```

The main portion of this control is very common practice for ASP.NET development. Careful use of the `ValidationGroup` attribute ensures that the module will be properly displayed if placed with other ASP.NET validators on the same page.

The name and comment fields are made a requirement by using the `RequiredFieldValidator` control. The website is constrained to a valid format using the default ASP.NET Regular Expression validator for Internet URLs. This creates the first level of interface needed to support the most basic structures of the module.

Code Behind

The code behind for this control is very straightforward. At this time, settings are validated on the first page load to ensure that the module is configured, *and,* if anonymous posting is not allowed, that the proper display is completed. Then code is implemented to handle the posting of a comment, including updating the module cache if needed. Listing 8-17 (C#) code and Listing 8-18 (VB) provide the full source code for the code behind.

Listing 8-17: SignGuestbook.ascx.cs Code Behind

```csharp
using System;
using System.Collections;
using System.Collections.Generic;
using System.Reflection;
using System.Web.UI;
using System.Web.UI.WebControls;
using DotNetNuke.Common.Utilities;
using DotNetNuke.Entities.Modules;
using DotNetNuke.Entities.Modules.Actions;
using DotNetNuke.Services.Exceptions;
using DotNetNuke.Services.Localization;

namespace WroxModules.GuestbookCS
{
    public partial class SignGuestbook : PortalModuleBase
    {
        protected void Page_Load(object sender, EventArgs e)
        {
            if (!IsPostBack)
            {
                object allowAnon = Settings["WROX_Guestbook_AllowAnon"];
                if (allowAnon != null)
                {
                    bool allowAnonPosting =
                        bool.Parse(allowAnon.ToString());

                    if (UserId == -1 && !allowAnonPosting)
                    {
                        pnlSignGuestbook.Visible = false;
                    }
                    else
                    {
                        pnlCannotSign.Visible = false;
                    }
                }
                else
                {
                    pnlCannotSign.Visible = false;
                    pnlSignGuestbook.Visible = false;
                    string oMessage = Localization.GetString
```

(continued)

Listing 8-17 *(continued)*

```
                              ("NotConfigured",
                              this.LocalResourceFile);
                    DotNetNuke.UI.Skins.Skin.AddModuleMessage
                              (this, oMessage,
        DotNetNuke.UI.Skins.Controls.
           ModuleMessage.ModuleMessageType.YellowWarning);
                }
            }
        }

        protected void btnSign_Click(object sender, EventArgs e)
        {
            if (Page.IsValid)
            {
                GuestbookCSController oController =
                    new GuestbookCSController();
                GuestbookEntryInfo oInfo = new GuestbookEntryInfo();
                oInfo.EntryId = -1;
                oInfo.ModuleId = this.ModuleId;
                oInfo.SubmissionDate = System.DateTime.Now;
                oInfo.SubmitterComment =
                    Server.HtmlEncode(txtComment.Text);
                oInfo.SubmitterName = Server.HtmlEncode(txtName.Text);
                oInfo.SubmitterWebsite =
                    Server.HtmlEncode(txtWebsite.Text);
                oInfo.IsApproved =
               !bool.Parse(Settings["WROX_Guestbook_ModerateEntries"].
                    ToString());
                oController.InsertGuestbookEntry(oInfo);

                string oMessage = "";

                if (oInfo.IsApproved)
                {
                    oMessage = Localization.GetString("Success",
                        this.LocalResourceFile);
                    ModuleController.SynchronizeModule(this.ModuleId);
                }
                else
                    oMessage =
                        Localization.GetString("SuccessModerated",
                            this.LocalResourceFile);

                DotNetNuke.UI.Skins.Skin.AddModuleMessage
                        (this, oMessage,
        DotNetNuke.UI.Skins.Controls.ModuleMessage.
           ModuleMessageType.GreenSuccess);
                }
            }
        }
    }
```

Listing 8-18: SignGuestbook.ascx.vb Code Behind

```vb
Imports DotNetNuke
Imports DotNetNuke.Common
Imports DotNetNuke.Entities.Modules
Imports DotNetNuke.Services.Exceptions
Imports DotNetNuke.Services.Localization

Namespace WroxModules.GuestbookVB
    Partial Class SignGuestbook
        Inherits Entities.Modules.PortalModuleBase

        Private Sub Page_Load(ByVal sender As System.Object, ByVal e As
                             System.EventArgs) Handles MyBase.Load
            If Page.IsPostBack = False Then
                If CType(Settings("WROX_Guestbook_AllowAnon"), String)
                    <> "" Then
                    Dim allowAnon As Boolean
                    allowAnon =
                 Boolean.Parse(CType(Settings("WROX_Guestbook_AllowAnon"),
                    String))

                    If UserId = -1 AndAlso Not allowAnon Then
                        pnlSignGuestbook.Visible = False
                    Else
                        pnlCannotSign.Visible = False
                    End If
                Else
                    pnlCannotSign.Visible = False
                    pnlSignGuestbook.Visible = False
                    Dim oMessage As String =
                     Localization.GetString("NotConfigured",
                        Me.LocalResourceFile)
                    DotNetNuke.UI.Skins.Skin.AddModuleMessage
                       (Me, oMessage, Skins.Controls.ModuleMessage.
                       ModuleMessageType.YellowWarning)
                End If
            End If
        End Sub

        Protected Sub btnSign_Click(ByVal sender As Object,
            ByVal e As EventArgs)
                       Handles btnSign.Click
            If Page.IsValid Then
                Dim oController As New GuestbookVBController
                Dim oInfo As New GuestbookEntryInfo
                oInfo.Entryid = -1
                oInfo.ModuleId = Me.ModuleId
                oInfo.SubmissionDate = System.DateTime.Now
                oInfo.SubmitterComment =
                    Server.HtmlEncode(txtComment.Text)
                oInfo.SubmitterName = Server.HtmlEncode(txtName.Text)
                oInfo.SubmitterWebsite =
```

(continued)

Listing 8-18 *(continued)*

```
                    Server.HtmlEncode(txtWebsite.Text)
            oInfo.IsApproved =
                Not Boolean.Parse(CType(Settings
                ("WROX_Guestbook_ModerateEntries"), String))
            oController.InsertGuestbookEntry(oInfo)

            Dim oMessage As String = ""
            If oInfo.IsApproved Then
                oMessage =
                    Localization.GetString("Success",
                    Me.LocalResourceFile)
                ModuleController.SynchronizeModule(Me.ModuleId)
            Else
                oMessage =
                    Localization.GetString("SuccessModerated",
                    Me.LocalResourceFile)
            End If

            DotNetNuke.UI.Skins.Skin.AddModuleMessage
                (Me, oMessage, Skins.Controls.ModuleMessage.
                ModuleMessageType.GreenSuccess)
        End If
    End Sub
End Class
End Namespace
```

The code presented for this control uses several items discussed in previous controls, including the retrieval of stored settings and the displaying of user feedback messages using the `AddModuleMessage` method. The most important element to understand and remember in terms of newly added items to this code is the use of `Server.HtmlEncode` on all input text. This process encodes the user input and protects against HTML and script injection, which are very common attack points in Guestbook modules. The additional use of stored procedures at the database level ensures that SQL script injection is prevented as well.

Localization File

As with all other controls, DotNetNuke localization is used to handle static text elements. It is necessary to add the new localization file to the project. This is done by right-clicking on the `App_LocalResources` folder and selecting Add New Item. The type of item is a resources file, and the name should be `SignGuestbook.ascx.resx`.

Table 8-7 shows the individual resource elements that should be added to this file. As with the other localization files, the comments are optional.

Table 8-7

Name	Value	Comment
lblName.Text	Your Name	Label for the name prompt
lblName.Help	Please provide your name for display in the guestbook	Help text for the name prompt
NameRequired.Text	You must supply your name	Error text for the missing name
lblWebsite.Text	Your Web site	Label for the website prompt
lblWebsite.Help	You may provide your Web site here, be sure to include http://	Help text for the website prompt
WebsiteFormat.Text	Must be a valid website address	Error text for an invalid website format
lblComment.Text	Comments	Label for the comments prompt
lblComment.Help	Your comments to list in the guestbook	Help text for the comments prompt
CommentRequired.Text	You must supply a comment to post to the guestbook	Error text for a missing comment
btnSign.Text	Add My Entry	Text for the Add button
lblCannotSign.Text	<p>You must be logged in to sign the guestbook. Please log in and return to this page to post an entry.</p>	Cannot sign text
NotConfigured.Text	<p>This module has not been configured and is not accepting input at this time.</p>	Not configured error text
Success.Text	<p>Your post was successfully added to the guestbook and is now visible.</p>	Success text for posting with automatic approval
SuccessModerated.Text	<p>Your post has been received. However, the approval of a site administrator is required before it will be visible on this site.</p>	Success text for posting to a moderated guestbook

This step completes the building of the initial user interface for the module. At this time, when you select Build Solution from the Build menu, you should see a success message.

Final Module Manifest Additions

Because the final step of interface creation involves the addition of the `SignGuestbook.ascx` user control, you must modify the `.dnn` files. Specifically, you must add an additional module definition, as well as two new files to the files section.

Adding Module Definitions

Listing 8-19 (C#) and Listing 8-20 (VB) show the module definition for the `Sign Guestbook` control that was added to the project. These definitions must be added to the `.dnn` file, after the last module definition but before the `</moduleDefinitions>` closing tag. You add this individual control as a new module in order to enable it to be displayed at the same time as the other module. This packages the modules together, and when one is selected from the control panel for addition to a page, both will be added.

Listing 8-19: C# Manifest Module Addition

```
<moduleDefinition>
  <friendlyName>Sign Guestbook CS</friendlyName>
  <defaultCacheTime>0</defaultCacheTime>
  <moduleControl>
    <controlKey />
    <controlSrc>DesktopModules/GuestbookCS/
        SignGuestbook.ascx</controlSrc>
    <supportsPartialRendering>false</supportsPartialRendering>
    <controlTitle>Sign Guestbook</controlTitle>
    <controlType>View</controlType>
    <iconFile />
    <helpUrl />
    <viewOrder>0</viewOrder>
  </moduleControl>
  <moduleControl>
    <controlKey>Settings</controlKey>
    <controlSrc>DesktopModules/GuestbookCS/Settings.ascx</controlSrc>
    <supportsPartialRendering>false</supportsPartialRendering>
    <controlTitle>Sign Guestbook Settings</controlTitle>
    <controlType>Edit</controlType>
    <iconFile />
    <helpUrl />
    <viewOrder>0</viewOrder>
  </moduleControl>
</moduleDefinition>
```

Listing 8-20: VB Manifest Module Addition

```
<moduleDefinition>
  <friendlyName>Sign Guestbook VB</friendlyName>
  <defaultCacheTime>0</defaultCacheTime>
  <moduleControl>
    <controlKey />
    <controlSrc>DesktopModules/GuestbookVB/
        SignGuestbook.ascx</controlSrc>
    <supportsPartialRendering>false</supportsPartialRendering>
    <controlTitle>Sign Guestbook</controlTitle>
    <controlType>View</controlType>
    <iconFile />
    <helpUrl />
    <viewOrder>0</viewOrder>
  </moduleControl>
  <moduleControl>
    <controlKey>Settings</controlKey>
    <controlSrc>DesktopModules/GuestbookCS/Settings.ascx</controlSrc>
    <supportsPartialRendering>false</supportsPartialRendering>
    <controlTitle>Sign Guestbook Settings</controlTitle>
    <controlType>Edit</controlType>
    <iconFile />
    <helpUrl />
    <viewOrder>0</viewOrder>
  </moduleControl>
</moduleDefinition>
```

Adding a File Listing

The final required addition to the manifest file is the indication of extra included files for processing. This is completed by adding the code from Listing 8-21 to the `<files>` section of the manifest. This code is the same for both the VB and C# versions of the module.

Listing 8-21: Files Addition

```
<file>
  <path>app_localresources</path>
  <name>SignGuestbook.ascx.resx</name>
</file>
<file>
  <path>app_localresources</path>
  <name>ViewSettings.ascx.resx</name>
</file>
<file>
  <name>SignGuestbook.ascx</name>
</file>
<file>
  </name>ViewSettings.ascx</name>
</file>
```

Chapter 9 introduces an automatic method to generate the DotNetNuke manifest file that helps avoid the tedious task of tracking all module files.

Modules and CSS

This chapter has used a few of the common DotNetNuke CSS classes such as the following:

❑   `SubHead`: Typically used for input labels

❑   `Normal`: Used for standard text

❑   `NormalTextbox`: Used for input boxes

❑   `NormalRed`: Used for error messages

A number of CSS classes such as these can be used by default. For more information on DotNetNuke skinning, you might want to take a look at *Beginning DotNetNuke Skinning and Design* by Andrew Hay and Shaun Walker (Wrox, 2007). A discussion of all the common elements is outside the scope of this book.

As a module developer, it is possible to include a custom CSS file with a module. You can do this simply by adding the file to your module package, and the file listing in the manifest called `module.css`. DotNetNuke will handle the automatic linking of the CSS file. This is very helpful when you are working with a module that has a complex layout.

Summary

This chapter introduced the process to create a localized DotNetNuke interface by building each of the needed controls for the C# and VB Guestbook modules. Common DotNetNuke localization practices were investigated, and individual DotNetNuke development techniques (including page navigation) were explored with examples.

At this point, you have a module that can be fully compiled. That sets the stage for Chapter 9, in which you will test the module, debug the module, and prepare it for deployment to other DotNetNuke installations.

Packaging, Installing, and Debugging the Module

In Chapter 8, you completed the first round of development for the Guestbook modules. Now it is time to test them and prepare them for deployment and distribution.

This chapter introduces the concepts of packaging, installation, and debugging of custom modules, using the Guestbook module as the demonstration tool. The chapter begins with a quick overview of how a DotNetNuke module is actually installed and viewed. You will then learn about the processes behind actually packaging a module for deployment, as well as the packaging debugging processes for those times when things are just not working. The chapter concludes with an examination of additional testing and best practices to help you prepare for deployment. By the end of this chapter, you should be familiar with all the aspects of installation, packaging, and debugging.

Module Installation

You should already be familiar with the standard DotNetNuke module installation process involving the use of a packaged module ZIP file. If you are not, you can visit the author's website at www.mitchelsellers.com for a detailed overview.

By now, you have developed and compiled the Guestbook modules, and they should be sitting inside the local test DotNetNuke environment. However, they are not ready to actually be tested. When installing a module that has been created locally and not using the standard installation procedures, you must first import the module manifest, which defines the structure of the module. You must also manually execute any SqlDataProvider scripts necessary to create database objects. The following sections examine this process.

Import Module Manifest

The process of importing the module manifests is exactly the same for both the C# and Visual Basic modules — the only difference is the file selected for importing. The following procedure uses the C# module for demonstration purposes.

To start the process, you must log in to the site as the host user and navigate to the Module Definitions page. Select Import Module Definition from the action menu, as shown in Figure 9-1.

Figure 9-1: Selecting Import Module Definition from the action menu

After selecting this option, you will see the Module Definitions page, as shown in Figure 9-2. From the Manifest drop-down list, select the .dnn file as the module you want to import (in this case, GuestbookCS.dnn). Click the Import Manifest link.

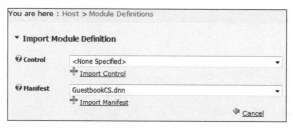

Figure 9-2: Import Module Definition page

You should now see a status update at the bottom of the page, similar in format to the one shown in Figure 9-3. This indicates the successful import of the manifest file. You can now select Cancel to return to the list of installed modules, where the newly imported Guestbook module will be displayed. Using the default text from the .dnn file, the entry in Module Definitions should look similar to the one shown in Figure 9-4 for the C# module.

```
StartJob Starting Installation
Info      Starting Installation - WROX_GuestbookCS
Info      Starting Installation - Script
Info      Begin Sql execution
Info      Finished Sql execution
Info      Component installed successfully - Script
Info      Starting Installation - Module
Info      Module registered successfully - WROX_GuestbookCS
Info      Component installed successfully - Module
Info      Starting Installation - Assembly
Info      Component installed successfully - Assembly
Info      Starting Installation - File
Info      Component installed successfully - File
Info      Installation committed
Info      Installation successful. - WROX_GuestbookCS
Info      Deleted temporary install folder
EndJob  Installation successful.
```

Figure 9-3: Import Manifest status display

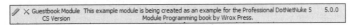

Figure 9-4: Module Definitions display of the installed module

Manually Execute SqlDataProvider files

Once the manifest has been imported, you must execute *all* necessary `.SqlDataProvider` files from your module, because the import manifest process does *not* execute them like the standard installation process. This is a very simple process. While you are still logged in as the host user, select SQL from the Host menu. You should see a screen similar to that shown in Figure 9-5. From here, you can click the Browse button to locate the SQL data provider file on your local system. Once you have located the file, click the Load link to load the file.

Figure 9-5: DotNetNuke SQL File page

After you click the link, the file is loaded into the textbox on the page, but the action does not yet execute the statement. Now that the query is loaded, it is *very* important for you to check the Run as Script option. This option ensures that DotNetNuke replaces any `{objectQualifier}` and `{databaseOwner}` values with the proper configuration elements. After this has been completed, click the Execute link and the scripts will be executed. You should then see a message that says "The Query completed successfully!" The final page displayed after completing this operation should look similar to the one shown in Figure 9-6.

147

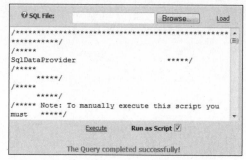

Figure 9-6: SQL page after successful script execution

> This step is one of the mostly commonly overlooked tasks when building and testing DotNetNuke modules locally. The testing notes at the end of this chapter provide more insight.

Testing the Module

Now that you have successfully installed the module to the portal, it is now possible to install and test the module's functionality. To do so, navigate to a test page inside the local DotNetNuke installation. On this page, you can select the GuestbookVB or GuestbookCS module from the "available modules" listing, where in Figure 9-7 the default control panel display is shown. Once you have selected the module, click Add on the right side of the control panel.

Figure 9-7

After you have completed this step, you should see the module displayed, similar in layout to the one shown in Figure 9-8. It is important to note that since the module is implemented using two controls site administrators have the ability to move the View and Sign controls to different locations on the page to match their desired layout.

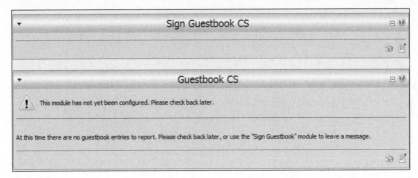

Figure 9-8

At this time, you should test the module, first by properly configuring it, and then by testing the addition of entries and the approval queue process. Once the module has passed the testing process, you are ready to move on to the packaging process to prepare the module to deploy to other DotNetNuke sites.

> If errors are encountered during testing, see the section "Debugging," later in this chapter, to learn how to hook up the Visual Studio debugger to the process.

Packaging the Module

One of the biggest changes in DotNetNuke between older versions and version 5.0 is in the module package system. In previous versions of DotNetNuke, the module package process did not support subfolders. Therefore, you couldn't have multiple files with the same name, and you had to ensure that everything fit well into the root of a ZIP package. With DotNetNuke 5.0, a new module manifest has been introduced, as discussed in previous chapters. Support has also been included for the addition of folders to the module package ZIP.

Following are a couple of key things to remember when it comes to DotNetNuke module packages:

❑ In one way or another, all files must be identified inside the .dnn file for the module.

❑ All items must be loaded into the ZIP file inside their own proper folder. Note that although the /bin directory is included in the root of the module, DotNetNuke will move it to the proper location.

In addition to these points, remember that when working with compiled (WAP) module projects (as the examples in this text are), you must also keep in mind the following:

❑ Never include an app_code folder with your project.

❑ Never deploy any .vb or .cs code with your module. It will not be used and will confuse users. If a source version is desired, distribute one as such.

With this in mind, you can use many different methods to actually package a module for deployment, as discussed in the following sections.

Manual File Creation

Thus far, you have used the manual method to create the samples. This is not an elegant solution but it works, and after you establish a routine it can be completed quickly.

With this method, you simply create a "package" folder somewhere (either inside the development environment or elsewhere), and copy the respective files and folders into the folder. That way, all files and folders can be selected and created as a ZIP file.

This method is more prone to error, but it can be a successful process for smaller modules.

Batch File Creation

When working with DotNetNuke 4.x module development, I created a batch file that performed XCOPY operations to move the necessary files from their source location to a "packages" folder. I could then put these in a ZIP file for installation.

> *You can read more about DotNetNuke 4.x module packaging at* www.mitchelsellers.com/blogs/
> articletype/articleview/articleid/200.aspx. *This article includes step-by-step instructions for automatic package creation by using Visual Studio Build Events to call the script, and it even includes command-line switches to pull debug/release* .dll *files, depending on the configuration.*

Listing 9-1 shows an example .bat script that will create the module package for the GuestbookCS module. Of course, it would be an additional exercise to implement the automated build process.

Listing 9-1: GuestbookCS Module Package Batch File (Debug Build)

```
@ECHO off
ECHO %1 Passed command is the debug/release flag
ECHO Declare paths needed, package path is cleaned at start
set project= "C:\inetpub\wwwroot\DotNetNuke\DesktopModules\GuestbookCS"
set package= "C:\DotNetNukePackages\GuestbookCS"

ECHO Delete Existing Files from package location!  CAREFUL!!!
ECHO Y | DEL %package%\*.*
ECHO Y | DEL %package%\App_LocalResources\*.*
ECHO Y | DEL %package%\Bin\*.*

ECHO Copy resource files
XCOPY %project%\App_LocalResources\*.resx %package%\App_LocalResources /I

REM Copy User Controls
XCOPY %project%\*.ascx %package%

REM Copy DNN File
XCOPY %project%\*.dnn %package%

REM Copy CSS
XCOPY %project%\*.css %package%

REM Copy Txt
```

```
XCOPY %project%\*.txt %package%

REM Copy SqlDataProvider files
XCOPY %project%\*.SqlDataProvider %package%

REM Copy DLL Files, note use of flag to grab debug/release depending
    on passed value
XCOPY%project%\obj\Debug\*.dll %package%\Bin /I
```

With this example, you can simply execute the `.bat` file to create the module package. However, you must create the package folders before running the script.

> **For assistance with this process, see the author's forum at** www.mitchelsellers
> .com/forums.aspx.

DotNetNuke-Generated Packages

When working with a local copy of DotNetNuke, it is possible to have DotNetNuke create the needed installation package automatically. This process works quite well if you simply want a ZIP file to distribute to clients, and you want to leave everything to DotNetNuke to handle.

To generate a module package from DotNetNuke, begin by logging in as the host user and navigating to the Module Definitions page. From the definitions listing, select the module for which you want to create a package. Then, scroll to the section titled Package Settings. From here, you can modify information regarding the configuration of the module package, including the name, description, version, license, and release notes. At the very bottom of this page, you can specify the owner, organization, URL, and contact e-mail for contact information.

In addition, at the bottom of this page is a Create Package option. When the package information has been properly updated, simply click the Create Package button. The Create Package wizard then displays the first step, as shown in Figure 9-9.

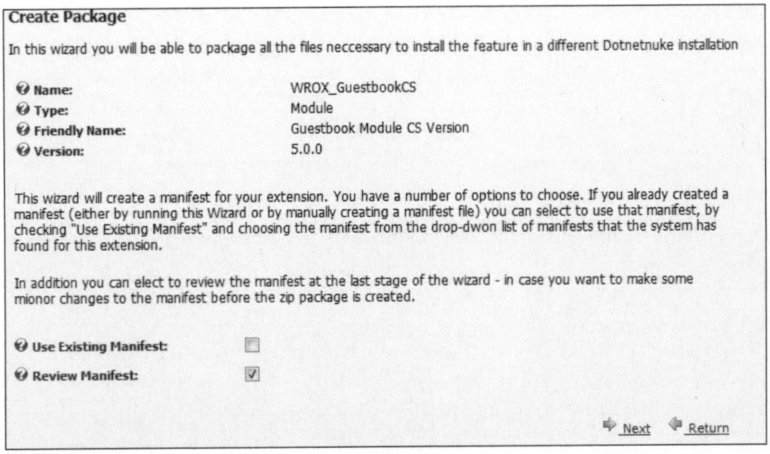

Create Package

In this wizard you will be able to package all the files neccessary to install the feature in a different Dotnetnuke installation

Name:	WROX_GuestbookCS
Type:	Module
Friendly Name:	Guestbook Module CS Version
Version:	5.0.0

This wizard will create a manifest for your extension. You have a number of options to choose. If you already created a manifest (either by running this Wizard or by manually creating a manifest file) you can select to use that manifest, by checking "Use Existing Manifest" and choosing the manifest from the drop-dwon list of manifests that the system has found for this extension.

In addition you can elect to review the manifest at the last stage of the wizard - in case you want to make some mionor changes to the manifest before the zip package is created.

Use Existing Manifest:	☐
Review Manifest:	☑

➡ Next ◀ Return

Figure 9-9: First step of the Create Package wizard

151

This first step provides an overview of what will be completed, and gives you the options to use the existing manifest and to review the manifest. If you know that the current manifest is correct, select the Use Existing Manifest option; otherwise, leave this unchecked and DotNetNuke will generate the manifest for you.

Click Next to continue with the wizard's file-selection step. DotNetNuke attempts to get all needed files for the module, which, by default, is *all* files. If you use the templates (as we have done in this book), a few additional files are added by default. Figure 9-10 shows the Choose Files to Include window, showing the default display for the `GuestbookCS` package. To remove files, simply delete them from the textbox. In this example, all items in the `/documentation/` folder must be removed. The Include Source option enables you to create a package that distributes the source code. Click Next to continue with the wizard.

Choose Files to include

At this step you can choose the files to include in your package. The wizard has attempted to determine the files to include, but you can add or delete files from the list. In addition you decide whether to include the source files, by checking the "Include Source" checkbox.

Folder DesktopModules\GuestbookCS   Refresh File List

Include Source: ☐

```
01.00.00.sqldataprovider
guestbookcs.sqldataprovider
uninstall.sqldataprovider
guestbookcs.dnn
documentation\documentation.css
documentation\documentation.html
documentation\logo.gif
app_localresources\editguestbookcs.ascx.resx
app_localresources\settings.ascx.resx
app_localresources\viewguestbookcs.ascx.resx
editguestbookcs.ascx
settings.ascx
signguestbook.ascx
viewguestbookcs.ascx
app_localresources\signguestbook.ascx.resx
```

Previous   Next   Return

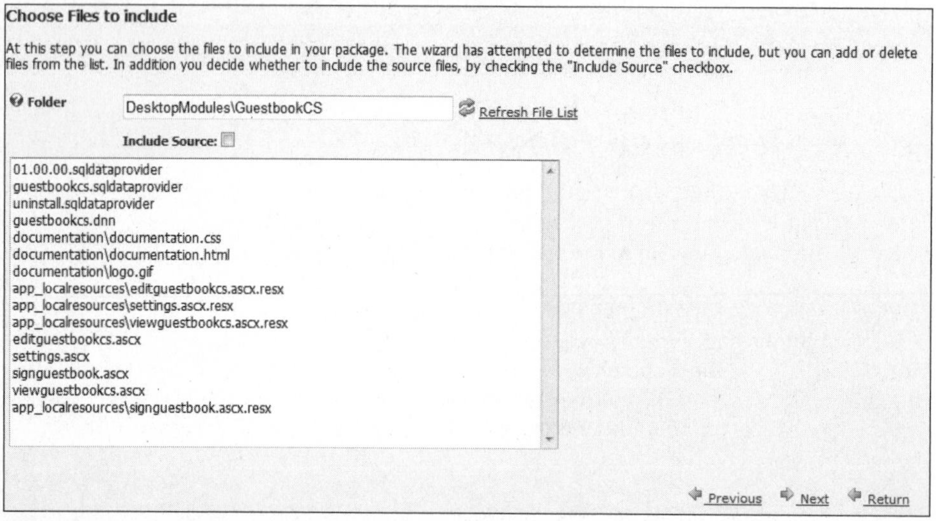

Figure 9-10: File-selection step with the Create Package wizard

The third step of the wizard process enables you to add any needed assemblies to the distribution, as shown in Figure 9-11. From here, you can simply use the default values and click Next to continue. Because you checked the Review Manifest option at the beginning of the wizard process, you are now allowed to review (edit) the manifest file that will be created, as shown in Figure 9-12. Click Next to continue with the wizard.

Choose Assemblies to include

At this step you can add the assemblies to include in your package. If there is a project file in the Package folder, the wizard has attempted to determine the assemblies to include, but you can add or delete assembliess from the list.

```
bin\wroxmodules.guestbookcs.dll
```

Previous   Next   Return

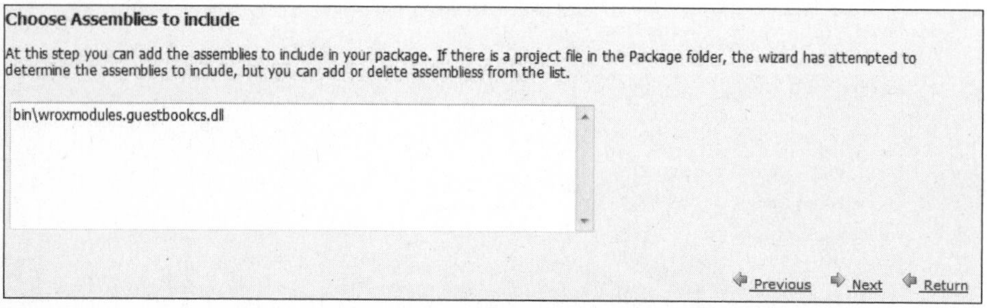

Figure 9-11: Adding needed assemblies with the Create Package wizard

Create Manifest

Based on your selections the wizard has created the manifest for the package. The manifest is displayed in the text box below. You can edit the manifest, before creating the package.

```
<description>
    This example module is being created as an example for the Professional DotNetNuke 5 Module Programming
book by Wrox Press.
    </description>
    <owner>
      <name>Mitchel Sellers</name>
      <organization>None</organization>
      <url />
      <email>msellers@iowacomputergurus.com</email>
    </owner>
    <license>
      &lt;p&gt;Permission is hereby granted, free of charge, to any person obtaining a copy of this software and
associated
      documentation files (the "Software"), to deal in the Software without restriction, including without limitation
      the rights to use, copy, modify, merge, publish, distribute, sublicense, and/or sell copies of the Software,
and
      to permit persons to whom the Software is furnished to do so, subject to the following conditions:
      The above copyright notice and this permission notice shall be included in all copies or substantial portions
      of the Software.&lt;/p&gt;&lt;p&gt;THE SOFTWARE IS PROVIDED "AS IS", WITHOUT WARRANTY OF ANY
KIND, EXPRESS OR IMPLIED, INCLUDING BUT NOT LIMITED
      TO THE WARRANTIES OF MERCHANTABILITY, FITNESS FOR A PARTICULAR PURPOSE AND
```

 Previous Next Return

Figure 9-12: Reviewing (or editing) the manifest file with the Create Package wizard

After you have completed the first four steps of the process, the final step is to specify the installation package's name. Here you may also save a copy of the manifest. Figure 9-13 shows the selections needed to create the `Guestbook CS` installation package with a name of `GuestbookCSInstallation`. Click Next to generate the package inside the `Packages` folder, where it can be downloaded and distributed.

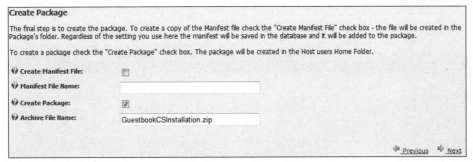

Figure 9-13: Creating the package with the Create Package wizard

Other Options

You still have many other options when creating a DotNetNuke module package. Many individuals use NAnt to create a custom build event that will create the package, while others use `MSBuild` to accomplish the same task. Any tool can be used for module package creation as long as the result is properly formatted with all necessary files and no extras are included.

Debugging

As you have learned, one disadvantage of the WAP development model for DotNetNuke modules is that you can't simply select Run from the Debug menu to start the debugging process. However, it is still very simple to start the debugging of custom-created DotNetNuke modules.

After a module has been properly installed to the local DotNetNuke system and the site has been loaded, you can use Visual Studio's Attach to Process option from the Debug menu to start debugging. To start this debugging process, it is assumed that the module has been developed on the local system, in debug mode, and deployed to the local DotNetNuke installation. Without a debug build (which creates a `pdb` file), it is not possible to debug the module. Once you select this option, a screen similar to the one shown in Figure 9-14 will be displayed, listing the available processes currently running on the system.

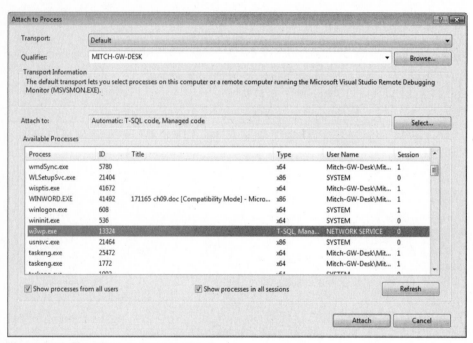

Figure 9-14: The Attach to Process dialog

Ensure that the "Show processes from all users" option is selected, and then look for an entry for `w3wp` `.exe` (for Windows 2003, 2008, and Vista operating systems) or `aspnet_wp.exe` (for Windows 2000 and XP). If multiple entries appear for either process, then be sure to select the entry with a type of "T-SQL, Managed," because this is the proper stream for debugging.

> If more than one process is listed with the T-SQL, Managed type, it is possible to select all instances. Doing this will attach the debugger to all processes at the same time, allowing them to be monitored for debugging, regardless of which is the specific process for the environment. This is common when operating on a server with sites running in multiple application pools.

Once you have selected this entry, click Attach and the debugger will start. At this point, you can debug the module just like any other .NET application, including the addition of breakpoints.

Distribution and Testing Considerations

With a module developed and tested, you may be anxious to deploy the module into the wild. However, you should be aware of some important issues before going down this path.

When you are creating modules for distribution to the diverse DotNetNuke community, keep in mind that the module will be exposed to various DotNetNuke installation versions, skins, containers, and other modules. After local testing, it is in the best interests of module developers to deploy the module to at least one other location. First of all, this enables you to fully test the package that was created. Second, it ensures that proper configuration is actually occurring in environments other than the development environment.

In addition to testing on another isolated installation, you should also perform an installation on DotNetNuke's minimum supported version, as well as the most current version. This wide base of testing scenarios can help to minimize the number of support requests that appear later in the development cycle when the modules are deployed into the vast community.

Summary

Having reviewed the process to install, package, debug, and test a module, the first round of development has been completed for the custom Guestbook modules. Now that the basics of DotNetNuke module development have been covered, it is time to start focusing on the more advanced topics of DotNetNuke development.

Chapter 10 introduces DotNetNuke interfaces that can be implemented to help improve site functionality.

10

Implementing Optional DotNetNuke Interfaces

With the standard module build out of the way, let's start investigating the methods that can be used to more tightly integrate the Guestbook and other custom modules to the DotNetNuke system. To accomplish this integration, the DotNetNuke framework presents a number of very helpful interfaces that can be implemented in various locations within the module code.

This chapter examines five of the key interfaces that can be used, along with sample code, and provides a look at implementation in the Guestbook module (if applicable). By the end of this chapter, you will have the information you need to make proper business judgments regarding which interfaces should be implemented.

IPortable

The IPortable interface provides users with the capability to import and export content from one module instance (or portal) to another. Although many developers may decide that their modules don't need to export content, it is typically a good idea to support this interface because it can be helpful to site administrators in the long run.

When a module implements IPortable, two options are added to the module action menu: Import Content and Export Content. Additionally, if a module supports IPortable and a site administrator creates a site template with the "With data" option enabled, the module's content will also be exported. This is functionality that most users simply expect as part of the process.

Implementation

The `IPortable` interface is implemented in the `BusinessControllerClass` of your module project. In the case of the Guestbook module being built in this book, it will be added to either the `GuestbookCSController.cs` file or the `GuestbookVBController.vb` file.

The process to implement the interface is very simple. First, you add a statement indicating that the module implements the interface. Listing 10-1 shows the modified C# code and Listing 10-2 shows the VB class declarations needed to perform this step.

Listing 10-1: New C# Controller Definition

```
public class GuestbookCSController : IPortable
```

Listing 10-2: New VB Controller Definition

```
Public Class GuestbookVBController
    Implements IPortable
```

Once this is completed, you simply implement the two methods required by the interface.

`ExportModule` accepts a single parameter for `ModuleId`. This method must return a string literal containing XML-formatted information about the module. A simple string builder process can be used to create the XML string. The module ID provides information regarding the content to export.

The `ImportModule` method provides input values for `ModuleId`, which is the ID of the new module instance to populate. `Content` is the XML string that contains the module's contents. `Version` indicates the version of the module from which the content was retrieved. (This is helpful to ensure that module code is processed using the right format if content structures are ever changed in the future.) The final parameter is the `userId` of the importing user, to be used if tracking "Created by" users.

Listings 10-3 shows the C# implementation and Listing 10-4 shows the VB implementation of `IPortable` for the Guestbook module.

> These listings assume that `using`/`imports` **statements have been added for** `System.Text` **and** `System.Xml`. **If these are not added, errors may be encountered.**

Listing 10-3: C# IPortable Implementation

```
#region IPortable Implementation
public string ExportModule(int ModuleID)
{
    StringBuilder sb = new StringBuilder();
    List<GuestbookEntryInfo> entries = GetAllEntries(ModuleID);

    if (entries.Count > 0)
```

```
        {
            sb.Append("<GuestbookCS>");
            foreach (GuestbookEntryInfo entry in entries)
            {
                sb.Append("<entry>");
                sb.Append("<submitterName>");
                sb.Append(XmlUtils.XMLEncode(entry.SubmitterName));
                sb.Append("</submitterName>");
                sb.Append("<submitterWebsite>");
                sb.Append(XmlUtils.XMLEncode(entry.SubmitterWebsite));
                sb.Append("</submitterWebsite>");
                sb.Append("<submitterComment>");
                sb.Append(XmlUtils.XMLEncode(entry.SubmitterComment));
                sb.Append("</submitterComment>");
                sb.Append("<submissionDate>");
                sb.Append(XmlUtils.XMLEncode(entry.SubmissionDate.ToString()));
                sb.Append("</submissionDate>");
                sb.Append("<isApproved>");
                sb.Append(XmlUtils.XMLEncode(entry.IsApproved.ToString()));
                sb.Append("</isApproved>");
                sb.Append("</entry>");
            }
            sb.Append("</GuestbookCS>");
        }

    return sb.ToString();
}

public void ImportModule(int ModuleID, string Content,
    string Version, int UserID)
{
    XmlNode entries = DotNetNuke.Common.Globals.GetContent
        (Content, "GuestbookCS");
    foreach (XmlNode entry in entries.SelectNodes("entry"))
    {
        GuestbookEntryInfo oInfo = new GuestbookEntryInfo();
        oInfo.ModuleId = ModuleID;
        oInfo.SubmitterName =
            entry.SelectSingleNode("submitterName").InnerText;
        oInfo.SubmitterWebsite =
            entry.SelectSingleNode("submitterWebsite").InnerText;
        oInfo.SubmitterComment =
            entry.SelectSingleNode("submitterComment").InnerText;
        oInfo.SubmissionDate =
            DateTime.Parse(entry.SelectSingleNode
            ("submissionDate").InnerText);
        oInfo.IsApproved =
            bool.Parse(entry.SelectSingleNode
            ("isApproved").InnerText);
        InsertGuestbookEntry(oInfo);

    }
}
#endregion
```

Listing 10-4: VB IPortable Implementation

```vb
#Region "IPortable Implementation"
        Public Function ExportModule(ByVal ModuleID As Integer)
          As String Implements IPortable.ExportModule
            Dim sb As New StringBuilder
            Dim entries As List(Of GuestbookEntryInfo) =
                GetAllEntries(ModuleID)
            Dim entry As GuestbookEntryInfo

            If (entries.Count > 0) Then
                sb.Append("<GuestbookVB>")
                For Each entry In entries
                    sb.Append("<entry>")
                    sb.Append("<submitterName>")
                    sb.Append(XmlUtils.XMLEncode(entry.SubmitterName))
                    sb.Append("</submitterName>")
                    sb.Append("<submitterWebsite>")
                    sb.Append(XmlUtils.XMLEncode
                        (entry.SubmitterWebsite))
                    sb.Append("</submitterWebsite>")
                    sb.Append("<submitterComment>")
                    sb.Append(XmlUtils.XMLEncode
                        (entry.SubmitterComment))
                    sb.Append("</submitterComment>")
                    sb.Append("<submissionDate>")
                    sb.Append(XmlUtils.XMLEncode
                        (entry.SubmissionDate.ToString()))
                    sb.Append("</submissionDate>")
                    sb.Append("<isApproved>")
                    sb.Append(XmlUtils.XMLEncode
                        (entry.IsApproved.ToString()))
                    sb.Append("</isApproved>")
                    sb.Append("</entry>")
                Next
                sb.Append("</GuestbookVB>")
            End If

            Return sb.ToString()
        End Function


        Public Sub ImportModule(ByVal ModuleID As Integer,
            ByVal Content As String, ByVal Version As String,
            ByVal UserID As Integer) Implements IPortable.ImportModule
            Dim entries As XmlNode =
                DotNetNuke.Common.Globals.GetContent
                (Content, "GuestbookVB")
            Dim entry As XmlNode
            For Each entry In entries.SelectNodes("entry")
                Dim oInfo As New GuestbookEntryInfo
                oInfo.ModuleId = ModuleID
                oInfo.SubmitterName =
                    entry.SelectSingleNode("submitterName").InnerText
```

```
                   oInfo.SubmitterWebsite =
                       entry.SelectSingleNode
                       ("submitterWebsite").InnerText
                   oInfo.SubmitterComment =
                       entry.SelectSingleNode
                       ("submitterComment").InnerText
                   oInfo.SubmissionDate =
                       DateTime.Parse(entry.SelectSingleNode
                       ("submissionDate").InnerText)
                   oInfo.IsApproved =
                       Boolean.Parse(entry.SelectSingleNode
                       ("isApproved").InnerText)
                   InsertGuestbookEntry(oInfo)
           Next
       End Sub
   #End Region
```

IHydratable

The IHydratable interface was added to DotNetNuke in version 4.6.0 to help improve performance of database operations for modules using the CBO class for data hydration. Prior to the existence of the IHydratable interface, developers could still call code such as CBO.FillCollection<MyClass> (MyDataReader) and retrieve their formatted collection, and this process worked very well. However, it used reflection to obtain the class information for hydration. With IHydratable, if an information object implements this interface, CBO will call the class's internal Fill method (defined by the developer), which can specifically map the columns, thus eliminating the need for reflection.

Basic performance testing has shown that objects implementing the IHydratable interface are substantially faster. In some cases, reductions in load time of more than 60 seconds were achieved.

Implementation

The implementation of the IHydratable interface is complete on the individual information object level. Current limitations of the IHydratable interface only allow for support when the information object has a primary key that is an integer value.

You must make a few configuration changes for the individual information object classes to implement IHydratable. First, the GuestbookCSInfo.cs and GuestbookVBInfo.vb files must be updated to include additional references. This can be completed by adding the code from Listing 10-5 (C#) or Listing 10-6 (VB) to the bottom of the existing Using or Imports statements. These add the references needed for data processing and interface implementation.

> Depending on the template versions used, one or more using/import **statement might exist. Only add these if they do not already exist.**

Listing 10-5: Additional using statements for C#

```
using DotNetNuke.Entities.Modules;
using System.Data;
```

Listing 10-6: Additional Imports statements for VB

```
Imports System.Data;
Imports DotNetNuke.Entities.Modules
```

With this completed, you can add the necessary code to the class declaration that indicates that the module implements the interface. Listings 10-7 (C#) and Listing 10-8 (VB) show the new class declarations.

Listing 10-7: New info Class Declaration (C#)

```
public class GuestbookEntryInfo : IHydratable
```

Listing 10-8: New info class declaration (VB)

```
Public Class GuestbookEntryInfo
    Implements IHydratable
```

The final step to implement the interface is to implement the KeyID public property. This property provides the CBO class with a unique identifier. You must also implement the Fill method, which provides a DataReader, and simply hydrate the object with the needed values. Listing 10-9 (C#) and Listing 10-10 (VB) show the code needed to implement the interface.

Listing 10-9: C# IHydratable Implementation

```
#region IHydratable Implementation
public int KeyID
{
    get { return _entryId; }
    set { _entryId = value; }
}

public void Fill(IDataReader oReader)
{
    _entryId = int.Parse(oReader["EntryId"].ToString());
    _isApproved = bool.Parse(oReader["IsApproved"].ToString());
    _moduleId = int.Parse(oReader["ModuleId"].ToString());
    _submissionDate = DateTime.Parse(oReader["SubmissionDate"].ToString());
    _submitterComment = Convert.ToString(oReader["SubmitterComment"]);
    _submitterName = Convert.ToString(oReader["SubmitterName"]);
    _submitterWebsite = Convert.ToString(oReader["SubmitterWebsite"]);
}
#endregion
```

Listing 10-10: VB IHydratable Implementation

```vb
#Region "IHydratable Implementation"
        Public Property KeyId() As Integer Implements
          IHydratable.KeyID
          Get
              Return _entryId
          End Get
          Set(ByVal value As Integer)
              _entryId = value
          End Set
        End Property

        Public Sub Fill(ByVal oReader As IDataReader)
          Implements IHydratable.Fill
          _entryId = Integer.Parse(oReader("EntryId").ToString())
          _isApproved =
              Boolean.Parse(oReader("IsApproved").ToString())
          _moduleId = Integer.Parse(oReader("ModuleId").ToString())
          _submissionDate =
              DateTime.Parse(oReader("SubmissionDate").ToString())
          _submitterComment =
              Convert.ToString(oReader("SubmitterComment"))
          _submitterName = Convert.ToString(oReader("SubmitterName"))
          _submitterWebsite =
              Convert.ToString(oReader("SubmitterWebsite"))
        End Sub
#End Region
```

This is a *very* simple interface to implement and one that provides a noticeable performance improvement. Its usage in modules is highly recommended.

ISearchable

DotNetNuke has a search facility built into the core system, and ISearchable is the method by which custom modules can expose their information to the search indexer. The example Guestbook module doesn't implement this because enabling users to search user-supplied comments is unlikely to be a valuable feature and has no bearing on the overall functionality of the site. Nonetheless, the following discussion provides all the necessary implementation information for other module development projects that may benefit from this feature.

Implementation

Implementation of the ISearchable interface is completed inside the BusinessControllerClass because it is a global facility. A single method is needed to meet the contract of the ISearchable interface, and from there you must feed the method *all* content from your module so that it can update the index accordingly.

If you wanted to implement ISearchable for the Guestbook module, then you would use code similar to that shown in Listing 10-11 (C#) or Listing 10-12 (VB). The key point to note here is that the method must return a collection of SearchItemInformation objects.

Listing 10-11: C# ISearchable Implementation

```csharp
#region ISearchable Implementation
public SearchItemInfoCollection GetSearchItems(ModuleInfo modInfo)
{
    SearchItemInfoCollection searchItems =
        new SearchItemInfoCollection();
    List<GuestbookEntryInfo> items = GetAllEntries(modInfo.ModuleID);

    foreach (GuestbookEntryInfo item in items)
    {
        SearchItemInfo searchItem = new SearchItemInfo();
        searchItem.Author = 2; //Default to admin
        searchItem.Content = item.SubmitterComment;
        searchItem.Description = item.SubmitterComment;
        searchItem.ModuleId = modInfo.ModuleID;
        searchItem.PubDate = item.SubmissionDate;
        searchItem.SearchItemId = item.EntryId;
        searchItem.SearchKey = item.EntryId.ToString();
        searchItem.Title = "Guestbook Comment";
        searchItems.Add(searchItem);
    }
    return searchItems;
}
#endregion
```

Listing 10-12: VB ISearchable Implementation

```vb
#Region "ISearchable Implementation"
        Public Function GetSearchItems(ByVal modInfo As ModuleInfo)
                As SearchItemInfoCollection Implements
                ISearchable.GetSearchItems
            Dim searchItems As New SearchItemInfoCollection
            Dim item As GuestbookEntryInfo
            Dim items As List(Of GuestbookEntryInfo) =
                GetAllEntries(modInfo.ModuleID)

            For Each item In items
                Dim searchItem As New SearchItemInfo
                searchItem.Author = 2 'Default to admin
                searchItem.Content = item.SubmitterComment
                searchItem.Description = item.SubmitterComment
                searchItem.ModuleId = modInfo.ModuleID
                searchItem.PubDate = item.SubmissionDate
                searchItem.SearchItemId = item.Entryid
                searchItem.SearchKey = item.Entryid.ToString()
                searchItem.Title = "Guestbook Comment"
                searchItems.Add(searchItem)
            Next
            Return searchItems
        End Function
#End Region
```

Table 10-1 provides a summary of each of the search item properties.

Table 10-1

Property	Description
Author	The userId of the person adding or updating the content. This can default to 2 for the standard DNN administrator.
Content	This is the text that should actually be indexed for searching.
Description	This is the description displayed in the search results.
ModuleId	This is the module ID in which the content is displayed.
PubDate	This is the date of the last update. This is used to ensure that the search doesn't waste effort by re-indexing unchanged content.
Searchitemid	This is the unique ID for this item in this module instance (typically your info object's unique ID).
Search Key	This is the key value.
Title	This is the title used in all search results.

IUpgradable

IUpgradeable is an interface that enables module developers to execute custom bits of code after a successful module upgrade. Be careful when using this interface because it is not an exact science that guarantees the code will be executed. However, if a simple SQL script is not enough to take care of module upgrades, this is a valid option. There is no need for implementations of this within the Guestbook module, however, so the following discussion addresses general implementation details for use with future project needs.

Implementation

Implementation of the IUpgradeable interface is completed in the BusinessControllerClass because it is a globally defined process and is called once per upgraded version. To implement this interface, you decorate the controller to indicate that it implements IUpgradable. This is done just as with other interfaces. Once this is complete, you add the UpgradeModule method, which accepts a string parameter for the module version. You can then take action based on the version. Listing 10-13 (C#) and Listing 10-14 (VB) show an example of how this would be implemented.

Listing 10-13: IUpgradable C# Example

```csharp
#region IUpgradable Implementation
public string UpgradeModule(string moduleVersion)
{
    switch (moduleVersion)
    {
        case "05.01.00":
            //Take action for this version
            break;
    }

    return "True";
}
#endregion
```

Listing 10-14: IUpgradable VB Example

```vb
#Region "IUpgradable Implementation Example"
        Public Function UpgradeModule(ByVal moduleVersion As String)
          As String
            Implements IUpgradeable.UpgradeModule
          Select Case moduleVersion
              Case "05.01.00"
                    'Do your stuff here
          End Select
          Return "True"
        End Function
#End Region
```

IActionable

The IActionable interface enables a developer to add custom elements to the action menu that can be displayed for any module within a DotNetNuke site. Of all the DotNetNuke interfaces, this is by far the most heavily implemented. For example, a large percentage of modules implement this interface on at least one control to provide access to an "edit" or "add item" screen. The example Guestbook module does not provide any reason to implement this interface, however, so the following discussion addresses general implementations.

Implementation

Implementation of this interface is completed in the code-behind file for each module that must add elements to the action menu. This is accomplished by simply adding a public property called ModuleActions that meets the requirements of the IActionable interface. Listing 10-15 (C#) and Listing 10-16 (VB) show an example of how to add an item to the action menu to link to Google.com for admin users only.

Listing 10-15: C# IActionable Implementation

```csharp
#region IActionable Implementation
public DotNetNuke.Entities.Modules.Actions.
     ModuleActionCollection ModuleActions
{
    get
    {
        ModuleActionCollection oActions = new ModuleActionCollection();
        oActions.Add(GetNextActionID(), "Google", "", "", "",
            "http://www.google.com", false,
            DotNetNuke.Security.SecurityAccessLevel.Edit, true, true);
        return oActions;
    }
}
#endregion
```

Listing 10-16: VB IActionable Implementation

```vb
#Region "IActionable Demo"
        Public ReadOnly Property ModuleActions()
            As DotNetNuke.Entities.Modules.Actions.
            ModuleActionCollection Implements
                IActionable.ModuleActions
          Get
                Dim oActions As New
                        DotNetNuke.Entities.Modules.Actions.
                        ModuleActionCollection
                oActions.Add(GetNextActionID(), "Google", "", "", "",
                    "http://www.google.com", False,
                    SecurityAccessLevel.Edit, True, False)
                Return oActions
            End Get
        End Property
#End Region
```

Table 10-2 provides a list of parameter items.

Table 10-2

Property Name	Description
Id	This is the unique ID of the action. Use the `GetNextActionId()` method to retrieve the proper value.
Title	This is the title of the menu item, typically loaded from localization files using `Localization.GetString("Key", LocalResourceFile)`.
CommandName	This is the name of the command, used when implementing an action event, rather than a simple redirection.
CommandArgument	This is the argument passed to the method when implementing an action event.
Icon	This is a string path to an icon to be displayed next to the menu item.
Url	This is the fully qualified URL to which the user is directed.
UseActionEvent	This is a Boolean value indicating whether it should be an action event. If it is, then rather than use redirection, a postback will occur.
SecurityAccessLevel	This is a value from the `DotNetNuke.Security.SecurityAccessLevel` enumeration. Possible values include the following: `Admin`: Users in administrator role `Anonymous`: Unauthenticated users `Control Panel`: Users who can see the control panel `Edit`: Users with edit permissions to the module `Host`: Host users `View`: Users with view permissions to the module
Visible	This is a Boolean value indicating whether the entry is visible or not.
NewWindow	This is a Boolean value indicating whether the link should be opened in a new window.

IPropertyAccess

This interface enables information objects to implement methods, allowing for the use of standard DotNetNuke token-replacement methods. Rather than implement your own tokenizing process (as done previously in Chapter 8), DotNetNuke methods can be leveraged to speed the development process. The following sections show the implementation of this interface as used by the Announcements module within the DotNetNuke core projects.

Implementation

Implementing this interface is as simple as adding a few items to the information object class and building a `Token Replacement` class that sits along with the information object.

First you need a `using/imports` statement to reference the `DotNetNuke.Services.Tokens` namespace. After that, you must modify the class declaration to note that it implements the

`IPropertyAccess` interface. This is completed in a manner similar to all other code provided in this book. Listing 10-17 shows the `IPropertyAccess` implementation for the Announcements module information object.

> For brevity, some items have been removed from the `Select Case` statement.

Listing 10-17: Announcements Module IPropertyAccess Implementation

```
        Public Function GetProperty(ByVal strPropertyName As String, ByVal
strFormat As String, ByVal formatProvider As System.Globalization.CultureInfo,
ByVal AccessingUser As Entities.Users.UserInfo, ByVal AccessLevel As
Services.Tokens.Scope, ByRef PropertyNotFound As Boolean) As String
        Implements Services.Tokens.IPropertyAccess.GetProperty
            Dim OutputFormat As String = String.Empty
            Dim portalSettings As PortalSettings =
                    PortalController.GetCurrentPortalSettings()
            If strFormat = String.Empty Then
                OutputFormat = "D"
            Else
                OutputFormat = strFormat
            End If
            Select Case strPropertyName.ToLower
                Case "edit"
                    Dim userInfo As UserInfo =
        CType(HttpContext.Current.Items("UserInfo"), UserInfo)
                    Dim moduleConfiguration As ModuleInfo = New
                        ModuleController().GetModule(ModuleId,
                        portalSettings.ActiveTab.TabID)
                    If IsEditable Then
                        Return "<a href=""" +
                          Common.Globals.NavigateURL
                          (portalSettings.ActiveTab.TabID, False,
                          portalSettings,
"Edit", Globalization.CultureInfo.CurrentCulture.Name,
        "mid=" + ModuleId.ToString,
        "itemid=" + ItemId.ToString) + """><img border=""0"" src=""" +
        Common.Globals.ApplicationPath + "/images/edit.gif"" alt=""" +
        Localization.GetString("EditAnnouncement.Text",
        LocalResourceFile) + """ /></a>"
                    Else
                        Return String.Empty
                    End If
                Case "itemid"
                    Return (Me.ItemId.ToString(OutputFormat,
                        formatProvider))
                Case "moduleid"
                    Return (Me.ModuleId.ToString(OutputFormat,
```

(continued)

Listing 10-17 *(continued)*

```
                                formatProvider))
                    Case "title"
                        Return PropertyAccess.FormatString(Me.Title,
                            strFormat)
                    Case "description"
                        Return HttpUtility.HtmlDecode(Me.Description)
                    Case "vieworder"
                        Return (Me.ViewOrder.ToString(OutputFormat,
                            formatProvider))
                    Case "createddate"
                        Return (Me.CreatedDate.ToString(OutputFormat,
                            formatProvider))
                    Case "publishdate"
                        Return (Me.PublishDate.ToString(OutputFormat,
                            formatProvider))
                    Case "expiredate"
                        Return (Me.ExpireDate.ToString(OutputFormat,
                            formatProvider))
                    Case "more"
                        Return Localization.GetString("More.Text",
                            LocalResourceFile)
                    Case Else
                        PropertyNotFound = True
                End Select

            Return Null.NullString
        End Function

        Public ReadOnly Property Cacheability() As
            Services.Tokens.CacheLevel
                Implements Services.Tokens.IPropertyAccess.Cacheability
            Get
                Return CacheLevel.fullyCacheable
            End Get
        End Property
```

As you can see from this listing, one method and property is implemented: `GetProperty`, which is simply used to obtain a property value. A `Select Case` statement defines the lookup to get to the specific element. Note that any processing to format the element can be done at this time.

The implemented property sets the `Cacheability` level of the resulting replacements and is defined using the `CacheLevel` options provided by DotNetNuke.

Once this has been implemented, the final implementation step is to create an `Announcements TokenReplace` function that will actually perform the replacements using the core implementation. This is accomplished using the code provided in Listing 10-18.

Listing 10-18: AnnouncementsTokenReplace Code

```
Public Class AnnouncementsTokenReplace
    Inherits TokenReplace
    Public Sub New(ByVal announcement As AnnouncementInfo)
        MyBase.new(Services.Tokens.Scope.DefaultSettings)
        Me.UseObjectLessExpression = True
        Me.PropertySource(ObjectLessToken) = announcement
    End Sub

    Protected Overrides Function replacedTokenValue
        (ByVal strObjectName As
        String, ByVal strPropertyName As String, ByVal strFormat
        As String) As String
        Return MyBase.replacedTokenValue(strObjectName,
              strPropertyName, strFormat)
    End Function

    Public Function ReplaceAnnouncmentTokens
        (ByVal strSourceText As String)
            As String
        Return MyBase.ReplaceTokens(strSourceText)
    End Function

End Class
```

The purpose of this method is to provide the new customized `ReplaceAnnouncementTokens` method that will actually replace the token values. The advantage is that other token values can also be used, such as `Portal:PortalName` to reflect the name of the portal!

Usage

With the implementation of the interface on the information object, as well as the creation of the `Token Replacement` class, it is a very simple process to replace tokens with object values. Listing 10-19 provides an example, using an empty Announcements module object as an example.

Listing 10-19: Example Token Replacement

```
Dim announcementInstance As New AnnouncementInfo
Dim oTokenReplace As New
    AnnouncementsTokenReplace(announcementInstance)

'Perform replacement
string updatedText = oTokenReplace.ReplaceAnnouncementTokens("[TITLE]")
```

This is another good example of using the core components to provide a consistent user interface experience. A great exercise to become more familiar with this process would be to implement this replacement methodology in the Guestbook module.

Summary

This chapter introduced some of the most common DotNetNuke integration interfaces that enable custom modules to leverage the power of the DotNetNuke framework. The elements examined here are invaluable to any module developer because they provide the information needed to provide tight DotNetNuke integration. More important, they provide an implementation as it is meant to be. No custom menus are needed, and the administrative actions match what administrators are accustomed.

Chapter 11 introduces the concept of DotNetNuke scheduled tasks, and examines how you can use them to provide robust module functionality.

DotNetNuke Scheduled Tasks

In addition to the standard module development tasks and processes, DotNetNuke provides a scheduling engine that you can use to execute tasks at a specific interval. For example, you might use DotNetNuke scheduled tasks to clean up the site log or to re-index the search index for site search. Third-party modules (such as forum modules) use scheduled tasks to process e-mail from queues, rather than from inside the application process.

Although there is no relevant scheduled task item for this book's sample Guestbook module, this chapter introduces you nonetheless to the concept of DotNetNuke scheduled tasks. The chapter begins with an overview of the scheduled task system, including important points to consider to ensure that code written as tasks can execute as desired. You will also examine a sample written in both C# and VB code that demonstrates processing for scheduled tasks. The chapter concludes with an overview of installation procedures, schedule options, and the process to check on task success or failure.

Scheduling System Overview

DotNetNuke provides a scheduling system that can execute any code that uses the `SchedulerClient` base class provided by the DotNetNuke framework. This class contains two methods that must be defined in each implementation.

The first method is a constructor that accepts a `ScheduleHistoryItem` parameter. This parameter (passed by the core) is used to mark success and failure. In addition, it exposes a method for users to use when writing entries to the log. The second method is an override of the `DoWork` method. This method is the actual working portion of the task, and all processing code is included here.

The scheduling system works in one of two modes. The default functionality, request mode, is for task items to be triggered via a check on page requests. If tasks are needed, then they are triggered as a result of the request. The second mode is known as the *timer method*. With the timer method, on application startup, a separate thread is created that is used to handle the scheduling and execution of scheduled tasks.

In addition to these options (which affect all scheduled tasks), administrators can create many customizations to control the frequency and dependency of multiple scheduled tasks. Details on each of the scheduled task options are provided later in this chapter.

Considerations with Scheduled Tasks

It is very important that you fully understand the differences between the two modes under which the scheduler can operate. These have a dramatic impact on what you can and cannot do within the `DoWork` methods of the task items.

If the scheduler mode is set to request, then you have access to the `HttpContext` and can use all items that come with it, including `Server.MapPath`. However, if the scheduler is running using the timer method, it will execute events outside of the scope of the request. This leaves two options if you must access the file system or URLs in any manner:

❑   You can create an `HttpContext` yourself.

❑   You can have your module persist the needed information inside a configuration that you can then access from the scheduled task.

The other important thing to consider is that the DotNetNuke scheduler is a process that exists inside the ASP.NET application. Therefore, it is *not* an exact science, and it is *not* 100 percent guaranteed that your process will execute every single time or on time! This is because of the manner in which ASP.NET applications run. After a certain period of inactivity (20 minutes by default), the application will shut down. This prevents the scheduler from executing any tasks. If you have a mission-critical task that must be executed exactly on time, regardless of application state, you should probably consider a solution outside the context of ASP.NET.

> **A common solution to resolve the timing issue is to use a keep-alive technique or service such as `Pingdom.com` or `Host-Tracker.com` to ping the site on a regular activity. These services are the exact external process needed to keep the application running. Users on a dedicated server may also reconfigure the default timeout to prevent routine shutdowns.**

Sample Task Creation

To illustrate the process that must be followed, and to introduce best practices in development, let's add a scheduled task to the Guestbook service, a task that simulates a small amount of processing. Once this is done, you will learn how to perform the configuration within DotNetNuke to execute the task:

1. To create the class, add a new file inside the `Components` folder of the `GuestbookCS` or `GuestbookVB` project. Do this by right-clicking on the folder and selecting Add ⇨ Class.

2. In the dialog that appears, input the following filename, with the proper extension for the project type:

`DemoScheduledTask`

3. Once this is created, replace the auto-added code with the proper code from Listing 11-1 (C#) or Listing 11-2 (VB) to create the sample task.

Listing 11-1: C# Sample Schedule Task Code

```csharp
using System;
using System.Collections.Generic;
using System.Web;
using DotNetNuke;
using DotNetNuke.Common.Utilities;
using DotNetNuke.Entities.Modules;
using DotNetNuke.Services.Scheduling;

namespace WroxModules.GuestbookCS
{
    public class DemoScheduledTask : SchedulerClient
    {
        public DemoScheduledTask(ScheduleHistoryItem oItem)
            : base()
        {
            this.ScheduleHistoryItem = oItem;
        }

        public override void DoWork()
        {
            try
            {
                //Mark as progressing
                this.Progressing();

                //Note
                this.ScheduleHistoryItem.AddLogNote("Starting Task:<br />");

                System.Threading.Thread.Sleep(5000);

                //Note
                this.ScheduleHistoryItem.AddLogNote("Task Completed:");

                //Show success
                this.ScheduleHistoryItem.Succeeded = true;
            }
            catch (Exception ex)
            {
                this.ScheduleHistoryItem.Succeeded = false;
```

(continued)

175

Listing 11-1 *(continued)*

```
                    this.ScheduleHistoryItem.AddLogNote("Exception: " + ex.Message);
                    this.Errored(ref ex);
                    DotNetNuke.Services.Exceptions.Exceptions.LogException(ex);
                }
            }
        }
    }
```

Listing 11-2: VB Sample Schedule Task Code

```vb
Imports System
Imports System.Collections.Generic
Imports System.Web
Imports DotNetNuke
Imports DotNetNuke.Common.Utilities
Imports DotNetNuke.Entities.Modules
Imports DotNetNuke.Services.Scheduling

Namespace WroxModules.GuestbookVB
    Public Class DemoScheduledTask
        Inherits SchedulerClient

        Public Sub New(ByVal oItem As ScheduleHistoryItem)
            Me.ScheduleHistoryItem = oItem
        End Sub

        Public Overrides Sub DoWork()
            Try
                'Mark as progressing
                Me.Progressing()

                'Note
                Me.ScheduleHistoryItem.AddLogNote("Startiing Task:<br />")

                System.Threading.Thread.Sleep(5000)

                'Note
                Me.ScheduleHistoryItem.AddLogNote("Task Completed")

                'Show success
                Me.ScheduleHistoryItem.Succeeded = True
            Catch ex As Exception
                Me.ScheduleHistoryItem.Succeeded = False
                Me.ScheduleHistoryItem.AddLogNote("Exception: " & ex.Message)
                Me.Errored(ex)
                DotNetNuke.Services.Exceptions.Exceptions.LogException(ex)
            End Try
        End Sub
    End Class
End Namespace
```

Once you have this code implemented, build the project to update the compiled .dll file. This sample scheduled task simply creates an item that inserts a few log entries, waits for five seconds, and then exits.

Although it is not performing any task of value, DemoScheduledTask does demonstrate all of the best practices recommended for use with custom scheduled tasks, including the following:

❑ *All* work is performed inside a try/catch block. This ensures that a status can *always* be returned to the scheduler to keep administrators updated.

❑ The progressing method is used to indicate that the task is working.

❑ The AddLogNote method is used to add information to the scheduler log. This information is demonstrated later in this chapter when the task is scheduled and added.

The key point here is that any code can be added inside this DoWork method, and it will be called once per scheduled instance of the task.

Working with the Scheduler

Now that the scheduled task has been created and the module assembly has been recompiled to include the new addition, you are ready to add the scheduled task to the scheduler and then investigate the logging and other functionality provided by the DotNetNuke system.

To work with the scheduler in any capacity, you must log in to the DotNetNuke site as a host-level user. After you are logged in, you can navigate to the Host ⇨ Scheduler page to access the page. From here you can see a listing of all scheduled items, as well as some general information regarding their status, last run time, and other related information.

To add the sample custom task, select Add Schedule Item from the action menu; you will see a page similar to the one shown in Figure 11-1. Table 11-1 shows the values that should be set to schedule the DemoScheduledTask item, as well as a general description of each scheduled task setting.

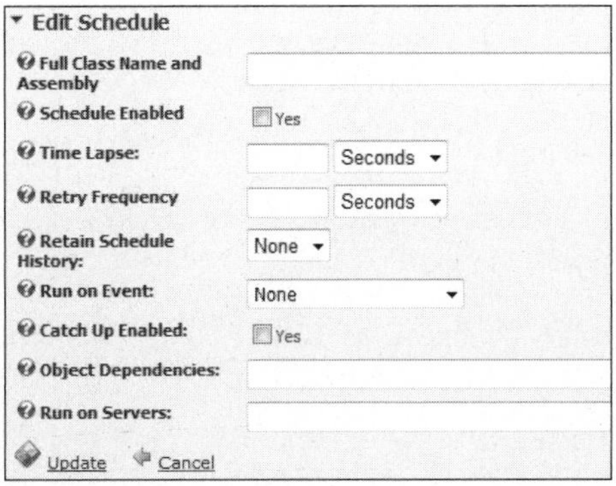

Figure 11-1

Table 11-1: Settings to Add DemoScheduledTask

Setting	Description	DemoScheduledTask Value
Full Class/Assembly	This is the full class and assembly name used to point the scheduler to the proper class to execute.	For C#, `WroxModules.GuestbookCS.DemoScheduledTask, WroxModules.GuestbookCS` For VB, `WroxModules.GuestbookVB.DemoScheduledTask, WroxModules.GuestbookVB`
Schedule Enabled	Enables and disables the scheduled task item	Yes
Time Lapse	Sets the duration between runs of the task. This can be set in seconds, minutes, hours, or days.	5 minutes
Retry Frequency	Sets the duration for re-attempts if the task fails. This can be set in seconds, minutes, hours, or days.	10 minutes
Retain Schedule History	Specifies how many history items should be retained	10
Run on Event	This allows an item to run when the application starts	None
Catch Up Enabled	If enabled, skipped schedule items will be executed as well. For example, if two instances were missed, the next run will occur three times.	No
Object Dependencies	This is where you can set dependencies (e.g., to ensure that objects needed are available).	Leave blank
Run on Servers	In a Web-farm scenario (or other scenario in which items are running on multiple servers), this ensures that the task only runs on a specific server(s).	Leave blank

With the task scheduled, you can view the schedule history. From the Schedule page, click the History link to the right of the newly added `DemoScheduledTask` item. Clicking this link takes you to the Schedule History page, which provides a detailed listing of the history, as shown in Figure 11-2.

Schedule History			
Description	**Duration (seconds)**	**Succeeded**	**Start/End/Next Start**
WroxModules.GuestbookCS.DemoScheduledTask,WroxModules.GuestbookCS Starting Task: Task Completed:	5.017	True	S: 10/19/2008 9:05:37 PM E: 10/19/2008 9:05:42 PM N: 10/19/2008 9:10:37 PM
Cancel			

Figure 11-2

This schedule history provides information regarding the specific class executed, all custom log entries, as well as the duration and success of the task. Start, End, and Next Run times are also displayed.

Summary

DotNetNuke scheduled tasks are a must-know for any module developer because they enable modules to contain more advanced functionality and can help offload some responsibility from the presentation code. Scheduled tasks are most commonly implemented for behind-the-scenes behaviors such as cleanup routines and the queued sending of e-mail messages. The sample task provided in this chapter provides a full implementation that can easily be modified to perform task processing for any module.

Chapter 12 introduces some common DotNetNuke controls that can be used to improve the functionality of your module. For the guestbook example, you will learn how the CAPTCHA control can provide the final piece of functionality.

DotNetNuke User Controls

In the Guestbook module you have created so far, you have already used one of the DotNetNuke user controls, the `Label` control. The DotNetNuke core provides many more helpful controls that can be used to provide a robust, user-friendly interface.

This chapter introduces a few of these items, and, when possible, implements them in the Guestbook modules to demonstrate proper use. The chapter begins by providing information about how to register the tags for all of the DotNetNuke user controls. After that, you'll learn about each of the controls, with implementation examples provided along the way, including demonstrations of when you might use the control. The chapter concludes with a summary of the benefits of using these controls.

Registering the Controls

With the exception of `Label` and a handful of other controls, all DotNetNuke Web controls are contained as compiled controls inside the `DotNetNuke.UI.WebControls` namespace. Therefore, a single `Register` tag can handle registering them for use. This `Register` tag must be added at the top of *any* `.ascx` control that needs to use the controls. As illustrated by the following, the code is the same for C# and VB:

```
<%@ Register TagPrefix="dnn" Assembly="DotNetNuke"
    Namespace="DotNetNuke.UI.WebControls" %>
```

This single `Register` tag grants access to all controls inside the `DotNetNuke.UI.WebControls` namespace. Inside the modified `.ascx` file, if you now type **<dnn:**, you will see IntelliSense information on all available controls.

The following sections take a look at the implementation of a few controls.

CAPTCHA Control

One of the most commonly used DotNetNuke Web controls is the CAPTCHA control. (The word "CAPTCHA" is actually an acronym standing for "completely automated public Turing test to tell computers and humans apart.") This control provides a form of human verification, and in the case of the Guestbook module, it is designed to prevent bots (computer robots) from posting to the guestbook. The CAPTCHA control is very easy to implement after the `Register` tag has been added to the top of the `SignGuestbook.ascx` control.

Listing 12-1 shows the code that should be added to the control to define the row containing the CAPTCHA. The new text is in bold.

Listing 12-1: CAPTCHA Definition

```
    </tr>
    <tr runat="server" id="trCaptcha">
        <td class="SubHead">
            <dnn:Label ID="lblCaptcha" runat="server"
                ControlName="ctlCaptcha"
                Suffix=":" />
        </td>
        <td>
            <dnn:CaptchaControl runat="server" CssClass="normal"
                CaptchaLength="5"  />
        </td>
    </tr>
    <tr>
        <td colspan="2"> </td>
    </tr>
```

This code sample shows a very minimal configuration of the CAPTCHA control, with the specification of a total number of characters. Table 12-1 provides a list of other helpful properties that can be set on the CAPTCHA control.

Table 12-1

Property Name	Description
CaptchaChars	The set of characters that could be used to create the CAPTCHA
CaptchaHeight	Height of the CAPTCHA
CaptchaLength	Total number of characters to use in the CAPTCHA
CaptchaWidth	Width of the CAPTCHA
CssClass	The CSS class used by the control
Text	The prompt Text used

With the CAPTCHA control added to the Guestbook module, you can now hook it up on the back end. Inside the `Page_Load` method of the `SignGuestbook` module, you must validate the CAPTCHA. Once you have established the settings, you set the visibility on the CAPTCHA control row.

To do this, add the following code to the `Page_Load` method. Listing 12-2 shows the C# implementation and Listing 12-3 shows the code additions for the VB module. The new code appears in bold.

Listing 12-2: C# Code Addition for Page_Load

```
bool allowAnonPosting = bool.Parse(allowAnon.ToString());
bool useCaptcha =
    bool.Parse(Settings["WROX_Guestbook_EnableCaptcha"].ToString());
trCaptcha.Visible = useCaptcha;

if (UserId == -1 && !allowAnonPosting)
```

Listing 12-3: VB Code Addition for Page_Load

```
Dim allowAnon As Boolean
allowAnon = Boolean.Parse(CType(Settings
    ("WROX_Guestbook_AllowAnon"), String))
Dim useCaptcha As Boolean
useCaptcha = Boolean.Parse
    (CType(Settings("WROX_Guestbook_EnableCaptcha"), String))
trCaptcha.Visible = useCaptcha

If UserId = -1 AndAlso Not allowAnon Then
```

The final step of the process is to modify the code inside the `btnSign_Click` event to check for the CAPTCHA's `IsValid` property (in addition to `Page.IsValid`) if the CAPTCHA is enabled. This is done by adding the code shown in Listing 12-4 (C#) or Listing 12-5 (VB) to the modules. As before, the additions appear in bold. This is a simple conditional check. Now the module can be secured from malicious use.

Listing 12-4: C# CAPTCHA Check Code

```
bool useCaptcha = bool.Parse
    (Settings["WROX_Guestbook_EnableCaptcha"].ToString());

if (Page.IsValid &&
    (!useCaptcha || (useCaptcha && ctlCaptcha.IsValid)))
{
```

Listing 12-5: VB CAPTCHA Check Code

```
Dim useCaptcha As Boolean
useCaptcha = Boolean.Parse
    (CType(Settings("WROX_Guestbook_EnableCaptcha"), String))

If Page.IsValid AndAlso (Not useCaptcha Or
    (useCaptcha And ctlCaptcha.IsValid)) Then
```

Overall, this is a very simple control to use. After building the changes and enabling the CAPTCHA for the guestbook, you can see a new control on the page prompting for the input of the code, as shown in Figure 12-1. This control must be used for any system that accepts input from unauthenticated users.

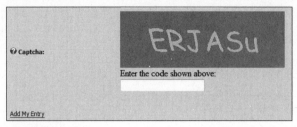

Figure 12-1

TextEditor Control

Another commonly used DotNetNuke control is the `TextEditor` control. Most people know this control as the Rich Text Editor. This control provides site users with the capability to format their input using a common Microsoft Word–styled editor, complete with toolbars and other action items for assistance. Figure 12-2 shows a sample of the default display for the `TextEditor` control.

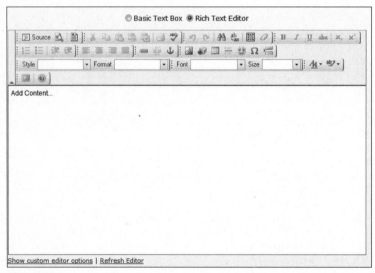

Figure 12-2

The TextEditor control is another one of the controls that is referenced outside of the compiled .dll. Therefore, in order to use the TextEditor control, you must register it at the top of each control in which it should be used. The following code snippet shows the script needed to register the control:

```
<%@ Register TagPrefix="dnn" TagName="TextEditor" Src="~/controls/TextEditor.ascx"
    %>
```

Now you can add this control to your site anywhere you desire by using code similar to the following:

```
<dnn:TextEditor id="myId" runat="server" />
```

As with the CAPTCHA control, you will want to set a few key properties. Table 12-2 provides a list of some of the common elements.

Table 12-2

Property Name	Description
Height	Specifies the height of the editor. If you specify this value, a minimum of 300 pixels is recommended to ensure that all visual elements are rendered.
HtmlEncode	This Boolean indicates whether the user-supplied text should be HTML-encoded. If this is set to true (the default), then all text will be encoded before being stored in the database. Doing this protects against the injection of malicious code. However, in certain administrative situations, it will be necessary to disable this.
Width	Specifies the width of the editor. If you specify this value, a minimum of 300 pixels is recommended to ensure that all visual elements are rendered.

This control is widely used in modules of all kinds. However, it is very important that you understand that this control does allow users to include JavaScript and other components that could be unsafe. Therefore, careful consideration must be taken when making this control available to untrusted, or less-privileged, users.

SectionHead Control

The SectionHead control is another control that is found in multiple places in a DotNetNuke site. However, many developers are unaware that this is a default DotNetNuke control. The SectionHead control is simply a header that can expand and collapse the content provided on a page. Figure 12-3 shows an example of how this control is used under the DotNetNuke Host Settings page. It is simply implemented as a header along with plus/minus icons, depending on the action needed.

⊟ Configuration

Figure 12-3

The `SectionHead` control is another of the controls provided inside the DotNetNuke installation package. Therefore, you must manually register the control at the top of the page. This is accomplished by using the following `Register` script:

```
<%@ Register TagPrefix="dnn" TagName="SectionHeadControl"
    Src="~/controls/SectionHeadControl.ascx" %>
```

Once this is completed, you can add the control to the page using the following syntax:

```
<dnn:SectionHeadControl id="dnnSh" runat='server' />
```

Table 12-3 provides a list of all available properties for the control, and specifies which items are required for proper module usage.

Table 12-3: DNN SectionHead Control Properties

Property Name	Description	Required
CssClass	Allows the specification of a different CSS class. By default, the control uses `Head`.	No
IncludeRule	Indicates whether a horizontal rule should be added below the title of the header	No
MaxImageUrl	The URL for the maximized image can be used to specify a custom maximized image.	No
MinImageUrl	The URL for the minimized image can be used to specify a custom minimized image.	No
ResourceKey	The resource key, used to find the localized text for the section head	No (but should be specified, rather than using `Text`)
Text	The text of the header	No (should not be used because a resource key provides auto localization)
Section	The ID of the control that is to be used as the expand/collapse section. Should be a `Panel` control or an HTML table.	Yes

Overall, this control is very helpful if you have large amounts of input or content and you want to expand/collapse that content in response to a client request.

Paging Control

The final control to be discussed here is the DNN paging control. This control provides an interface for use with a Search Engine Optimization (SEO) friendly paging control. When implemented, the DNN paging control renders an interface similar to that shown in Figure 12-4. The links generated by this control are all standard HTML links. This control does *not* use a postback to perform paging by default. Although it causes a reload of the page, this is the *only* method to fully ensure that search engines accessing your site can view all content. Therefore, it is highly recommended that you use this control.

Page 1 of 8	First Previous [1] 2 3 4 5 6 7 8 Next Last

Figure 12-4

Note that this control provides the interface only for managing the pages and selecting the pages. It is the responsibility of other controls on the page to handle the actual paging of the resulting dataset. This can be done in various manners — something as simple as using a data grid and setting the page values, or as complex as using SQL Server data paging.

This control provides a number of properties, many of which must be specified in order for the control to work properly. Table 12-4 provides a list of the most common properties, and identifies those that are required.

Table 12-4

Property Name	Definition	Required
Current Page	The current page number, starting at 1. You can re-specify this if you must change the page.	No
Mode	Accepts values of URL or Postback, allowing the paging behavior to be changed	No (It is recommended to leave at default of URL)
PageSize	The total number of records per page. This is needed for the control to calculate the total number of pages needed.	Yes
QuerystringParameters	A listing of additional query string parameters needed to return to the current page, or to be able to load the next set of data. If the implementing control needs any query string values, they must be re-specified here so that the control can generate the proper paging URLs.	Yes, if needed by the module
TotalRecords	The total number of records to display. This is used in conjunction with PageSize to calculate the total number of pages.	Yes
TabId	The ID of the tab that the module is currently on. This is used to generate the paging URLs.	Yes

The required properties for this control can be specified in the .ascx file or via the code-behind file. The key thing to remember is that the control must be configured during the page-load process. If it is not, then users won't see the proper display setup. When using this control in the default URL mode, paging operations will return the user to the same page, but with a currentPage query string value passed, which can then be used to load the new user content.

A large amount of business logic has been implemented inside the DotNetNuke paging control that can save a significant amount of time when you want to provide a search-engine-friendly paging model for module results.

Url and UrlTracking Controls

Two of the most commonly visible controls in third-party modules are the Url and UrlTracking controls. These controls offer users an easy-to-use method for selecting files or uploading new files (Url control) and for optionally viewing file tracking information if enabled for a specific file. Figures 12-5 and 12-6 show the Url and UrlTracking controls in action.

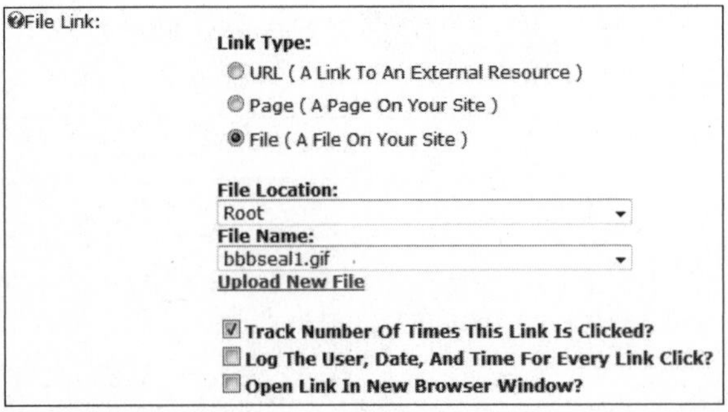

Figure 12-5

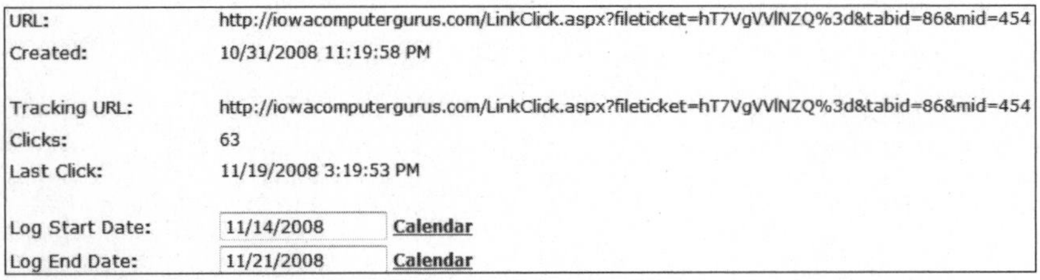

Figure 12-6

As you can see, these two controls complement each other. If tracking is enabled within the Url control, then a UrlTracking module instance is needed to successfully track and view information.

Similar to the `TextEditor` control, the `Url` and `UrlTracking` controls are actual `.ascx` files contained within the DotNetNuke installation. Therefore, the first step to take to use these controls is to register them on the page. This can be done using the following code:

```
3<%@ Register TagPrefix="dnn" TagName="UrlControl"
    Src="~/controls/UrlControl.ascx" %>
<%@ Register TagPrefix="dnn" TagName="Tracking"
    Src="~/controls/URLTrackingControl.ascx" %>
```

Once the controls have been registered, they can be added using the default format for user controls. A fairly common configuration for both controls is illustrated in the following code sample:

```
<dnn:UrlControl ID="fleSelector"
    runat="server"
    ShowFiles="true"
    ShowLog="true"
    ShowTrack="true"
    ShowUpLoad="true"
    ShowNewWindow="True"
    UrlType="F" />

<dnn:tracking id="ctlTracking" runat="server"></dnn:tracking>
```

Table 12-5 and Table 12-6 show some of the most common properties that can be set on these controls.

Table 12-5

Property Name	Definition
ShowFiles	If set to `true`, allows users to select files for upload. If not set to `true`, users will not be able to select files.
ShowLog	If set to `true`, allows users to select the "Log the user, date, and time for every link click" option, which will log user information on all clicks if the user was authenticated at the time of the click.
ShowTrack	If set to `true`, allows users to select the "Track number of times this link is clicked" option, which will record count information on download.
ShowUpload	If set to `true`, allows users to upload files to folders to which they currently have permission.
ShowNewWindow	If set to `true`, allows users to select the "Open in new window" option when creating links.
UrlType	Can be set to `F`, `U`, or `P`. This simply defaults the link type selection for the user.
Url	The URL that has been selected by the user. This is used to get the user's selection; or, for updates, it is used to set the control to the current URL.
Log	Boolean indicator showing whether the user has selected the "Log" option
Track	Boolean indicator showing whether the user has selected the "Track" option
NewWindow	Boolean indicator showing whether the user has selected the "New Window" option

Table 12-6

Property Name	Definition
Url	The URL that is being tracked and for which information should be displayed
ModuleId	The ID of the module that has been generating links to the resource

One important behavior that is commonly overlooked with these controls is the proper saving and creation of the links when used to link to other resources, such as files. Saving the Url portion is as simple as saving the value of the Url property of the Url control. However, you must additionally make one call to the UpdateTracking method of the UrlControl. Table 12-7 shows the parameters and implementation details.

Table 12-7

Parameter Name	Description/Implementation
PortalId	The ID of the portal (for C#, this.portalId; for VB, me.portalId)
Url	The selected URL, obtained from the Url control
UrlType	The type of URL, obtained from the Url control
LogActivity	The value of the Log property from the Url control
TrackClicks	The value of the Track property from the Url control
ModuleId	The ID of the module (for C#, this.moduleId; for VB, me.moduleId)
NewWindow	The value of the New Window property from the Url control

Given the information needed to call the UpdateTracking method, this is typically completed just after saving other information. Forgetting to complete this method call will result in URL items not being tracked correctly.

Now that you have properly recorded all the necessary information and, via some method, saved the URL that you are tracking, you can link the resource code anywhere inside the module by using the code shown in Listing 12-6 (C#) or Listing 12-7 (VB), depending on the language used.

Listing 12-6: C# LinkClick Link Generation

```
DotNetNuke.Common.Globals.LinkClick(oInfo.FileUrl, this.TabId,
    this.ModuleId);
```

Listing 12-7: VB LinkClick Link Generation

```
DotNetNuke.Common.Globals.LinkClick(oInfo.FileUrl, me.TabId,
  me.ModuleId)
```

As you can see from the screen captures and minimal code needed, these controls are very valuable items, as they allow full access to files on the site, and user upload access, with less than 10 lines of code to implement the entire solution. With the added benefits of logging and tracking, these are an invaluable resource for module developers.

Other Controls

This chapter has just scratched the surface of the controls available for use as part of the DotNetNuke framework. The framework developers were very careful to create controls whenever they started to see functionality duplicated across administrative sections of the framework. Therefore, many common elements have been created over the life cycle of the project, exposing numerous time-saving controls to the greater development community.

One of the easiest methods to use when learning about the wide collection of controls is to simply create a test module and experiment with the controls to see what they do. Because of the large number of controls, it would be impossible for this book to cover them all. Another great resource for learning about the various DotNetNuke controls is the `http://webcontrols.dotnetnuke.com` website, which contains a collection of control examples and sample code.

Summary

This chapter introduced some of the various controls that are available to module developers. Although it has provided only a brief overview of the most commonly used control elements, this chapter indicates the direction in which to look for custom control implementations. The benefits of using these controls should be very apparent when you consider the time that it would take to create a custom control to duplicate the functionality discussed here.

Chapter 13 introduces one more common DotNetNuke development scenario: How to get modules to talk with one another.

13

Module Navigation and Communication

The examples provided in previous chapters have examined a few of the basic DotNetNuke module navigation and communication methods that can be used. This chapter takes a deeper dive into the various methods for navigation and communication between modules, as well as controls within a specific module, with special attention paid to pointing out common "gotcha" items.

This chapter begins with a look at the two most common utilities for navigation within DotNetNuke: NavigateUrl and EditUrl. Some of the most common overloads and examples of usage are provided throughout the discussion, including information about common "gotcha" moments when navigating from control to control.

The chapter then progresses with a discussion about module isolation and how it can affect the development of custom modules, and methods that can be used to get around this limitation in the DotNetNuke framework.

The chapter concludes with a discussion of inter-module communication using two helpful interfaces built into DotNetNuke: IModuleCommunicator and IModuleListener.

Module Navigation

As mentioned earlier, the two common mechanisms for managing navigation within a DotNetNuke installation are NavigateUrl and EditUrl. This section takes a look at the differences between the two, their usage, and the limitations of each method.

NavigateUrl

The NavigateUrl method exists inside the DotNetNuke.Common.Globals class. It is a method of generating standard links to individual pages, or specific view controls of a DotNetNuke module. Figure 13-1 shows the available overloads for the NavigateUrl method.

```
NavigateURL() As String
NavigateURL(Integer) As String
NavigateURL(Integer, Boolean) As String
NavigateURL(Integer, Boolean, DotNetNuke.Entities.Portals.PortalSettings, String, ParamArray String()) As String
NavigateURL(Integer, Boolean, DotNetNuke.Entities.Portals.PortalSettings, String, String, ParamArray String()) As String
NavigateURL(Integer, DotNetNuke.Entities.Portals.PortalSettings, String, ParamArray String()) As String
NavigateURL(Integer, String) As String
NavigateURL(Integer, String, ParamArray String()) As String
NavigateURL(String) As String
NavigateURL(String, ParamArray String()) As String
```

Figure 13-1

The most commonly used overloads are NavigateUrl(Integer) and NavigateUrl(Integer, String, ParamArray String()).

NavigateUrl(Integer) generates a link to a specific page in a DotNetNuke portal and takes the TabId as the only parameter. This is the most basic linking method, and it can be used to generate a link to any page inside a portal. It is often used in combination with the TabId property of PortalModuleBase to perform redirection back to the current page in a portal. Listing 13-1 (C#) and Listing 13-2 (VB) show the code needed to redirect the user to the current page.

Listing 13-1: C# Redirect Example

```
Response.Redirect(DotNetNuke.Globals.NavigateUrl(this.TabId));
```

Listing 13-2: VB Redirect Example

```
Response.Redirect(DotNetNuke.Globals.NavigateUrl(Me.TabId))
```

This most basic form of navigation is very helpful when working with DotNetNuke because you can gain access to page listings and perform redirects. However, if you have a module that contains multiple user controls, then it is necessary to use a different overload of NavigateUrl to create a usable link.

NavigateUrl(Integer, String, ParamArray String()) accepts an integer parameter, which, again, is the target page's TabId. In addition to the tab ID, a string for the control key and a parameter array for additional URL parameters are accepted. Working with a module that contains multiple view controls using this overload is the only proper way to navigate from control to control.

If you were working with a module that had a second view control with a key value of Control2, you could use the code shown in Listing 13-3 (C#) or Listing 13-4 (VB) to direct users to the proper view layout.

Listing 13-3: C# Secondary View Redirect Example

```
Response.Redirect(DotNetNuke.Globals.NavigateUrl(this.TabId,
    "Control2", "mid=" +     this.ModuleId));
```

Listing 13-4: VB Secondary View Redirect Example

```
Response.Redirect(DotNetNuke.Globals.NavigateUrl(Me.TabId, "Control2",
    "mid=" & Me.ModuleId))
```

Note in these examples that not only are you passing the control key as the secondary parameter, you are also adding a third parameter, mid, in the parameters section of the call to NavigateUrl. This is done to tell DotNetNuke that you are loading the Control2 control for a specific module. The generated URL might look something like the following if the TabId were 36 and the ModuleId were 200:

```
http://localhost/dotnetnuke/home/tabid/36/ctl/Control2/mid/200/default.aspx
```

You can see how the individual values are written into the URL. Forgetting to include the mid parameter ID your URL will result in a blank page being displayed.

Note that this limitation of DotNetNuke does present a situation that may need to be considered and worked around. See the section "Module Isolation" later in this chapter for more detailed information.

EditUrl

The NavigateUrl method is great for those times when you are navigating to another page or another view control. However, as you edit content, the EditUrl method is more helpful. The EditUrl method also has many overloads that are designed to help a developer pass information to edit controls on a page. Four of these overloads, shown in Figure 13-2, are particularly helpful, each of which is discussed in the following sections.

```
EditUrl(String) As String
EditUrl(String, String) As String
EditUrl(String, String, String) As String
EditUrl(String, String, String, ParamArray String()) As String
```

Figure 13-2

EditUrl()

The most basic call to EditUrl is EditUrl(). This call generates a standard edit link to a standard edit control of Edit. This is very helpful if you must get to the edit control of a module and don't need to pass any information to it. For example, in a default module scenario, with a TabId of 36 and a ModuleId of 200, you would get a URL similar to this:

```
http://localhost/dotnetnuke/home/tabid/36/mid/200/ctl/edit/default.aspx
```

The key thing to note here is that this default overload of EditUrl automatically inserts the TabId, ModuleId, and control key values. This information is made available because EditUrl is part of PortalModule Base and has the current ModuleContext information, which includes ModuleId and TabId. This is simply a shortcut designed to save time, rather than use NavigateUrl, which can generate the exact same resulting URL by passing the proper query string values.

EditUrl(string)

Another common overload for the EditUrl method is EditUrl(string), which accepts a single string parameter that is the control key value. This is the overload that would be used when working with an edit control that has a key other than Edit.

EditUrl(string, string, string)

EditUrl(string, string, string) is the most common overload used on a regular basis. The first parameter is the string keyName that is passed to the edit page. The second parameter is the string keyValue, forming the edit information that is sent to the edit page. The final parameter in this overload is the control key of the edit control.

As an example, to obtain the URL for an edit page by passing an `EntryId` value of `0` to the `"EditEntries"` control, code similar to the following would be used:

```
EditUrl("EntryId", "0", "EditEntries")
```

This will generate a link with all the proper information, and an `"EntryId=0"` query string value that can be used by the edit page to properly handle the edit operations.

EditUrl(string, string, string ParamArray string())

The `EditUrl(string, string, string ParamArray string())` overload is just like `EditUrl(string, string, string)` but is capable of handling more optional parameters. Building on the previous example, which required passing an `EntryId` of `0`, let's say that you also must pass a parameter called `Action` with a value of `Edit`. You can use the following overload to successfully pass the information. Table 13-1 includes a detailed list of the parameters.

```
EditUrl("EntryId", "0", "EditEntries", "Action=Edit")
```

Table 13-1

Position	Type	Description
1	String	This is the query string key for the value being passed to the resulting page.
2	String	This is the query string value for the value being passed to the resulting page.
3	String	This is the control key for the edit page, as defined in the .dnn manifest.
4	ParamArray string()	A collection of string objects. Each string object must represent a full query string key/value pair. For example, action=edit is a valid entry in the array.

You can see from this example that the form used for URL construction is very similar. Although it is possible to use `NavigateUrl` to produce the same links as `EditUrl`, `EditUrl` provides the benefit of pre-filling many of the parameters needed by `NavigateUrl` so that developers can focus on passing their information, as opposed to the default DotNetNuke information.

Module Isolation

As shown in all of the previous navigation examples, when moving around a site, and from individual control to control, module developers must constantly provide the `ModuleId` inside the URL. This is done because when navigating to a nondefault view or edit control, the module is loaded into the `Admin` site skin, and other modules that exist on the page are *not* rendered.

Figure 13-3 and Figure 13-4 show examples of this. Figure 13-3 represents the view of the default DotNetNuke site template for 5.0, and Figure 13-4 shows the view after clicking Edit Text for the first Text/HTML module, which displays the welcome text.

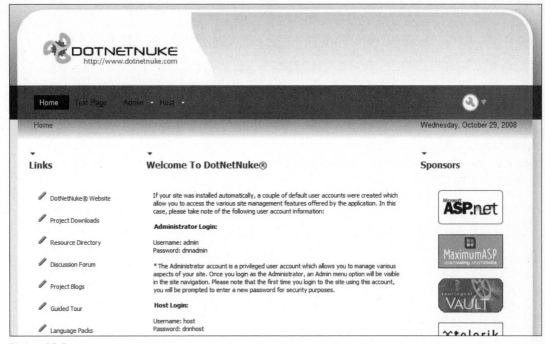

Figure 13-3

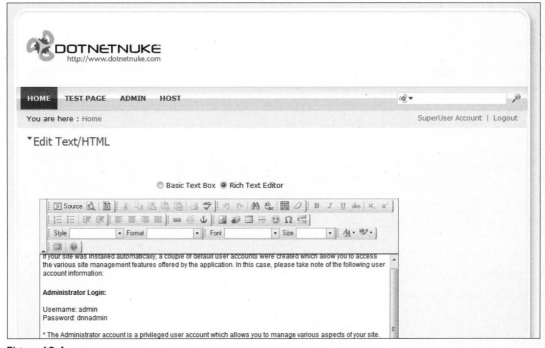

Figure 13-4

When you visit the edit page for the Text/HTML module, DotNetNuke removes all other modules from the page, leaving only the current control visible. This is a default behavior that works in *any* situation when not viewing the default view control of a module, because DotNetNuke must have a way of processing the control selection process. Therefore, at face value, it seems that you can only have one usable view control. This isn't necessarily the case, but it is something to take into consideration.

You have a few options for getting around the situation by handling the control selection and display in code, rather than relying on DotNetNuke to perform the selection. The following sections discuss three of the available scenarios, including the merits and disadvantages of each method.

Dynamically Loaded Controls

The first option that comes to mind would be to use a placeholder control as the primary view control, and simply dynamically load each of the individual controls when needed — either based on control actions on the page or via specific query string parameters.

This method has the benefit of being very easy to implement, with a few straightforward steps to load the control and add it to the placeholder. However, there are many drawbacks. With dynamically loaded controls, it is not possible to have `viewstate` information saved. Thus, postbacks and other actions inside the control are much more complex, if not impossible. Third-party placeholders are available that can grant the capability to persist `viewstate`, but as of this writing none seems to be good enough for most solutions.

MultiView Control

The .NET Framework provides a `MultiView` control that enables developers to simply create a control that can have multiple views and which provides a simple method for switching between controls. Using a `MultiView` control is a very common approach to resolving the module isolation issue. It is very easy to add the control to your User Control, and even easier to simply switch between views, depending on the specific actions needed. Listing 13-5 shows a very brief example of a `MultiView` control's ASCX markup. (The markup is the same for C# and VB.)

Listing 13-5: MultiView Control Example

```
<asp:MultiView ID="MultiView" runat="server" ActiveViewIndex="0">
    <asp:View ID="View1" runat="server">
        This is View Number 1<br />
        <br />
        <table border="0" cellpadding="4" cellspacing="4" width="90%">
            <tr>
                <td style="width: 25%">
                    <asp:Label ID="lblAge" runat="server" Text=
                        "Your Age:"
                            Font-Bold="True"></asp:Label>
                    <br />
                    <br />
                    <asp:RadioButtonList ID="rblAge" runat="server">
                        <asp:ListItem>0-20</asp:ListItem>
                        <asp:ListItem>21-40</asp:ListItem>
                        <asp:ListItem>41-99</asp:ListItem>
```

```
                            </asp:RadioButtonList></td>
            </tr>
        </table>
    <asp:button id="btnGoToTwo" runat="server" text="[Go To View 2]" />
        <br />
        <br />
        <br />
    </asp:View>
    <asp:View ID="View2" runat="server">
        This is View Number 2<br />
        <br />
        <br />
        Age selected on View 1:
        <asp:Label ID="lblAgeDisplay" runat="server"></asp:Label>
        <br />
        <asp:Button ID="btnResetAge" runat="server"
            Text="[Reset Age Control]" />
        <br />
        </asp:View>
    <asp:View ID="View3" runat="server">
        This is View Number 3<br />
        <br />
        <br />
    </asp:View>
    </asp:MultiView>
```

This listing demonstrates that when using the `MultiView` control, all controls are placed in the same location. Controls can access the values of any other view directly, making wizard-style interfaces very easy to accomplish. Depending on the requirements and/or the developer's preferences, view changes can be completed via a postback or via redirection to the same page, with a `PageLoad` method to call the proper display format.

As with any method, though, using a multi-view control has its associated disadvantages. You can have only one view visible at a time; and with larger setups, the process of maintaining it can be a bit cumbersome.

Multiple User Controls

The last method to examine here is a sort of hybrid — one that can be very useful and that represents a best-of-both-worlds approach. Earlier, you saw that dynamic loading has its disadvantages, in particular the lack of the capability to use `viewstate` to preserve values. You also learned about the limitations of the multi-view control, with the one-at-a-time display.

A very simple approach using *subcontrols* is the best way to go. Using this method, you can create a single control for each of the "views" and reference them on the actual DotNetNuke view control. By doing this, you have a centralized location, which can drive the individual views, and show or hide any or all controls as needed.

This method is just like what would be used outside of DotNetNuke, but for some reason many developers fail to apply the practice to DotNetNuke module development. It is important to remember that DotNetNuke is provided as a core framework on top of which you can build modules. Developers are not 100 percent bound to do everything "as the core does it." The only requirement is that the final solution must be compatible with the core at the key integration points.

Inter-Module Communication

Now that you understand how to navigate between modules, and get from point A to point B, let's take a look at methods of communication between modules. The most common method of communication between modules is to simply pass relevant information across via the query string of the destination links. If the first module completes a task and must notify a second module, a simple redirect with an added query string parameter will do the trick.

Unfortunately, that doesn't always result in what you want. If you happen to have two modules that must communicate when they are located on the same page, DotNetNuke provides two helpful interfaces that can facilitate the communication: IModuleCommunicator and IModuleListener. The following sections examine what these interfaces provide, and offer some sample implementation code for each.

IModuleCommunicator

The IModuleCommunicator interface is used to publish communication events. Inter-module communication is implemented in DotNetNuke using a simple publisher/listener model. In this model, a module makes a communication, and any module on the page can listen to it, if it implements the IModuleListener interface.

The process of meeting the constructs of the IModuleCommunicator interface is very simple. First and foremost, you must add IModuleCommunicator as an implemented interface to the class definition, and you must define a public event ModuleCommunication that uses the ModuleCommunicationEventHandler. Listing 13-6 (C#) and Listing 13-7 (VB) show minimal class declarations for implementations of IModuleListener All other class code has been removed for brevity.

Listing 13-6: C# IModuleCommunicator Implementation

```
public partial class CommunicationSample :
    PortalModuleBase, IModuleCommunicator
{
    public event ModuleCommunicationEventHandler ModuleCommunication;
}
```

Listing 13-7: VB IModuleCommunicator Implementation

```
Partial Class CommunicationSample
    Inherits PortalModuleBase
    Implements IModuleCommunicator

    Public Event ModuleCommunication(ByVal sender As Object, _
        ByVal e As ModuleCommunicationEventArgs) _
        Implements IModuleCommunicator.ModuleCommunication

End Class
```

With the event defined, the only remaining step to fully implement IModuleCommunicator is to build a method that will actually raise the event if necessary. Listing 13-8 (C#) and Listing 13-9 (VB) provide code samples showing how to send a communication via the interface implementation.

Listing 13-8: C# Send Information Implementation

```
if (ModuleCommunication != null)
{
    ModuleCommunicationEventArgs args =
        new ModuleCommunicationEventArgs();
    args.Sender = "CommunicationSampleModule";
    args.Target = "Any String";
    args.Text = "Any String";
    args.Type = "Any String";
    args.Value = new Object();

    //Raise event
    ModuleCommunication(this, args);
}
```

Listing 13-9: VB Send Information Implementation

```
Dim args As ModuleCommunicationEventArgs _
    = New ModuleCommunicationEventArgs()

args.Sender = "CommunicationSampleModule"
args.Target = "Any String"
args.Text = "Any String"
args.Type = "Any String"
args.Value = new Object()

RaiseEvent ModuleCommunication(Me, args)
```

Note a few things about the values and items provided in these listings. The Sender value should be a descriptive, unique name for the module so that the listener (which will be created later) can successfully identify messages from the module. The Target, Text, and Type fields are all string fields that can be used to pass information. The final Value field is provided to enable communication with any other object. Custom information classes and any other object may be passed via the Value field.

With this implementation, a communication event will be raised, passing the provided event arguments, which IModuleListener can then use to take action. This provides a very flexible implementation for passing information of all types.

IModuleListener

With the IModuleCommunicator actually publishing the "update" information, it is time to set up the code needed to listen for module messages. The process for doing this is very similar to what you have just done.

First, the class declaration for the module must be modified to show that it implements the IModuleListener interface. Listing 13-10 (C#) and Listing 13-11 (VB) show the base code for the ListenerSample control definition, including the single method that must be defined to meet the rules of the interface. Other supporting code has been removed for clarity.

Listing 13-10: C# ListenerSample Class Code

```csharp
public partial class ListenerSample :
    PortalModuleBase, IModuleListener
{
    public void OnModuleCommunication(object s,
        ModuleCommunicationEventArgs e)
    {
        //Code goes here
    }
}
```

Listing 13-11: VB ListenerSample Class Code

```vb
Partial Class ListenerSample
    Inherits PortalModuleBase
    Implements IModuleListener

    Sub OnModuleCommunication(ByVal s As Object, _
                        ByVal e As ModuleCommunicationEventArgs) _
        Implements IModuleListener.OnModuleCommunication
  'Code goes here
    End Sub
End Class
```

The code that is inserted into the //Code goes here sections of these examples represents the key point of implementation. The ModuleCommunicationEventArgs class provides the information needed. It is the responsibility of the implemented code to successfully take action on the passed information. Typically, a comparison will be made to e.sender to ensure that the sending module is the one that should be listened to. If that is the case, further action is taken based on the values passed in the IModuleCommunicator code.

Considerations

The use of inter-module communication is very simple. However, it is important to take a few items into consideration before deciding that inter-module communication is the end-all solution for business needs. One of the main things to consider when evaluating and using inter-module communication is that it only works between modules located on the same page. Therefore, if an action must trigger something on another page, other communication mechanisms must be considered.

Another key consideration is the use of Ajax. If inter-module communication is used inside a module that uses Ajax to perform postbacks asynchronously, then it is more than likely that the events will fire and the other module will process the messages. However, because the Listener modules are not part of the update panel, there will be no difference in visible content.

The last consideration is that events raised via inter-module communication are sent to *any* module that implements the IModuleListener interface. This is a key point to remember in order to avoid accidentally processing messages sent by other modules. In addition, keep in mind that other modules *could* listen to the messages sent by the newly developed module.

Summary

This chapter provided an introduction to module navigation, display, and communication. You learned about required elements of the DotNetNuke framework that have been used in previous chapters in order to gain a full understanding. You also learned about special considerations in regard to modules with multiple view controls, as well as methods of communicating between modules.

Now that you have an understanding of navigation and communication, Chapter 14 introduces important points of consideration when using third-party .dll files with your custom modules.

14

Third-Party Components and Controls

Because all DotNetNuke modules, skins, and skin objects are created with .NET code and languages, it is very common for individuals to incorporate third-party components and control suites into their DotNetNuke components. Third-party controls enable you to quickly take your existing module and add functional bits that dress it up, or start a new module and use third-party components to quickly create a highly robust module.

However, there are special considerations that must be investigated when incorporating those third-party controls into custom DotNetNuke modules. This chapter focuses on these DotNetNuke-specific considerations that must be handled to ensure appropriate third-party integration. In addition, it is very important to remember to consider standard third-party component restrictions such as licensing and source code ownership.

The chapter starts out with a look at compatibility concerns, and when DotNetNuke as a platform might become an issue for controls. The discussion then examines deployment issues and conflict resolution, focusing on cascading failure potentials when deploying third-party applications. The chapter concludes with a review of developer responsibility and end-user expectations when it comes to custom module development.

Compatibility

On the surface, you would think that a .NET component is a .NET component, and that it can work in any .NET application. However, this is not 100 percent true. Compatibility must be looked at as more than just "can it run in .NET?" The whole picture and target audience must be considered prior to embarking on component integration.

For example, by default, DotNetNuke can be configured to run in a partial trust environment, which does not require full permissions from the .NET run-time. However, some components require full trust environments. If you are working toward an individual deployment, then this isn't an issue; but if you are developing a module that is slated for sale to the widespread DotNetNuke community, then it is entirely possible that many customers would not be able to utilize a module that requires full trust, even if it is distributed with the module. Many hosting providers such as GoDaddy do not allow user applications to run in full trust.

Another consideration is skin compatibility. An increasing number of third-party components (including ASP.NET AJAX) require that the implemented site include a doc type of XHTML. Many DotNetNuke skins in the DNN ecosystem (at minimum) do not contain the needed doc type declaration, and, in many cases, do not properly function with an XHTML doc type. You should investigate this issue, depending on the target audience for the custom-created modules.

Deployment/Maintenance Issues

In addition to adding a few new compatibility concerns, DotNetNuke also introduces an interesting set of deployment and maintenance issues that can affect developers and third-party components, not only for public development efforts, but also internal development efforts as well. When incorporating a third-party component in a DotNetNuke module, various .dll file(s) must be deployed with the module to ensure that the third-party component functions properly.

In the case of a single custom module inside a DotNetNuke installation, there is no issue with deployment or maintenance of the site. However, once you start introducing other modules, skins, and providers that contain third-party utilities, you can quickly create a situation in which more than one module uses the same third-party components.

There are actually two very severe and different compatibility issues that can arise from multiple modules sharing the same assemblies: incompatible assembly versions and removed assembly files.

> Note that the risk of the following two issues has been minimized in DotNetNuke 5.0 and later for modules *installed* using the DotNetNuke 5.x installation framework. This is accomplished by registering all installed assemblies and managing their usage; only upgrading when needed; and only deleting files when no extension is using it. However, this is still something to be aware of, because it is an exposure point for upgraded sites, as well as modules built using the DotNetNuke 4.x manifest.

Incompatible Assembly Versions

Incompatible assembly version issues can be encountered when an existing module is installed and working with a specific version of a third-party module and a new module is installed with a different version. Typically, these issues only arise when the new module contains an assembly version that is older than the existing module.

For example, suppose that Module A has a dependency on the most current version of Component Z (2.1.0), a third-party .dll, and Module B has a dependency on version 1.0.0 of the same component. If Module A is installed, then the newest version of Component Z is copied to the bin directory, and everything functions as expected. However, if later Module B is installed, then the dll in the bin directory will be overwritten with the older version included in the installation package. Typically, in this scenario, Module B will now be functioning correctly, but module A will be generating errors.

This is an important item to consider, because it is not always known to site administrators what third-party components are included. When you are developing modules for internal use only, this is a less common issue; but for commercial developers, these types of situations happen on a regular basis.

Removed Assembly Files

If two installed modules happen to rely on the same version of a third-party component, no issues will be experienced while each of the modules is still installed and not upgraded. However, if an administrator elects to remove a module and selects the option to "delete files," in addition to the module assembly being removed, the third-party assembly will be removed, breaking all other modules and components that rely on that functionality.

To provide a real-world example, consider a DotNetNuke site that contains a skin using the Telerik RadMenu component, and a DotNetNuke module that also uses the RadMenu component. Frustrated with the performance of the third-party module, the site administrator uninstalls it to remove all traces of it from the system. After uninstalling this, the entire skin falls apart. Every page view logs more than ten errors, and the system reverts to the DNN blue skin. Not knowing the issue, the administrator spends hours trying to diagnose the problem, just to discover that the module removal was the root cause.

Developer Responsibility

Now that you are familiar with some of the issues, how do they impact module developers? Some people might suggest that they are not an issue at all, that it is the responsibility of the site administrator to know what is being installed on the systems. However, I would caution that it is always in the best interests of module developers to be honest and up front with customers, because there is nothing worse than having a module that you created be the cause of a site outage, regardless of fault.

Developer responsibility (especially when distributing modules and other DotNetNuke components that rely on potentially shared resources) is a must-consider item for all developers. Providing a quality product is one thing, and your users will be happy for it, but providing users with the information they need to avoid making a change that will break your module (or even worse, their site) not only benefits the customer, but also reduces the total number of support calls.

Summary

This chapter took a brief look at DotNetNuke development when working with third-party components. Two of the most common DotNetNuke-specific compatibility issues were examined, as well as issues related to deployment and module conflicts. You also learned why these topics are important to developers.

Chapter 15 introduces the various ways to distribute the custom DotNetNuke modules that you have created. A focus on the various distribution channels, module review programs, and even a quick highlight of different licensing considerations will bring this book to a close.

DotNetNuke, Modules, and Ajax Functionality

DotNetNuke 4.6.0 was the first version of DotNetNuke to fully support Microsoft's ASP.NET Ajax library. That version changed the expectations of end users by enabling developers to quickly add Ajax functionality to any and all modules developed for use within DotNetNuke. After 4.6.0, subsequent releases refined the Microsoft Ajax functionality, and it became an integral part of the toolkits used by most developers, even allowing for easy implementation and usage of the Ajax Control Toolkit.

Then, in September 2008, when Microsoft announced that it would start shipping the Open Source jQuery JavaScript/Ajax library, DotNetNuke Corporation was quick to include support for jQuery starting with DotNetNuke 5.0 RC1. This additional support provides DotNetNuke developers with numerous tools that can be leveraged to implement rich, interactive, client-facing modules and sites.

This chapter focuses on the integration between DotNetNuke, modules, and the Ajax libraries. The chapter starts out with demonstrations on basic ASP.NET Ajax, and then discusses the ASP.NET Ajax Control Toolkit, including how it can be leveraged to add even more functionality to the Microsoft offering. This chapter concludes with a brief overview of the jQuery support options available in DNN 5.0 RC1 and later.

ASP.NET Ajax

As mentioned previously, support for ASP.NET Ajax was added in DotNetNuke version 4.6.0. It provides a very robust and easy-to-implement framework for DotNetNuke developers to use. Because ASP.NET Ajax is part of the framework, developers are not required to make any `web.config` changes or to use any other nonstandard implementation processes.

There are typically two key methods of integrating Ajax support for DotNetNuke modules: enabling by control and manually enabling. The following discussion looks at each of these options, and explains when and why you should use each of them. This section of the chapter includes a brief summary of considerations that are important to remember.

Enabling by Control

One of the most common methods to enable ASP.NET Ajax is to simply select a control and enable Ajax for that control. This process is completed on a control-by-control basis using the Host ➪ Module Definitions page.

Using the guestbook example, you can click the Edit icon next to the Guestbook module listed in Module Definitions, as shown in Figure 15-1. Once the module has been selected, an information page displays each of the controls for the module, as shown in Figure 15-2. Click the Edit icon next to the "Sign Guestbook (DesktopModules/GuestbookCS/SignGuestbook.ascx)" entry. If SignGuestbook.ascx is not immediately available, then you must first select the Sign Guestbook option from the Select Definition drop-down list.

Figure 15-1

Figure 15-2

Now you have opened the detailed information for the SignGuestbook.ascx control, the control used to sign the guestbook. Figure 15-3 shows the default display for this control. Notice the final checkbox in the list of options, Supports Partial Rendering? When enabled, this option causes DotNetNuke to wrap the control in an ASP.NET Ajax Update Panel before rending it to the user's browser, effectively enabling Ajax without any code. This option can also be defaulted in the .dnn file by adding <supportspartialrendering>true</supportspartialrendering> inside the control definition.

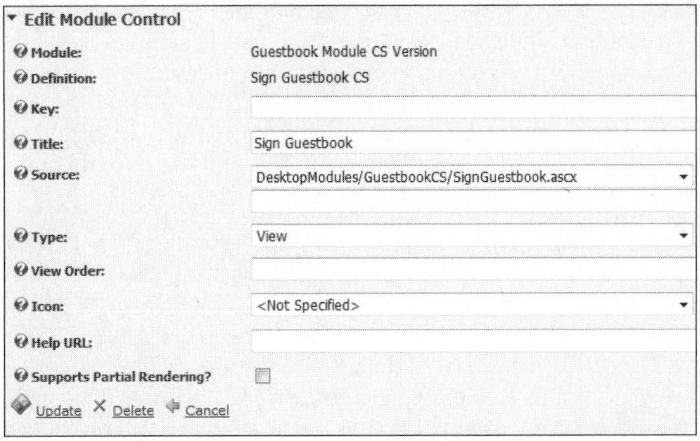

Figure 15-3

Now, if the user clicks to sign the guestbook, an Ajax request will be performed, rather than a postback. This can be a very helpful way to improve the overall performance of a module without getting deeply involved with the ins and outs of Ajax implementation as a module developer. Certain scenarios, though, do not support this implementation, such as when sending a file to the user via the response stream. See the section "Considerations When Using ASP.NET Ajax" later in this chapter for more information on the proper times to use this method to enable Ajax.

Manually Enabling

DotNetNuke provides a number of helpful items inside the `DotNetNuke.Framework.Ajax` class that allow access to determine whether Ajax is installed, and to learn about methods to register individual components to become Ajax-enabled regions. This method provides a much more granular method of adding or modifying support for ASP.NET Ajax. This method does not require the manual insertion of control markup in the `.ascx` file, such as `ScriptManagers` or `UpdatePanels`.

Listing 15-1 (C# code) and Listing 15-2 (VB code) show the code necessary to wrap a panel inside of an ASP.NET Ajax update panel using the DotNetNuke framework methods. This code must be put inside the `Page_Load` or `Page_Init` method handlers, and *must* execute on every page request to ensure that it is enabled at all times.

Listing 15-1: C# Wrap in Update Panel Code

```
if (DotNetNuke.Framework.AJAX.IsInstalled())
{
    DotNetNuke.Framework.AJAX.RegisterScriptManager();
    DotNetNuke.Framework.AJAX.WrapUpdatePanelControl(pnlName, true);
}
```

Listing 15-2: VB Wrap in Update Panel Code

```
If DotNetNuke.Framework.AJAX.IsInstalled Then
    DotNetNuke.Framework.AJAX.RegisterScriptManager()
    DotNetNuke.Framework.AJAX.WrapUpdatePanelControl(pnlName, True)
End If
```

This is very simple code. First, a conditional check is completed to ensure that Ajax has been installed and enabled. This covers cases when a DotNetNuke Host user has disabled Ajax functionality via the Host settings. If Ajax is enabled, then the script manager is registered.

Next, the `WrapUpdatePanelControl` method is called. This method accepts two parameters. The first parameter is the name of the panel that should be wrapped, and the second parameter is a Boolean flag that indicates whether a progress bar should be shown.

> In DotNetNuke 5.x, the `IsInstalled` check is no longer necessary because DotNetNuke 5.0 requires Ajax to operate.

At this point, it should be obvious how easy it can be to quickly wrap sections of a module in update panels, enabling the granular progression of updates. However, this still doesn't address the issue of a control that must perform a postback inside the registered update panel.

Luckily, DotNetNuke provides another method, `RegisterPostBackControl`, that accepts a single parameter, which is the control name. Using this method, it is possible to wrap a section of a control in an update panel, and still have a button inside it that performs a postback. This provides the true flexibility needed to enable and disable Ajax, but still follow the framework's functionality. Listing 15-3 (C#) and Listing 15-4 (VB) show modified Ajax-enabling routines that incorporate `RegisterPostbackControl` to force a button named `btnPostback` to cause a postback.

Listing 15-3: C# Wrap in Update Panel Code w/Postback Control

```
if (DotNetNuke.Framework.AJAX.IsInstalled())
{
    DotNetNuke.Framework.AJAX.RegisterScriptManager();
    DotNetNuke.Framework.AJAX.WrapUpdatePanelControl(pnlName, true);
    DotNetNuke.Framework.AJAX.RegisterPostBackControl(btnPostback);
}
```

Listing 15-4: VB Wrap in Update Panel Code w/Postback Control

```
If DotNetNuke.Framework.AJAX.IsInstalled Then
    DotNetNuke.Framework.AJAX.RegisterScriptManager()
    DotNetNuke.Framework.AJAX.WrapUpdatePanelControl(pnlName, True)
    DotNetNuke.Framework.AJAX.RegisterPostBackControl(btnPostback)
End If
```

You may be wondering why you would implement granular Ajax in this manner, rather than simply add the necessary `<asp:updatepanel ...>` elements to the actual markup in the `.ascx` file. This is a valid question, and the answer is simple. By utilizing the DotNetNuke framework methods and checking the `IsInstalled` property of the Ajax object, it is possible to determine whether the site administrator (for one reason or another) wanted to turn off Ajax. If so, it is possible for custom modules to follow that practice, therefore acting like a good citizen in the DotNetNuke environment.

Considerations When Using ASP.NET Ajax

As a module developer, you can appreciate how easy the DotNetNuke framework makes it for you to implement Ajax functionality inside your modules. However, with this ease of use comes a few items to consider when you are deciding which solution is most appropriate for your application. Table 15-1 shows a simple comparison that should help illustrate different business requirements, and which of the three available methods can support it. The asp:updatepanel items are included only for illustration purposes, and should be considered a last-ditch effort.

Table 15-1

Requirement	Supports Partial Rendering Option	Using DotNetNuke .Framework.Ajax Methods	Including <asp:updatepanel> Code in ascx
Entire control uses Ajax	X	X	X
No coding needed	X		
Capability to have some controls postback (such as file export, and so on)		X	X
Capability to have multiple UpdatePanels in a single control		X	X
Supports Ajax Disabled option	X	X	

If you are using the DotNetNuke.Framework.Ajax methods to enable Ajax, then it is also very important to remember that those operations must be completed on each and every page load. If they are performed only on the first page load, then the first request will use Ajax, but all future requests will be standard postbacks.

ASP.NET Ajax Control Toolkit

In addition to releasing the standard ASP.NET Ajax support, the ASP.NET team has also released the ASP.NET Ajax Control Toolkit (www.asp.net/ajax/ajaxcontroltoolkit/). This is a collection of new controls and extenders that can help improve the overall look and feel of your application.

Using this toolkit inside a DotNetNuke installation is very simple. Once the Ajax Control Toolkit has been downloaded and installed to the development machine, simply add a reference to the AjaxControlToolkit.dll file. After this has been done, the controls can be used just like they are in the examples provided on the ASP.NET website.

Figure 15-4 and Figure 15-5 show examples of two of the more common Toolkit controls. The first is the Modal Popup Extender, which enables developers to create modal dialogs to display information to users. The second is a Validation Callout Extender, which provides a nicer look and feel to your standard ASP.NET validators.

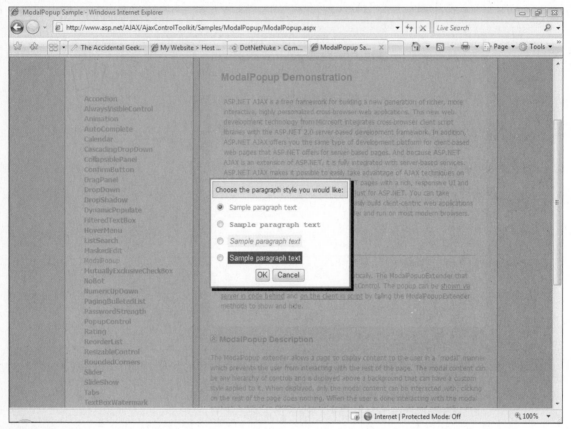

Figure 15-4

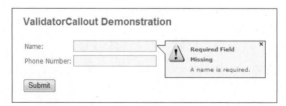

Figure 15-5

As you can see, these types of additional controls can add style and an overall better user experience, all at an extremely minimal development cost. Developers only need to take a few minutes to add references and configure the display.

Considerations with Ajax Control Toolkit

It is important to take into consideration the items noted in Chapter 14 about third-party `.dll` distribution when using items such as the Ajax Control Toolkit. There is some risk of `.dll` conflicts if multiple modules are using the same assembly, because you cannot use two installations of the same controls.

With the Ajax Control Toolkit, there are surprisingly few "gotcha" moments when working with the default DotNetNuke setup. The only known issue as of this writing is that some content positioning is incorrect with certain skin layouts. This can be resolved by adding `position:absolute` to the table cell containing the Ajax Control Toolkit items.

> **For assistance using the Ajax Control Toolkit items, consult the ASP.NET website.**

jQuery Support

Late in the third quarter of 2008, Microsoft announced that the open-source jQuery JavaScript library would be included in a future service pack of Visual Studio, including full support for IntelliSense. Quickly after this announcement, DotNetNuke Corporation added an enhancement to DotNetNuke 5.0 RC1 providing support for jQuery in the framework. This is a great feature for developers because it adds another framework that can be used to improve the client-side experience. With the combination of jQuery and ASP.NET Ajax, the options are truly endless. The following discussion examines jQuery configuration and usage inside a DotNetNuke module.

> **This information is based on the DotNetNuke 5.0 RC1 build. Minor implementation changes may occur during final release processes of DNN 5.**

jQuery Configuration

In DotNetNuke 5.0, the integration settings for jQuery are stored in the host settings area of the portal in a similar manner to that of the ASP.NET Ajax settings. The key difference is that the settings have been pulled out from other areas, and are contained in their own group within the Advanced Settings section. To configure jQuery when logged in as the host user, you can navigate to the Host ⇨ Host Settings menu option. From there, under Advanced Settings, you should find a collection of settings that looks like what is shown in Figure 15-6.

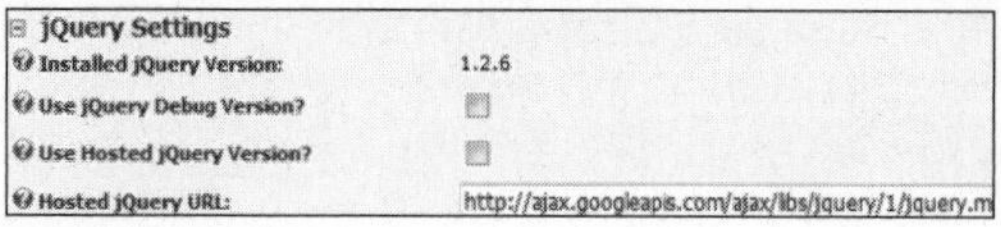

Figure 15-6

The first setting, Installed jQuery Versions, is for informational purposes only, and designates the current version of jQuery that is loaded by default into the DotNetNuke Installation (1.2.6 in Figure 15-6). The next two options are used to determine which versions of the jQuery scripts should be included for use in the site.

The first of these options, Use jQuery Debug Versions?, uses the full-size version of jQuery. This is "non-minified" and much easier to use for debugging purposes, but it is much larger in overall size. This option should most likely be used only in cases where debugging is needed.

The next option, Use Hosted jQuery Version?, enables you to optionally use a "hosted" version of jQuery, rather than a local copy that is installed with DotNetNuke. This option has a couple of key benefits. If enabled, the user's cache retains a copy of the jQuery file based on the requesting URL. If other sites are using jQuery, the library will already be in the user's cache, and the user won't have to download the file. This also makes the process of adopting newer versions much easier. The key item to remember here is that this does introduce an external dependency on your installation system.

The final option, Hosted jQuery URL:, reflects the URL that is used when loading jQuery from a hosted URL.

Overall, this is a very simple configuration. Notice that unlike ASP.NET Ajax, there is *no* Enable/Disable option for jQuery configuration. This is because, unlike ASP.NET Ajax, DotNetNuke utilizes a load-when-needed method, and only includes jQuery references when at least one module (or skin object) requires it. This helps to reduce page footprints on those pages without any jQuery usage.

jQuery Usage

Because DotNetNuke uses a "load only when necessary" model for jQuery inclusion, module developers must complete one small step before they can use jQuery. This step simply calls the following code, once per page request, regardless of postback or not:

```
DotNetNuke.Framework.jQuery.RequestRegistration()
```

This method call will result in DotNetNuke registering the required jQuery items on the page in accordance with the options selected by the site administrator. The most common stumbling block with jQuery usage inside of DotNetNuke is only calling the RequestRegistration() method on the first page load. If this happens, jQuery events will work until the first postback.

Summary

This chapter introduced the basic types of Ajax support available for DotNetNuke developers. No specific implementations on any of the individual Ajax libraries have been included because there are hundreds of other resources out there that developers can use to get a better understanding of their usage. The discussions in this chapter simply highlighted the implementation differences that are exposed when using the respective libraries with DotNetNuke.

If you are looking for more information on the individual Ajax libraries, start with `http://ajax.asp.net` (for the .NET implementation) and `http://www.jquery.com` (for the jQuery implementation).

Chapter 16 examines DotNetNuke skin object creation, which is simply another method of extending the DotNetNuke framework. However, rather than build a module that is loaded to a page, you will create an object that is added to the skin.

Creating Skin Objects

The discussions in the earlier chapters of this book were specifically geared toward the development of DotNetNuke modules, which, for many implementations, is the right way to go when adding needed functionality. However, it isn't the only solution available to help extend DotNetNuke.

This chapter begins an examination that focuses on some of the other methods for adding functionality to a DotNetNuke site. It is dedicated to *skin objects*, elements that are added and configured in the skin and not via the control panel.

The chapter begins with an overview of when it would be a good idea to use a skin object (instead of a module) to accomplish the desired functionality. The discussion then progresses to the development, installation, and configuration of a new skin object. The chapter concludes with a short overview of the purpose and process of creating a skin object.

When to Use Skin Objects

After working with DotNetNuke for a while, you start to notice the elements that appear on each and every page — items such as Login, Register, and Copyright are the most common. How do they get there? These elements are all implemented as skin objects, and are added by the administrator to the skin of the site, rather than on individual pages. DotNetNuke does allow an administrator to set a module to "display on all pages," but that option does not show the modules in the case of a different module running in Isolated mode.

Figure 16-1 shows a screen with the Logo, Login, Register, and Search skin objects visible from a default DotNetNuke installation. These skin objects are present on each page of a DotNetNuke site, and their positions are defined in the skin, as opposed to being modified by the site administrator when adding or editing content.

Figure 16-1

Skin objects are typically items that should be limited in complexity because they are items that will be executed on every page load. However, they provide a great place to add additional functionality. Google Analytics is a well-known example of third-party skin objects. These modules inject Google tracking code, as well as third-party menu controls.

In this chapter, you will create a rudimentary skin object that simply outputs the current date and time to the browser. This simple example illustrates the concepts needed to fully understand the process of creating skin objects.

Creating a "Current Time" Skin Object

Creating a skin object is a very simple process. In many ways, it is similar to creating a DotNetNuke module. Therefore, the easiest starting point is to simply create a new DotNetNuke module project, as described in Chapter 5. This will create the shell of the project, after which it can be manipulated to meet the needs as items progress.

To get started, create a new project called `CurrentTimeSkinObject` in the language of choice following the instructions in Chapter 5. For this example, create the Visual Basic object inside the `CurrentTimeSkinObject` folder, and the C# version under the `CurrentTimeSkinObjectCS` folder. This will enable the same filenames to be used for both projects.

Cleaning the Solution

With a default solution created, a large project structure is most likely present, complete with `Component` folders, multiple code files, and `SqlDataProvider` files. The skin object being created is very simple, and only four main files are needed. Following are the files to retain:

```
/App_LocalResources/ViewCurrentTimeSkinObject.ascx.resx
/CurrentTimeSkinObject.dnn
/ViewCurrentTimeSkinObject.ascx
/ViewCurrentTimeSkinObject.ascx (.cs or .vb)
```

All other files can be removed from the project. This leaves a single view control with an associated localization file and a single .dnn file for installation. Again, this is a minimal configuration of a skin object. Therefore, it is a lightweight solution.

The final step is to clean the solution by ensuring that the assembly name is set correctly inside the properties of the project. The assembly name should be `WroxModules.CurrentTimeSkinObjectCS` for the C# project, and `WroxModules.CurrentTimeSkinObjectVB` for the VB.NET project. It is very important to remember to correct these values. (Many developers forget to do so.)

Coding the Object

With the project properly configured, it is now time to configure the skin object code. Skin objects are configured in a similar manner to modules, as they are implemented as user controls. The key difference is that instead of inheriting from the `PortalModuleBase` class, skin objects inherit from the `SkinObjectBase` class. This base class, though, provides many of the common functionalities that were introduced in previous chapters. The following sections provide the code and text elements needed to complete the example object file by file. The `.dnn` file will be completed in the section "Installing the Skin Object (Locally)," later in this chapter, where a different method of creating the DotNetNuke manifest is explained.

Adding Elements to ViewCurrentTimeSkinObject.ascx.resx

Because you are creating a simple skin object, you only need to add one item to the localization file. This value is the display format to be used to control what is actually displayed on the page to the user when the skin object is rendered. Table 16-1 shows the exact information as it should be added into the `.resx` file.

Table 16-1

Key	Value	Comment
`DisplayTemplate.Text`	`Today is: [TODAY]`	Display template; `[TODAY]` is replaced with the current date

This completes the setup of the `.resx` file. Note the use of the `[TODAY]` token. This enables users to fully control the layout by simply rendering the date and time when replacing the token.

Coding ViewCurrentTimeSkinObject.ascx

The front-end display of the skin object is also very simple. It contains a single `asp:literal` control that will be used to relay the information to the user. Listing 16-1 shows the C# code and Listing 16-2 shows the VB code that should be added to the respective versions of the file.

Listing 16-1: C# ViewCurrentTimeSkinObject.ascx code

```
<%@ Control Language="C#" AutoEventWireup="false"
    CodeBehind="ViewCurrentTimeSkinObject.ascx.cs"
    Inherits="WroxModules.CurrentTimeSkinObject.
        ViewCurrentTimeSkinObject" %>

<asp:Literal ID="litContent" runat="server" Mode="PassThrough"
    EnableViewState="false" />
```

Listing 16-2: VB ViewCurrentTimeSkinObject.ascx code

```
<%@ Control Language="vb" AutoEventWireup="false"
    CodeBehind="ViewCurrentTimeSkinObject.ascx.vb"
    Inherits="WroxModules.CurrentTimeSkinObject.
        ViewCurrentTimeSkinObject" %>

<asp:Literal ID="litContent" runat="server" Mode="PassThrough"
    EnableViewState="false" />
```

Notice the configuration of the Mode on the Literal control. Setting this to PassThrough prevents ASP.NET from adding extra code around (or modifying) the values passed by the user. In addition to this configuration item, you also disable viewstate on the Literal control. With each page load, you update the value. Thus, viewstate would be unnecessary overhead for the page.

This is the only code needed here because the template will be used to actually send the display to the user.

Coding ViewCurrentTimeSkinObject.ascx (.cs/.vb)

The final piece needed is to specify the code that actually configures the display for the control. You will also add a public property for "Show Date Only" to allow a bit more flexibility in the display of the control. Listing 16-3 (C#) and Listing 16-4 (VB) provide the code needed for the skin object.

Listing 16-3: C# ViewCurrentTimeSkinObject.ascx.cs

```
using System;
using System.Web;
using System.Web.UI;
using System.Web.UI.WebControls;
using DotNetNuke.UI.Skins;
using DotNetNuke.Services.Localization;

namespace WroxModules.CurrentTimeSkinObjectCS
{
    public partial class ViewCurrentTimeSkinObject : SkinObjectBase
    {
        #region Private Members
        private bool _dateOnly = false;
        private const string _myFileName =
            "ViewCurrentTimeSkinObject.ascx";
        #endregion

        #region Public Properties
        public bool DateOnly
        {
            get { return _dateOnly; }
            set { _dateOnly = value; }
        }
        #endregion

        protected void Page_Load(object sender, EventArgs e)
```

```
        {
            //Get template
            string templateText = Localization.GetString("DisplayTemplate",
                              Localization.GetResourceFile
                              (this, _myFileName));

            //Load proper format
            if (_dateOnly)
                templateText = templateText.Replace("[TODAY]",
                                   System.DateTime.Now.ToShortDateString());
            else
                templateText = templateText.Replace("[TODAY]",
                                   System.DateTime.Now.ToString());

            //Load to user
            litContent.Text = templateText;
        }
    }
}
```

Listing 16-4: VB ViewCurrentTimeSkinObject.ascx.vb

```
Namespace WroxModules.CurrentTimeSkinObject

    Partial Class ViewCurrentTimeSkinObject

        Inherits DotNetNuke.UI.Skins.SkinObjectBase

        ' private members
        Private _dateOnly As Boolean = False
        Private Const _myFileName as String =
            "ViewCurrentTimeSkinObject.ascx"

#Region "Public Properties"
        Public Property DateOnly() As Boolean
            Get
                Return _dateOnly
            End Get
            Set(ByVal Value As Boolean)
                _dateOnly = Value
            End Set
        End Property
#End Region

        Private Sub Page_Load(ByVal sender As System.Object, ByVal e
            As System.EventArgs) Handles MyBase.Load
            'Load template
            Dim templateText As String = Localization.GetString("DisplayTemplate",
                              Localization.GetResourceFile(Me,_myFileName))

            'Replace with proper date
            If _dateOnly Then
                templateText = templateText.Replace("[TODAY]",
```

(continued)

Listing 16-4 *(continued)*

```
System.DateTime.Now.ToShortDateString())
        Else
            templateText = templateText.Replace("[TODAY]",
System.DateTime.Now.ToString())
        End If

        'Load to literal

        litContent.Text = templateText
    End Sub

End Class
End Namespace
```

As you can see, this is incredibly simple and common ASP.NET code. The important thing to remember here is that you must ensure that the object inherits from `SkinObjectBase` and not any other control. This is the key integration point for DotNetNuke.

Completion of the Code

With the previous sections of code added to the project, it is time to build the project. No build errors should be encountered. If they are, ensure that you have followed the steps correctly, and that all other default files from the template have been removed.

Installing the Skin Object (Locally)

In the earlier chapters, when working with installing a module on the local machine, the "Import Manifest" functionality was used to pull in the configuration. That functionality was then re-used when packaging the module. Because you have already learned about that method of extension creation, we will step through the process of using DotNetNuke to actually create the entire definition — installing the skin object locally and providing the formatted code that needs to be added to the .dnn file stored inside the solution. This method can be very easily leveraged to quickly create manifest files for skin objects and other files.

To start the process, log in to the DotNetNuke portal with Host access. After logging in, navigate to the Host ⇨ Extensions area. The default extensions view shown in Figure 16-2 then appears, listing all the installed extensions in the current portal. This includes skin objects, skins, containers, modules, and authentication providers. The move to DotNetNuke unified all the items and created one encompassing extensions system.

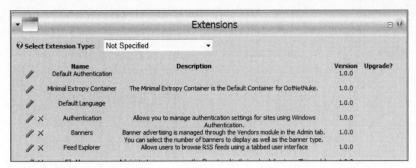

Figure 16-2

From the action menu in the upper-left corner, select Create New Extension. You will then see a dialog similar to the one shown in Figure 16-3. Fill in the information per Table 16-2. The table also provides detailed information about each option and how it should be configured. Note that the only items needed are the ones with the red circled arrows appearing on the right, as shown in Figure 16-3 (minus the color, of course).

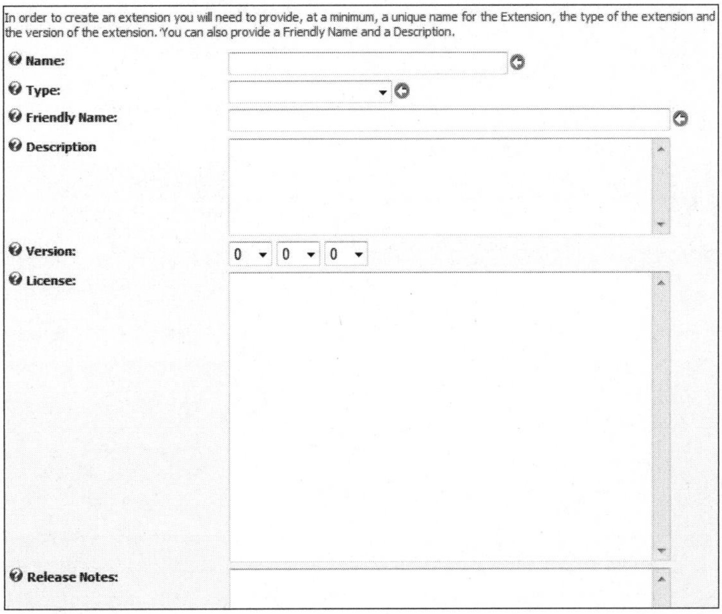

Figure 16-3

Table 16-2

Setting	Value	Notes
Name	`CurrentTimeSkinObject`	This is the name of the unique folder being used inside the `DesktopModules` folder.
Type	`SkinObject`	This selection defines what type of extension you are creating.
Friendly Name	Current Time Skin Object VB	This is the friendly name that is shown to the users. It can contain spaces and is more for display purposes.
Description	The Visual Basic version of the Current Time Skin Object as demonstration	This is a description of your extension, and is a free-form text input.
Version	1.0.0	This is the version information for your extension. No specific rules exist for starting or incrementing.
License	None	This is where the license terms that are presented to the user during installation can be displayed.
Release Notes	None	This is where a collection of release notes (or important "updates") can be provided to extension users.
Owner		This is the owner of the extension, typically a developer name. This is optional, and for support purposes only.
Organization		This is the organization responsible for the development of the extension.
Url		This is the URL to the party responsible for the development of the extension.
Email Address		This is the contact e-mail address for the party responsible for the extension.

After filling in this information, click the Add New Extension link to display the dialog shown in Figure 16-4. (Note that this figure has been cropped.) The final step to the configuration process is to set up the skin object-specific settings. To do this, you must set values for the three new options shown in Figure 16-4.

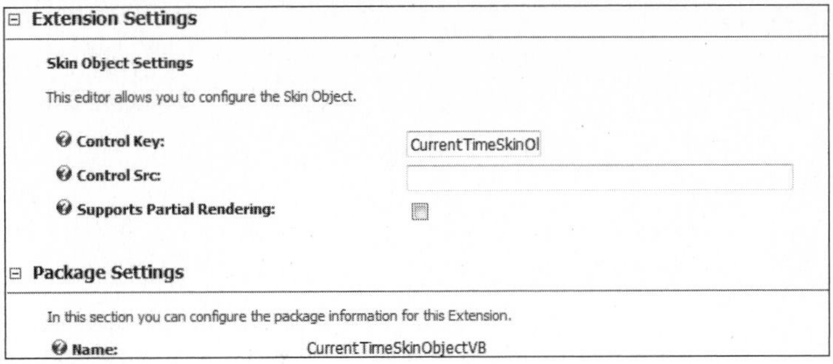

Figure 16-4

The first configuration item, the Control Key, is the unique key used to identify the skin object when adding it to a skin. You should try to keep this as simple as possible, but also as unique as possible. You cannot have spaces or special characters in the field. For this example, use `CurrentTimeCS` for the C# version, or `CurrentTimeVB` for the VB version.

The second configuration item, the control source (Control Src), is the path to the user control that implements the skin object base class. In this example, the value for the C# version is `/DesktopModules/CurrentTimeSkinObjectCS/ViewCurrentTimeSKinObject.ascx`. The VB version is `/DesktopModules/CurrentTimeSkinObject/ViewCurrentTimeSKinObject.ascx`. This tells DotNetNuke where to find the skin object.

The final configuration option is the Supports Partial Rendering checkbox. When checked, this will wrap the object inside an Ajax update panel, similar to the functionality for modules. Because this control does not have any user interaction, leave it blank for this example.

After filling out all fields, click Update Extension at the bottom of the page to update the extension. This completes the installation of the skin object on the local DotNetNuke installation.

Let's now take a look at the method necessary to actually add the skin object to a skin. We begin by quickly examining the process of creating the package, and the format of the resulting .dnn manifest.

Creating the Installation Package

You can use built-in DotNetNuke functionality to create the resulting installation package that is used in other DotNetNuke installations. You can also use this created package to generate the needed .dnn manifest.

To start this process, when viewing the skin object inside the Extensions Settings section, click Create Package to display the Create Package wizard dialog shown in Figure 16-5, which provides a summary of the package information. Because a .dnn file has not yet been configured, you do not want to select the Use Existing Manifest option shown in the lower portion of the figure. Instead, you want to review the created manifest, so leave that option selected. Click Next to continue to the next step.

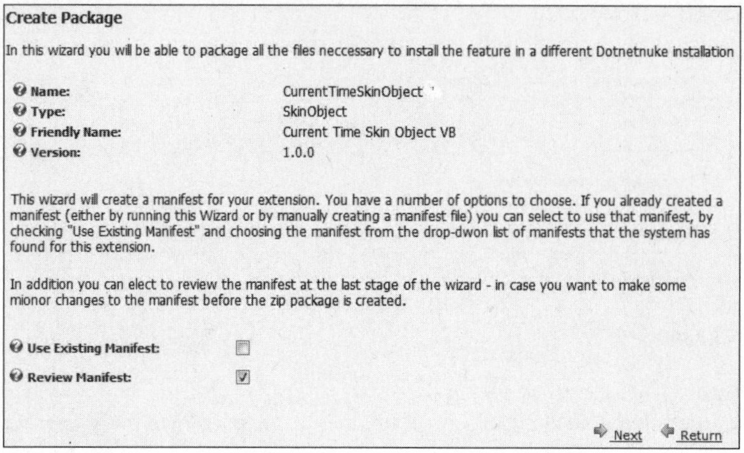

Create Package

In this wizard you will be able to package all the files neccessary to install the feature in a different Dotnetnuke installation

- **Name:** CurrentTimeSkinObject
- **Type:** SkinObject
- **Friendly Name:** Current Time Skin Object VB
- **Version:** 1.0.0

This wizard will create a manifest for your extension. You have a number of options to choose. If you already created a manifest (either by running this Wizard or by manually creating a manifest file) you can select to use that manifest, by checking "Use Existing Manifest" and choosing the manifest from the drop-dwon list of manifests that the system has found for this extension.

In addition you can elect to review the manifest at the last stage of the wizard - in case you want to make some mionor changes to the manifest before the zip package is created.

- **Use Existing Manifest:** ☐
- **Review Manifest:** ☑

→ Next ← Return

Figure 16-5

The next step in the process is to select the files to include with the package. For this example, DotNetNuke has already selected the correct files for the installation package. Figure 16-6 shows the default files selected for the VB version. Note that because the skin object was compiled, there is no need to include the source.

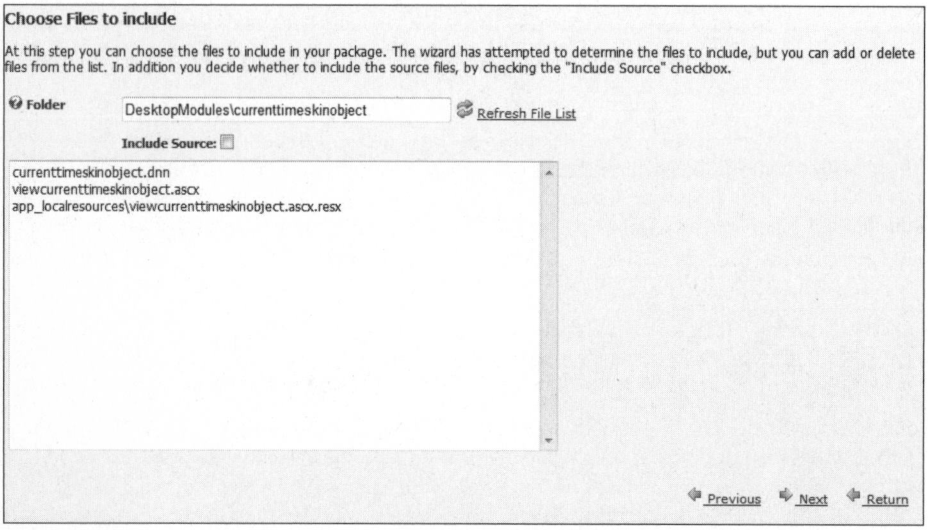

Choose Files to include

At this step you can choose the files to include in your package. The wizard has attempted to determine the files to include, but you can add or delete files from the list. In addition you decide whether to include the source files, by checking the "Include Source" checkbox.

Folder DesktopModules\currenttimeskinobject   ⟳ Refresh File List

Include Source: ☐

```
currenttimeskinobject.dnn
viewcurrenttimeskinobject.ascx
app_localresources\viewcurrenttimeskinobject.ascx.resx
```

← Previous → Next ← Return

Figure 16-6

The next step is to select the assemblies that must be included. DotNetNuke should properly select the `WroxModules.CurrentTimeSkinObjectVb.dll` or `WroxModules.CurrentTimeSkinObjectCs.dll`, depending on the version being created. Figure 16-7 provides an illustration of the default display. Click Next to continue with the package creation process.

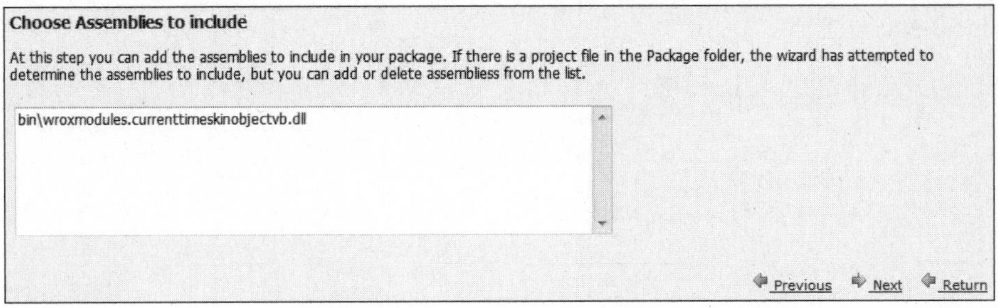

Choose Assemblies to include

At this step you can add the assemblies to include in your package. If there is a project file in the Package folder, the wizard has attempted to determine the assemblies to include, but you can add or delete assembliess from the list.

```
bin\wroxmodules.currenttimeskinobjectvb.dll
```

◄ Previous   ⇨ Next   ◄ Return

Figure 16-7

You should now see the manifest file for your review. This might be something helpful to record inside the Visual Studio project in the .dnn file that has yet to be modified. Listing 16-5 shows the generated manifest for the VB version of the skin object.

Listing 16-5: Generated VB Manifest

```
<dotnetnuke type="Package" version="5.0">
  <packages>
    <package name="CurrentTimeSkinObjectVB" type="SkinObject"
        version="1.0.0">
      <friendlyName>Current Time Skin Object VB</friendlyName>
      <description>The Visual Basic version of the Current Time Skin
        object as demonstration</description>
      <owner>
        <name>Mitchel Sellers</name>
        <organization>IowaComputerGurus Inc.</organization>
        <url>http://www.iowacomputergurus.com</url>
        <email>msellers@iowacomputergurus.com</email>
      </owner>
      <license>Your license goes here</license>
      <releaseNotes>New SKO</releaseNotes>
      <components>
        <component type="SkinObject">
          <moduleControl>
            <controlKey>CurrentTimeVB</controlKey>
            <controlSrc>
/DesktopModules/CurrentTimeSkinObject/ViewCurrentTimeSKinObject.ascx
            </controlSrc>
            <supportsPartialRendering>False</supportsPartialRendering>
          </moduleControl>
        </component>
        <component type="Assembly">
          <assemblies>
            <assembly>
              <path>bin</path>
              <name>wroxmodules.currenttimeskinobjectvb.dll</name>
            </assembly>
          </assemblies>
        </component>
```

(continued)

Listing 16-5 *(continued)*

```xml
            <component type="File">
              <files>
                <basePath>DesktopModules\currenttimeskinobjectvb</basePath>
                <file>
                  <name>currenttimeskinobject.dnn</name>
                </file>
                <file>
                  <name>viewcurrenttimeskinobject.ascx</name>
                </file>
                <file>
                  <path>app_localresources</path>
                  <name>viewcurrenttimeskinobject.ascx.resx</name>
                </file>
              </files>
            </component>
          </components>
        </package>
      </packages>
    </dotnetnuke>
```

If the format of this document seems similar to that of the module manifest file, that's because it contains many of the same header elements, as well as individual components (such as file and assembly). The only difference is that it contains additional items that are there to support SkinObjects (such as the skin object component). Appendix D provides more information about the available options and individual elements inside the manifest file.

Click Next to proceed past the manifest review. You may now create the necessary manifest and package files. Simply specify a name for the manifest and package. Figure 16-8 shows the values used to create the VB package.

Create Package

The final step is to create the package. To create a copy of the Manifest file check the "Create Manifest File" check box - the file will be created in the Package's folder. Regardless of the setting you use here the manifest will be saved in the database and it will be added to the package.

To create a package check the "Create Package" check box. The package will be created in the Host users Home Folder.

- **Create Manifest File:** ☑
- **Manifest File Name:** CurrentTimeSkinObjectVB.dnn
- **Create Package:** ☑
- **Archive File Name:** CurrentTimeSkinObjectVB.zip

Figure 16-8

Click Next to actually create the manifest and installation package. After it is successfully created, the package can be located in the /Portals/_default/ folder for easy download. The generated package can then be used to easily install the skin object on other DotNetNuke installations.

230

Adding a Skin Object to a Skin

Now that the skin object has been created, it is time to actually implement the skin object in the skin where it can be seen by users. To do this, you must find the skin file that is currently in use. For this example, the Portal skin from the Extropy package is being used. Therefore, the file needed to be modified can be found in /portals/_default/skins/extropy/portal.ascx. You must identify the skin in use and find its location in order to properly add a skin object to an existing skin.

After the skin has been located, you should note a section in the header that includes various Register sections. All you need to do to register the custom control is add a new Register element for the control. Listing 16-6 (C#) and Listing 16-7 (VB) show the required code for the skin object. As you can see, the TagPrefix value is always set to dnn. The TagName is the control key that was specified when the extension was created.

Listing 16-6: C# Register Code

```
<%@ Register TagPrefix="dnn" TagName="CurrentTimeCS"
    src="~/DesktopModules/CurrentTimeSkinObjectCS/
    ViewCurrentTimeSkinObject.ascx" %>
```

Listing 16-7: VB Register Code

```
<%@ Register TagPrefix="dnn" TagName="CurrentTimeVB"
    src="~/DesktopModules/CurrentTimeSkinObject/
    ViewCurrentTimeSkinObject.ascx" %>
```

With the Register code added, the final step is to actually place the control on the location on the page. To provide a full example, two instances will be placed, one in each format. Listing 16-8 (C#) and Listing 16-9 (VB) provide the code for both implementations.

Listing 16-8: C# Control Declarations

```
<dnn:CurrentTimeCS runat="server" id="WithTime" />
<dnn:CurrentTimeCS runat="server" id="DateOnly" DateOnly="true" />
```

Listing 16-9: VB Control Declarations

```
<dnn:CurrentTimeVB runat="server" id="WithTime" />
<dnn:CurrentTimeVB runat="server" id="DateOnly" DateOnly="true" />
```

This completes the process to use the skin object. Figure 16-9 shows the modified skin in the test installation that contains both declarations, just after the Login and Register skin objects.

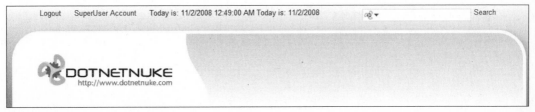

Figure 16-9

Summary

This chapter introduced the concept of skin object creation by providing a step-by-step example demonstrating how to create an incredibly simple skin object that can be used to display the current date and time. You should be able to extend this information easily to make it apply to any number of potential development solutions.

Chapter 17 dives into one more development type inside of DotNetNuke: the authentication provider. In Chapter 17, you will learn about the use of authentication providers using the Live ID provider as the model to dissect.

17

Creating Authentication Providers

To build a foundation for the discussion of various different extension options available within the DotNetNuke framework, Chapter 16 introduced you to the creation of the skin object. Authentication providers are the next integration method that will be discussed.

This chapter introduces authentication providers by starting with a brief overview of what they are and when it might be appropriate to use them. The chapter then continues with examples of authentication providers in use. The discussion then examines considerations that must be taken into account when working with authentication providers — most importantly, their limitations, including common "gotcha" moments that might be experienced. The chapter will then take a look at the code that implements the Live ID authentication provider that is included as part of the core DotNetNuke installation. The chapter wraps up with a brief note and warning about differences between DotNetNuke 4.x and 5.x installation processes for providers.

What Is an Authentication Provider?

Some developers may find the concept of an authentication provider difficult to grasp because many developers confuse authentication and membership. In DotNetNuke 4.6.0 and later, the authentication provider functionality has been implemented as a way to enable users to extend the authentication process to work with outside sources. An *authentication provider* simply provides the functionality to assert that users are who they say are.

This is a very helpful feature, because authentication providers can be used to help authenticate users to other systems, and even authenticate against federation-style systems such as Live ID or OpenID. An authentication provider's job is to log the user into the portal in question. This can be completed by doing the following:

❏ Signing the user in with an existing account

❏ Creating a new account based on external information

❑   Using underlying DotNetNuke authentication mechanisms for basic authentication and simply adding extra authentication factors to the base implementation

By default, DotNetNuke makes available providers for Active Directory, Windows Live ID, OpenID, and Windows Card Space. In the end, regardless of which authentication provider is used, the user must have a login created inside the DotNetNuke portal. This is accomplished in different manners, depending on which authentication provider is being used. For example, the Active Directory provider (which authenticates a user to a Windows Active Directory domain) uses a method whereby if the user doesn't exist, the user is added to the system, and passwords and all information are synchronized. The opposite of that is the Live ID provider, which simply creates a link to an existing account; if an account doesn't exist for the user to associate to, the user is forced to register for the site.

This differentiation between systems is very logical. The Active Directory provider is more of an authoritative source of the record — if users are domain users, they should be DotNetNuke users. The Active Directory provider can even synchronize roles from the domain to DotNetNuke. With the Live ID provider, it is a convenience, enabling users to log in with a standard login they use elsewhere. The point is that, depending on your needs, you have a high degree of control over how things are completed, as well as the level of integration.

Example of Authentication Provider Use

One of the key benefits of the DotNetNuke authentication provider system is that more than one provider can be used at any given time, which gives users flexibility when accessing a website. Figure 17-1 shows the DotNetNuke login page with the standard, Live ID, and OpenID providers enabled. By enabling multiple providers, users are given options when it comes to accessing the site.

Figure 17-1

Figure 17-2 shows the display for a user when logging in with Live ID. This screen shows one of the more simple processes. If the user's Live ID authentication values are not stored locally, the user is directed to the Live ID Login screen shown in Figure 17-3, where the user enters his or her familiar login information. The user is then returned to the DotNetNuke site and, as long as the user's account has been associated, the user is logged in.

Figure 17-2

Figure 17-3

Overall, for many users, this can be considered a much more simple process for authentication. Live ID remembers a user's authentication information based on the user's login settings, and can keep the user logged in for multiple sites at the same time. This is a very common implementation of an authentication provider.

Items to Consider When Creating a Provider

Authentication providers are a great extension option when working with DotNetNuke. However, it is important for developers to ensure that an authentication provider is the best solution when working with DotNetNuke. To help identify the right and wrong times to implement an authentication provider, consider the following issues when determining whether an authentication provider is the proper solution:

❑ Providing only authentication

❑ Co-existing with other providers

Providing Only Authentication

This is the most important consideration when evaluating the use of an authentication provider for a custom solution. An authentication provider alone provides *only* authentication services. If you are working with external systems, it is possible to synchronize information between DotNetNuke and the external system during the login and/or logout processes. However, there is no other integration/communication accomplished with an authentication provider. Therefore, profile information and other information that may be updated via standard user interactions within the DotNetNuke system will not be returned to the external system.

You can overcome some of this via synchronization methods in the login and logout processes, but be aware that it introduces a lag in communication times. If real-time integration of profile data is needed, then a custom membership provider would be a better solution because that enables control over the storage of all membership information.

Can Co-exist with Other Providers

It is also very important to remember that site administrators and users are not forced to use your authentication method exclusively. For example, with some custom authentication providers, developers may want to track all user logins, only to discover they do not see the desired results. The root cause of the issue may be that a site administrator re-enables one of the other authentication provider systems, thus enabling the users to log in via a separate process not tracked by the custom code.

This is an important distinction, because even with proper configuration in the beginning, it is possible later in the process for items to be disabled. Therefore, mission-critical data exchanges and pre-work for user login might not be appropriate here, or, at minimum, ensure very clear communication to end users.

Investigating Provider Code

The best way to understand the creation of a provider is simply to investigate the code of an existing authentication provider, one that will be familiar to users at some level. To do this, we'll examine the source code needed for the Live ID authentication provider. Earlier, Figure 17-2 showed the primary view from the authentication provider, which is the result of the primary user-facing code to be examined here. Figure 17-4 shows the administration configuration options available to those configuring the provider. This is a very common authentication scenario, and it provides a good basis for examining the code needed to create a provider.

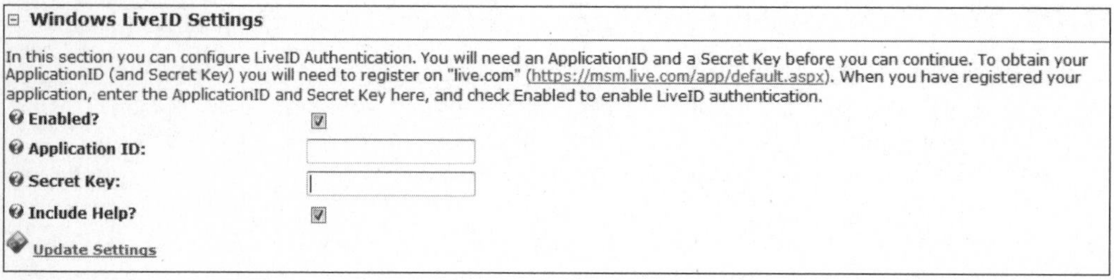

Figure 17-4

Code Location and Project Setup

The first piece of information that is important for developers to understand is that code for authentication providers is typically stored inside the `/desktopmodules/authenticationservices` folder. Each specific authentication provider system has a folder. This ensures that all authentication providers are stored in a common location. DotNetNuke's standard authentication system is stored in this location, as well as inside the `/dnn` folder.

Knowing this information, you must create a project to store the code for the custom provider. This can be done by simply using the existing templates that have been provided for the creation of modules and skin objects in earlier chapters of this book. However, note that you must make some modifications to properly reference the DotNetNuke assemblies. The Live ID provider, if installed, is located in `/desktopmodules/authenticationservices/liveid`.

Interface Code

At an interface level, authentication providers have the capability to create three controls. The first control is a `Login` control, and this is presented to the user when logging into the system. The second is the `Settings` control, which is the collection of settings that are available to site administrators inside the Authentication section in the site menu. The final control is a `Logoff` control, which is used for processing when a user logs off of a site. This can be used to ensure that cookies for external references are removed, or other activities are disabled after the user clicks Logoff.

The following sections explore these three controls for the Live ID provider. In the discussions that follow, you will learn about the new specific implementations that affect the development of custom providers.

> **Examples contained in remaining sections of this chapter are shown in C# only for brevity. This is the language used by the actual core component.**

Login.ascx

Listing 17-1 contains the full source code for the `Login` control's user interface. As you can see, it is a very simple collection with a label, a button, and a panel for identifying errors. Nothing specific is included in this code that is different from any .NET control.

Listing 17-1: Login.ascx Source Code

```
<%@ Control Language="C#" AutoEventWireup="true"
Codebehind="LogIn.ascx.cs"
  Inherits="DotNetNuke.Authentication.LiveID.Login,
             DotNetNuke.Authentication.LiveID" %>
<table id="tblLogin" runat="Server" cellspacing="0"
    cellpadding="3" border="0"
     summary="SignIn Design Table" width="160">
   <tr id="trHelp" runat="server">
      <td><asp:Label ID="lblHelp" runat="Server" cssClass="Normal"
                  resourcekey="Help" /></td>
   </tr>
```

(continued)

Listing 17-1 *(continued)*

```
      <tr>
       <td align="center"><asp:button id="cmdLogin"
resourcekey="cmdLogin"
                    cssclass="StandardButton" text="Login" runat=
       "server" /></td>
      </tr>
</table>
<asp:Panel ID="pnlError" runat="server" Visible="false"
     CssClass="Normal">
     <asp:Image ID="Image1" runat="server" ImageUrl="~/images/
        red-error.gif"
          ImageAlign="Left"   /><asp:Label ID="lblMessage"
             runat="Server"
          resourcekey="OpenIDError"/>
     <br />
</asp:Panel>
```

Login.ascx.cs

Listing 17-2 shows the code that implements the code-behind file for the Live ID provider key.
DotNetNuke integration points are noted following this listing.

Listing 17-2: Login.ascx.cs

```
using DotNetNuke.Services.Authentication;
using DotNetNuke.Entities.Modules;
using DotNetNuke.UI.Utilities;
using DotNetNuke;
using DotNetNuke.Entities.Users;
using DotNetNuke.Security.Membership;
using DotNetNuke.Common;
using DotNetNuke.Common.Utilities;

namespace DotNetNuke.Authentication.LiveID
{
    public partial class Login : AuthenticationLoginBase
    {
        private string appID;
        const string LoginCookie = "webauthtoken";
        static DateTime ExpireCookie = DateTime.Now.AddYears(-10);
        static DateTime PersistCookie = DateTime.Now.AddYears(10);

        #region Public Properties
        public string AppID
        {
            get { return appID; }
            set { appID = value; }
        }
        public override bool Enabled
```

```
{
    get { return Config.GetConfig(PortalId).Enabled; }
}
public string ReturnURL
{
    get
    {
        return Null.NullString;
    }
}
#endregion

#region Private Methods
private void loginUser(User user)
{
    //Try and Log User into DNN
    UserLoginStatus loginStatus =
        UserLoginStatus.LOGIN_FAILURE;
    UserInfo objUser =
        UserController.ValidateUser(PortalId, user.Id, "",
     "LiveID", "", PortalSettings.PortalName, IPAddress,
         ref loginStatus);

    //Raise UserAuthenticated Event
    UserAuthenticatedEventArgs eventArgs = new
     UserAuthenticatedEventArgs(objUser, user.Id,
         loginStatus, "LiveID");

    OnUserAuthenticated(eventArgs);
}
#endregion
#region Protected Methods
protected override void OnInit(EventArgs e)
{
    cmdLogin.Click += new EventHandler(cmdLogin_Click);
    base.OnInit(e);

    Config config = Config.GetConfig(PortalId);
    trHelp.Visible = config.IncludeHelp;
}
protected override void OnLoad(EventArgs e)
{
    HttpResponse res = HttpContext.Current.Response;
    HttpRequest req = HttpContext.Current.Request;
    HttpCookie loginCookie = req.Cookies[LoginCookie];

    try
    {
        //Initialize WindowsLiveLogin class
        WindowsLiveLogin wll = new WindowsLiveLogin(PortalId);

        if (loginCookie != null)
```

(continued)

Listing 17-2 *(continued)*

```
{
    string token = loginCookie.Value;

    if ((token != null) && (token.Length != 0))
    {
        User user = wll.ProcessToken(token);

        if (user != null)
        {
            //Try and Log User into DNN
            loginUser(user);
        }
    }
}
else
{
    string action = req.Params["action"];
    loginCookie = new HttpCookie(LoginCookie);
    switch (action)
    {
        case "logout":
            loginCookie.Expires = ExpireCookie;
            res.Cookies.Add(loginCookie);
            res.Redirect(AuthenticationController.
                GetLogoffRedirectURL
                (PortalSettings, Request));
            break;
        case "clearcookie":
            loginCookie.Expires = ExpireCookie;
            res.Cookies.Add(loginCookie);

            string type;
            byte[] content;
            wll.GetClearCookieResponse(out type,
                out content);
            res.ContentType = type;
            res.OutputStream.Write(content, 0,
                content.Length);
            break;
        case "login":
            User user = wll.ProcessLogin(req.Form);
            if (user != null)
            {
                loginCookie.Value = user.Token;

                if (user.UsePersistentCookie)
                {
                    loginCookie.Expires =
                        PersistCookie;
                }
```

```
                                        //Try and Log User into DNN
                                        loginUser(user);
                                }
                                else
                                {
                                        loginCookie.Expires = ExpireCookie;
                                }

                                res.Cookies.Add(loginCookie);
                                break;
                        default:
                                break;
                        }
                }

                tblLogin.Visible = true;
                pnlError.Visible = false;
        }
        catch (Exception exc)
        {
                tblLogin.Visible = false;
                pnlError.Visible = true;
        }
}
#endregion
protected void cmdLogin_Click(object sender, EventArgs e)
{
        //Initialize Windows Live Login
        WindowsLiveLogin wll = new WindowsLiveLogin(PortalId);

        Response.Redirect(wll.GetLoginUrl());
        }
    }
}
```

The first integration point to note in this listing is the fact that the Login control inherits from the AuthenticationLoginBase class. This is a requirement for all Login controls to ensure that DotNetNuke is able to properly load the control.

The second integration point is the call to the ValidateUser method provided inside of DotNetNuke's UserController class. This is a built-in method that enables developers to successfully validate a user's login. Figure 17-5 shows a few of the most common overloads to the ValidateUser method.

```
 ValidateUser(DotNetNuke.Entities.Users.UserInfo, Integer, Boolean) As DotNetNuke.Security.Membership.UserValidStatus
 ValidateUser(Integer, String, String, String, String, String, ByRef DotNetNuke.Security.Membership.UserLoginStatus) As DotNetNuke.Entities.Users.UserInfo
 ValidateUser(Integer, String, String, String, String, String, String, ByRef DotNetNuke.Security.Membership.UserLoginStatus) As DotNetNuke.Entities.Users.UserInfo
```

Figure 17-5

You can see from Figure 17-5 that it is easy to leverage the existing DotNetNuke framework methods to validate a user session. Table 17-1 provides detailed descriptions for each of the individual properties used in the various overloads.

Table 17-1

Name	Type	Description
PortalId	Integer	The ID of the portal to log in the user. This is used in both the second and third listed overloads.
Username	String	The username that is used to log in the user
Password	String	The password supplied by the user to log in
AuthType	String	The type of authentication provided. This is set to DNN to have it validate the login of the user against the DotNetNuke database.
VerificationCode	String	The user's verification code. This is typically left blank. However, if this is used in a verified registration portal configuration, then users may need to be prompted for the code.
PortalName	String	The name of the portal. This can be obtained using the PortalSettings.PortalName value that is provided by the base class implementation.
IP	String	The user's IP address. This is used for logging.
LoginStatus	UserLoginStatus	This is a value passed by reference that returns an enum value to indicate login success or failure.

Note that the first overload of the ValidateUser method, shown in Figure 7-5, simply validates the user's status in the portal. This is a very important and helpful integration element because it enables developers to focus on their external validation process, and *not* the process of actually saving the cookie information that will be used by DotNetNuke to remember the user and store the respective information.

The key piece of this functionality is the passing of the provider information. Passing the LiveId parameter simply tells DotNetNuke to log in the user. It does not go through password verification. As listing 17-2 shows, a blank password is used, yet login still occurs.

Settings.ascx

Listing 17-3 shows the source code for the Settings control. The interface for this control is very simple, and uses the DotNetNuke PropertyEditorControl to handle the interface elements of the settings. This property editor control relies on specifically formatted classes whereby it can generate the common user-interface experience that many users have come to expect inside of DotNetNuke. Specific additions to the class can enable developers to direct the placement of properties.

Listing 17-3: Settings.ascx Markup

```
<%@ Control Language="C#" AutoEventWireup="true"
       Codebehind="Settings.ascx.cs"
    Inherits="DotNetNuke.Authentication.LiveID.Settings,
                 DotNetNuke.Authentication.LiveID" %>
<%@ Register TagPrefix="dnn" Namespace="DotNetNuke.UI.WebControls"
    Assembly="DotNetNuke" %>
<asp:Label ID="lblHelp" runat="Server" resourcekey="LiveIDHelp"
     CssClass="Normal"
         />
<dnn:propertyeditorcontrol id="SettingsEditor" runat="Server"
    editcontrolwidth="200px"
    labelwidth="250px"
    width="450px"
    editcontrolstyle-cssclass="NormalTextBox"
    helpstyle-cssclass="Help"
    labelstyle-cssclass="SubHead"
    editmode="Edit"
    SortMode="SortOrderAttribute"
    />
<asp:Label ID="lblMessage" runat="Server" resourcekey="LiveIDMessage"
     CssClass="NormalRed" Visible="false" />
```

The key element to note in this code example is that public properties will all be given edit controls based on their data type, making the development process simple. For more details on this process, refer to Chapter 12, which discusses DotNetNuke controls, including the PropertyEditorControl.

Settings.ascx.cs

The Settings code-behind file is quite simple, with two method calls — one to load the settings and one to save the settings. Listing 17-4 provides the full source, with important integration elements for authentication providers appearing in bold. Just like the Settings control for modules created in previous chapters, authentication providers have an AuthenticationSettingsBase class that they must inherit from. This class exposes methods that can be overridden by the individual provider's methods, thus providing developers with the capability to perform needed actions.

Listing 17-4: Settings.ascx.cs File

```
using DotNetNuke;
using DotNetNuke.Entities.Modules;
using DotNetNuke.Entities.Profile;
using DotNetNuke.Services.Authentication;
using DotNetNuke.Services.Exceptions;


namespace DotNetNuke.Authentication.LiveID
{
    public partial class Settings : AuthenticationSettingsBase
    {

        #region Protected Methods
        protected override void OnLoad(EventArgs e)
```

(continued)

Listing 17-4 *(continued)*

```
        {
            //Call the base classes method
            base.OnLoad(e);

            try
            {
                Config config = Config.GetConfig(this.PortalId);

                SettingsEditor.DataSource = config;
                SettingsEditor.DataBind();
            }
            catch (Exception exc)
            {
                Exceptions.ProcessModuleLoadException(this, exc);
            }
        }

        #endregion

        #region Public Methods

        public override void UpdateSettings()
        {
            if (SettingsEditor.IsValid)
            {
                Config config = SettingsEditor.DataSource as Config;
                if (config.Enabled &&
        (String.IsNullOrEmpty(config.AppID) ||
         String.IsNullOrEmpty(config.SecretKey)))
                    lblMessage.Visible = true;
                else
                {
                    Config.UpdateConfig(SettingsEditor.DataSource
                        as Config);
                    lblMessage.Visible = false;
                }
            }
        }

        #endregion

    }
}
```

The Settings control is displayed in one of two manners. In DotNetNuke 5.0, it will be displayed on the Edit page of the extension via the Admin ⇨ Extensions menu options, where the control appears along with the other package settings. In DotNetNuke 4.x sites, the settings are accessed via the Authentication page accessible from the Admin menu. In the 4.x sites, settings for *all* authentication providers are displayed on the same page.

Logoff.ascx

The final user interface code is the `Logoff` control, shown in Listing 17-5. This is a very simple implementation for the user, providing a single Logoff button that will log out the user. Using this control, developers may take custom actions when the user leaves the application via a standard method. Depending on integration method and/or style, it might be possible to simply utilize the code provided with the DotNetNuke provider (`/dnn/logoff.ascx`) if all that is needed is to end the DotNetNuke session. Again, this is a consideration that must be evaluated on an application-by-application basis.

Listing 17-5: Logoff.ascx Markup

```
<%@ Control Language="C#" AutoEventWireup="true"
       CodeBehind="Logoff.ascx.cs"
   Inherits="DotNetNuke.Authentication.LiveID.Logoff,
                   DotNetNuke.Authentication.LiveID" %>
<table cellspacing="0" cellpadding="3" border="0" summary=
        "SignIn Design Table"
     width="160">
   <tr>
       <td><asp:Label ID="lblHelp" runat="Server" cssClass="Normal"
                    resourcekey="Help" /></td>
   </tr>
   <tr>
       <td><asp:CheckBox ID="chkLiveID" runat="Server"
          CssClass="NormalTextBox"
                 resourcekey="LiveID" Checked="true" /></td>
   </tr>
   <tr>
    <td align="center"><asp:button id="cmdLogoff"
           resourcekey="cmdLogoff"
                   cssclass="StandardButton" text="Logoff"
                        runat="server" /></td>
   </tr>
</table>
```

Logoff.ascx.cs

The code-behind file for the `Logoff` control is quite simple, as shown in Listing 17-6. The key thing to note here is that this must inherit from the `AuthetnicationLogoffBase` class. The only other important item is the call to `OnLogOff`. This is a method that processes the logout for the user from the DotNetNuke side of things, ensuring that DotNetNuke doesn't remember the user. The remainder of the code simply processes and logs off the user, based on the provided business rules for the provider-specific implementation.

Listing 17-6: Logoff.ascx.cs Code Behind

```
using DotNetNuke.Services.Localization;

namespace DotNetNuke.Authentication.LiveID
{
    public partial class Logoff : AuthenticationLogoffBase
    {
        protected void cmdLogoff_Click(object sender, EventArgs e)
        {
            //Log off DNN
            OnLogOff(EventArgs.Empty);

            if (chkLiveID.Checked)
            {
                //Initialize Windows Live Login
                WindowsLiveLogin wll = new WindowsLiveLogin(PortalId);
                //logoff Windows Live
                Response.Redirect(wll.GetLogoutUrl());
            }
            else
                //Redirect
                OnRedirect(EventArgs.Empty);
        }
    }
}
```

Interface Summary

As shown in the preceding code examples, the user interface portion of the custom provider is quite simple. The only major difference between developing modules and developing providers is the type of the base class that must be implemented. There is no single control base that can be used for all controls. Each of the three control types has its own specific base class. Omission of the proper base class is typically the most common error made when working with authentication providers, and something developers should be very careful about.

The other classes and components provided with the source package of the Live ID provider dive into the specifics of provider implementation. To keep the focus of this discussion on the development process for custom authentication providers, that code is not reviewed here because it does not relate to the development of general authentication providers.

DotNetNuke Manifest

Another key difference of authentication providers is their slightly different DotNetNuke manifest file information. The Create New Extension method demonstrated in Chapter 16 can be used to generate the proper manifest file. However, let's focus on the key differences between the module, skin object, and authentication provider manifests.

Listing 17-7 shows the complete manifest file for the installation version of the Live ID provider. The key difference is the inclusion of the AuthenticationSystem component and the type definition at the package level. These differences are shown in bold for clarity. This is the component that provides the specific bits and pieces that make up the provider definition.

Listing 17-7: Live ID Provider .dnn Manifest (DNN 5.x Format)

```
<dotnetnuke type="Package" version="4.0">
    <packages>
        <package name="DNN_LiveIDAuthentication"
            type="Authentication System"
    version="01.00.00">
            <friendlyname>DotNetNuke LiveID Authentication
                Project</friendlyname>
            <description>
                The DotNetNuke LiveID Authentication Project is an
                Authentication provider for DotNetNuke that
                uses the LiveID
                authentication protocol to authenticate users.
            </description>
            <vendor>
                <companyName>DotNetNuke Corporation</companyName>
                <contactInfo>support@dotnetnuke.com</contactInfo>
                <license src="license.txt" />
            </vendor>
            <dependencies />
            <components>
                <component type="AuthenticationSystem"
                    installOrder="1">
                    <authenticationService>
                        <type>LiveID</type>
                        <settingsControlSrc>
DesktopModules/AuthenticationServices/LiveID/Settings.ascx
                        </settingsControlSrc>
                        <loginControlSrc>
DesktopModules/AuthenticationServices/LiveID/Login.ascx
                        </loginControlSrc>
                        <logoffControlSrc>
DesktopModules/AuthenticationServices/LiveID/Logoff.ascx
                        </logoffControlSrc>
                    </authenticationService>
                </component>
                <component type="Assembly" installOrder="3">
                    <assemblies>
                        <assembly>
                            <path>bin\Providers</path>
                            <name>
DotNetNuke.Authentication.LiveID.dll
                            </name>
                            <version>01.00.00</version>
                        </assembly>
                    </assemblies>
                </component>
                <component type="File" installOrder="2">
                    <files>
                        <basePath>
DesktopModules/AuthenticationServices/LiveID
```

(continued)

Listing 17-7 *(continued)*

```xml
                        </basePath>
                        <file>
                            <path>App_LocalResources</path>
                            <name>Login.ascx.resx</name>
                        </file>
                        <file>
                            <path>App_LocalResources</path>
                            <name>Logoff.ascx.resx</name>
                        </file>
                        <file>
                            <path>App_LocalResources</path>
                            <name>Settings.ascx.resx</name>
                        </file>
                        <file>
                            <name>Login.ascx</name>
                        </file>
                        <file>
                            <name>Logoff.ascx</name>
                        </file>
                        <file>
                            <name>Settings.ascx</name>
                        </file>
                        <file>
                            <name>license.txt</name>
                        </file>
                    </files>
                </component>
            </components>
        </package>
    </packages>
</dotnetnuke>
```

> Note that DNN 4.x authentication providers have a type of `Authentication System`, whereas DNN 5.x authentication providers have a type of `Auth_System` at the package level. As of this writing, DNN 5.x will still support the `AuthenticationSystem` package type as of DNN 5.0 RC2 and later. However, the new `Auth_System` type is *not* supported on 4.x.

Four key pieces of information must be supplied for the `AuthenticationSystem` component. The first is the `type`, which is a unique identifier for your authentication provider, and is used in a similar manner to the module's `Definition` name. The last three settings are the source paths to the `Login`, `Logoff`, and `Settings` controls that provide the authentication provider functionality.

Looking at the remainder of the manifest file, notice the common components for the inclusion of files and assemblies. This is a key benefit of the new manifest system — the high degree of reusability and commonality between different providers. For more information on supported elements inside the new DotNetNuke manifest file, see Appendix D, which provides a more detailed look at options for the manifest.

Installation Package

Creating the installation package for a custom authentication provider is the exact same process that is used for modules and skin objects. If you are packaging elements manually, note that all files and folders must be created inside the package, and the `.dnn` file must be included. If you want to avoid creating the package manually, you can use the Create Package functionality to create not only the manifest, but also the fully functional installation package.

Aside from DLL reference issues for authentication providers, created installation packages are valid for DotNetNuke versions 4.6.0 and later. This is because upon the introduction of the authentication provider, the new manifest system has been included. This new manifest/package system only became fully operational in DotNetNuke 5.0. Let's now take a look at the differences between installations of DotNetNuke 4.x and 5.x.

Installation Differences (Versions 4.6.x Versus 5.x)

Because the authentication provider package type was supported in 4.6.x and followed a different installation process than standard modules, a few differences exist in the installation process for authentication provider packages between DotNetNuke version 4.x and version 5.x.

To install an authentication provider in DotNetNuke 4.x, you must first log in as the Host user, and then navigate to Host ⇨ Host Settings. You should see a dialog similar to the one shown in Figure 17-6, which includes a listing of currently installed authentication systems. From this dialog, select the Install New Authentication System link. When you click this link, the installation process is the same. When you are creating user documentation and other publishing materials, this might be a good item to identify.

	Type	Enabled	Settings Control Src	Login Control Src
⊟	**Authentication Settings**			
	DNN	☑	DesktopModules/AuthenticationServices/DNN//Settings.ascx	DesktopModules/AuthenticationServices/DNN//Login.ascx
X	LiveID	☑	DesktopModules/AuthenticationServices/LiveID/Settings.ascx	DesktopModules/AuthenticationServices/LiveID/Login.ascx
X	OpenID	☐	DesktopModules/AuthenticationServices/OpenID/Settings.ascx	DesktopModules/AuthenticationServices/OpenID/Login.ascx

✚ **Install New Authentication System**

Figure 17-6

The installation of an authentication provider in DotNetNuke 5.x follows the exact same process as that of a module. Simply navigate as Host to Host ⇨ Extensions and select Install Extension from the action menu, and follow the dialog.

Administration Differences (Versions 4.6.x Versus 5.x)

In addition to the installation differences, note that it was possible in DotNetNuke version 4.6.x to view the settings for all authentication providers via the Admin ⇨ Authentication menu option. This menu option has been removed in DotNetNuke version 5.x, and all settings administration for authentication providers are handled on a provider-by-provider basis. This process is completed by selecting Admin ⇨ Extensions from the navigation menu and clicking Edit next to the desired authentication providers.

Because this is a shift in user administration activities, it will be worth noting in user documentation to ensure a seamless integration process for all users.

Summary

This chapter introduced the concept of an authentication provider, and provided examples of potential uses for this method of extending DotNetNuke. A quick dive into the code for the Live ID provider offered a look into the code-specific items that must be implemented to fully create a new provider. The chapter concluded with a comparative look at packaging and installation between DotNetNuke versions and extension types.

Chapter 18 concludes the book by looking at some best practices that you should consider when developing DotNetNuke modules. The discussion examines considerations needed for testing, deployment, development, and release models.

18

DotNetNuke Development Best Practices

So far in this book, you have learned about various DotNetNuke integration techniques. Sprinkled throughout the various discussions in the book have been bits of best-practice information, as well as recommendations for proper development techniques when it comes to working with DotNetNuke.

This chapter provides a summary of best practices, and provides a few general overall recommendations when it comes to developing with DotNetNuke. The material is divided into two sections: things to do and things to avoid.

Things to Do

The following recommendations are items that, in general, are true best practices for development in the DotNetNuke ecosystem. These recommendations are geared toward developers working with provider modules, skin objects, and authentication providers with the intent of distributing the final application to the widespread DotNetNuke community. If you are working on one-time-use or custom solutions, not all of these recommendations will apply to your situation. For a broad distribution, however, these guidelines have all proven to deliver better quality modules that meet the needs of users.

Pick a Minimum Supported Version and Enforce It

When developers use the WAP development model, they must use a specific DotNetNuke version to build the module's DLL file. In the case of the examples of this book, these modules were all built against DotNetNuke 5.0.0. Therefore, these modules will work with DotNetNuke 5.0.0 and later versions of DotNetNuke, barring any breaking changes by the core team (which is something they strive very hard not to do).

Understanding this behavior is important, because installing a module built for version 5.0.0 on a 4.x DotNetNuke installation will result in an exception, and typically the entire site will be taken down. If you decide to support only installations greater than a specific DotNetNuke version, it is important to enforce this limitation by using the available options inside the `Package` element of the DotNetNuke manifest file. You can find details on the exact implementation of this limitation in Appendix D.

You might go through a number of different thought processes when weighing the factors to be considered when you decide upon the desired minimum DotNetNuke version. The most common determining factors for picking DotNetNuke 5.0.0 as the minimum version are to have the full capabilities to use the new manifest, and to allow easier integration into jQuery. The key is to evaluate the *minimum* required for the current project, and let those limitations steer you toward the proper DotNetNuke version.

Use the DotNetNuke API

Because DotNetNuke is a dynamic, database-driven framework, it is very common for developers to attempt to interact with DotNetNuke by modifying the database on their own. This practice is strongly discouraged because, just like modifying the core files, it places the site administrator at risk during an upgrade. If DotNetNuke modifies core database structures, it is possible that the custom module code that directly accesses these database objects will either fail after the updates or, even worse, stop DotNetNuke from successfully upgrading.

If your application must interact with the DotNetNuke framework for users, roles, or other common information, rather than directly access the database, use the respective controller classes that exist inside the `DotNetNuke.Entities` namespace of the framework. Utilizing DotNetNuke framework methods ensures that even with site upgrades and underlying database changes, the integration interface from DotNetNuke to the custom component will stay the same.

Reuse Common Controls

DotNetNuke provides a number of common controls. You learned about several of these controls and how they can be used in Chapter 12. You most certainly should utilize them when possible.

There are many benefits to using the DotNetNuke controls. Not only do they provide a common user interface, by using known components to build custom modules, the interfaces are familiar for the users managing the site. In addition to this, developers will notice a dramatic reduction in development time, as they no longer must spend time building controls that are localizable and reusable.

The DotNetNuke core team has strongly considered which controls to implement, and in most cases the controls provide complex functionality that would take many hours to recreate in such a flexible manner. A prime example of this would be the `DnnPagingControl`, which is a fairly simple module judging from the user display, but may pose many technical issues to resolve behind the scenes.

Test, Test, and Test Again

Given the nature of DotNetNuke, a module distributed to the broad community will be exposed to a wide variety of DotNetNuke installations. The differences between each of the installations will vary, but there is one overall constant: Not every site will be set up like the development environment used to create the module.

Because of this issue, when developing modules for distribution to the DotNetNuke community, you should keep in mind the following few simple testing rules to ensure that the highest quality code gets out there:

❑ **Test in both full and medium trust:** Most DotNetNuke modules can successfully run in a medium trust environment, which is great because many shared hosting providers do not allow code to execute in full trust on the shared hosting system. Certain operations, Web requests, and so on, always will require full trust, but because DotNetNuke runs in both environments, it is important to understand what is and isn't supported for each trust level, and how trust level affects the modules. The specification of full and medium trust can be handled via the `web.config` file by uncommenting the `trust` node within the default structure.

❑ **Test on multiple installations:** Testing a DotNetNuke installation package on a single DotNetNuke installation is not necessarily the most foolproof testing method. At a minimum, you should test on the minimum supported version and the most current version. If these versions can successfully run the module, it is usually a sign that the module is generally stable within the DotNetNuke integration points anyway.

❑ **Test both installation and upgrade:** After a first version of a module has been created and deployed into the DotNetNuke community, upgrades are the most important consideration when it comes to supporting the existing user base. Therefore, it is very important to fully test the upgrade process to ensure that the old module version can successfully upgrade to the most current version. In addition, it is equally important to ensure that the upgrade module can fully install on an installation that does not have existing versions. This is important because sometimes upgrade scripts are accidentally written in such a way that they rely on user data that would not be present in a default installation.

Following a comprehensive testing scenario that meets these requirements will help to ensure that the created module is functionally the best that it can be.

Support Localization and Globalization

The final item on the "things to do" list is to support localization and globalization to whatever extent possible. At a minimum, you should meet the same level that's adopted by the DotNetNuke core team. In practical terms, support of localization and globalization means two different things.

To support *localization*, your module must display content in the visitor's selected language. As of this writing, the DotNetNuke core team has implemented static text localization only. This is a great minimum standard of implementation, however. As more and more users implement DotNetNuke for sites using multiple languages, it will become very important to implement a method that allows for easy management of multiple languages for user-supplied content. Future releases from DotNetNuke Corporation promise to add new tools to help make that function easier to implement.

Globalization is building a module that is destined for worldwide distribution. To support globalization, the components should support the use of local text characters, even if they are nonstandard. Thus, in order to support this requirement, use of the NVARCHAR, NCHAR, and NTEXT column types is required at the database level to ensure that the user-supplied information is successfully retained.

Things to Avoid

Now that you understand a few things that should be done when working with DotNetNuke extensions, you should also be aware of what should typically be avoided. The following discussion provides general recommendations. Specific projects, business needs, or target audiences may dictate a different pattern. These are provided only as general guidelines.

Modification of web.config

Prior to DotNetNuke 5.0, it was not possible for a module to add or remove entries from the web.config file without implementing custom code to perform the operations (either via IUgradeable or some other facility). In addition to this, prior to DotNetNuke 4.6.2, DotNetNuke site administrators were required to manually merge custom web.config changes during core updates, something that was always tricky. Therefore, modifying the web.config was never a good idea, unless absolutely necessary.

This stance has been softened a little with recent DotNetNuke versions, because site administrators no longer must manually merge custom configuration settings, and the Config component is supported in the installation process (as described in Appendix D). It is now easier for developers to add/remove/modify items inside the web.config. However, web.config modifications should be limited to *only* those times where it is absolute necessary to achieve the desired functionality.

Modifying Core Components

This point has been repeated in multiple sections of this book, yet it bears repeating one last time: Including a core change as part of a customization is a highly discouraged practice. As soon as a core file has been modified, the DotNetNuke installation is taken out of the standard upgrade process, and you no longer have a guarantee that the site will successfully upgrade. Therefore, it is strongly recommended that all other options be fully considered, tried, tested, and disproved *before* settling with a core customization as a solution.

Requiring Nonstandard Implementation

With the advent of new items included in the DotNetNuke 5.0 Extensions system, developers now have much more control over the deployment of custom extensions. Given this expansive collection of options, developers should gear their efforts to a standard implementation system only. With the capability to run scripts, install assemblies, perform cleanup tasks, and even modify the web.config file through the module manifest, it would take a very unusual situation to require a deviation from the standard installation process.

Developers may experience many points of failure in nonstandard deployment scenarios. However, the most common point of failure is for a step to not be fully (or properly) implemented by the site administrator. When working with DotNetNuke, always keep in mind that the people running a site are often from varying backgrounds, some of whom have *no* technical experience at all. Therefore, general documentation that assumes a specific level of technological skills can make installation difficult, error-prone, or even impossible for many site administrators.

Summary

This chapter provided a brief summary of the best-practices information that has been provided throughout this book. Following these recommendations whenever possible will typically result in greater success for the implementation of DotNetNuke solutions targeted toward the broad DotNetNuke community.

The appendixes that follow provide supplemental information that will be helpful when implementing your DotNetNuke solutions.

Community Resources

DotNetNuke is supported by a large community. In many circumstances, the community provides numerous high-quality reference resources that are often overlooked. Some of these resources are free (such as personal blogs or tutorials), and some consist of paid services (such as video training sites designed to help get users quickly up to speed).

The sites listed in this appendix are merely a small sampling of the various sites and resources available in the DotNetNuke community. I have selected these sites for inclusion because they are time-tested resources in the community that have a good track record of providing quality content to users. Simple directed searches via Google or other search engines will result in the identification of hundreds of additional resources.

The resources shown here are divided into two categories:

❏   General resources

❏   Skinning resources

The resources listed in this appendix are provided as additional information only. The individual site owners have not requested to be listed here — these are simply sites that the author deems helpful for DotNetNuke module developers.

General Resources

The following resources are general community resources that contain a wide variety of information on DotNetNuke. Each resource is listed with a bit of information regarding the typical content found, as well as the normal frequency of updates.

DNN Creative Magazine

Lee Sykes, the creator of *DNN Creative Magazine* (www.dnncreative.com), maintains a subscription video tutorial magazine that provides hundreds of video tutorials covering all aspects of DotNetNuke administration and development. For those looking for video walk-throughs, the services offered by *DNN Creative Magazine* are second to none! New batches of videos are released each month.

DotNetNukeBlogs.com

DotNetNukeBlogs.com is a blog aggregation site maintained by Chris Hammond, a DotNetNuke core team member. This site was just launched in July of 2008, and is gaining new blog feeds on a regular basis. Serving merely as a centralized location to find DotNetNuke articles, it is a great resource for anyone who wants to stay current with the many individual bloggers focusing on creating DotNetNuke content.

Michael Washington's DotNetNuke Tutorials

Michael Washington, a DotNetNuke core team member, maintains a large collection of DotNetNuke module development tutorials on his website at www.adefwebserver.com/DotNetNukeHELP/. These free tutorials cover many aspects of module development, including LINQ and Silverlight. These are typically next-step recommendations for individuals looking for additional DotNetNuke tutorials.

This site is updated on a very regular basis with new content.

Mitchel Sellers' DotNetNuke Blog/Forums

The author of this book, who is also DotNetNuke Documents module project lead, maintains a mostly DotNetNuke blog on his website at www.mitchelsellers.com. This is a great resource for DotNetNuke tips and tricks of all types. Articles are available on installation, upgrade, emergency administration, and module development.

A support forum is additionally maintained at this site where individuals can ask targeted questions about .NET/DotNetNuke development, as well as custom modules created by the author. This site is updated at least once a week, if not more frequently.

Seablick Consulting DotNetNuke Blog

Tom Kraak, owner of Seablick Consulting, maintains a DotNetNuke-related blog at www.seablick.com. A key feature of blog postings found here is the typical focus on Search Engine Optimization (SEO) and usability inside DotNetNuke. Expect to find updates once every week to two weeks on this site.

SearchDotNetNuke.com

Although not a creator of DotNetNuke-specific content, SearchDotNetNuke.com is a targeted search starting point that will help you find valuable information on DotNetNuke. This site leverages the power of focused Google searches to provide quality search results against the DotNetNuke.com forums, as well as searches of specific sets of DotNetNuke sites.

Snapsis DotNetNuke Tips and Tricks

John Mitchell, a former DotNetNuke Core team member, maintains a DotNetNuke support forum at www.snapsis.com/DotNetNuke-Support-Forums.aspx. It contains both a tips-and-tricks section and a tutorials section. These two very helpful support resources provide a great deal of useful material that can help individuals with any level of DotNetNuke experience.

Skinning Resources

The following resources are known to provide good general information regarding DotNetNuke skin creation. Some sites duplicate resources listed in the "General Resources" category, but not all sites that provide general information provide information covering the DotNetNuke skinning process.

DNN Creative Magazine

As described earlier, *DNN Creative Magazine* is a subscription video tutorial service. In addition to developer- and administrator-specific topics, the videos also feature a robust collection of DotNetNuke skinning tutorials, designed to help users with all experience levels to understand DotNetNuke skinning.

SkinCovered

SkinCovered.com is a DotNetNuke skinning site maintained by Nina Meiers, a known resource in the DotNetNuke skinning community. This site contains a collection of free and for-purchase skins, as well as a great collection of "How to Skin" articles (www.skincovered.com/skinning.aspx). This site is a valuable resource because it contains many examples and walk-throughs that not only tell you about skinning, but also provide code samples and display examples for each element.

Think of Design Skinning Tools and Reference

Vasilis Terzopoulos, owner of ThinkOfDesign.com, is a well-known professional DotNetNuke skin designer who maintains a reference guide and tool collection for DotNetNuke skin creation. These tools can be found at www.thinkofdesign.com/dotnetnuke-skinning-tools.aspx. Additionally, on this site you can find free skins, even a few with entirely CSS-based layouts.

B

Additional web.config Options

When creating the DotNetNuke environment needed for development in Chapter 2, many default options were used to ensure that setup went smoothly for all readers. DotNetNuke contains many other optional configuration elements inside the `web.config` file that can be beneficial to users who want to customize their installations to meet individual business needs. This appendix introduces these additional configuration options. The topics presented are organized around their location inside the `web.config` section to help make locating settings easy.

appSettings

The `appSettings` section is the storage location for general application settings. These settings exist to enable individuals to customize the overall DotNetNuke installation environment. After installing some custom modules, additional settings might appear in this section as well.

Table B-1 shows the default DotNetNuke application settings and describes how they can be used to customize the installation.

Table B-1

Setting Name	Values	Purpose
AutoUpgrade	true/false	When set to `true`, this setting will cause DotNetNuke to automatically upgrade if a newer assembly version is detected. For security reasons, it is recommended that you set this to `false`.
UseInstallWizard	true/false	This setting is `true` by default, which means the installation uses the wizard installation mode. When set to `false`, a default installation using the "Auto" option is completed.
ShowMissingKeys	true/false	This setting is `false` by default. When set to `true`, it will show an indicator of missing localization keys. This is great for validating localization of custom modules.
EnableWebfarmSupport	true/false	This setting is used to enable Web farm support. If you are working in a Web farm, refer to the Web farm installation guide available from `www.dotnetnuke.com`.
HostHeader	String	When specified, the provided value will be removed from the request URL. For example `www.mysite.com/myfolder/default.aspx` would be treated as `www.mysite.com/default.aspx` if a `HostHeader` value of `myfolder` were specified.
PersistentCookieTimeout	Integer	When specified, this is the timeout (in minutes) for the cookie that is set when a user selects "Remember Me" on login to the DotNetNuke site.
UsePortNumber	true/false	When set to `true` and uncommented, this value ensures that DotNetNuke preserves the port number from all requests. This enables DotNetNuke to function correctly when IIS is running on a nonstandard port.

httpRuntime

The `httpRuntime` section is a single section inside the `web.config` file. By default, DotNetNuke is configured with the following values:

```
<httpRuntime useFullyQualifiedRedirectUrl="true" maxRequestLength="8192"
    requestLengthDiskThreshold="8192" />
```

This is a minimum configuration provided by DotNetNuke that specifies values relating to the HTTP processes. Table B-2 shows a list of the most popular httpRuntime settings that might help customize a DotNetNuke installation.

Table B-2

Setting Name	Values	Purpose
requestTimeout	Integer	This optional attribute (not included by default) can change the default request timeout. This allows for longer processing, if needed, for large uploads or other operations that might take longer than normal.
maxRequestLength	Integer	This setting specifies the maximum length of a request, in kilobytes. By default, DotNetNuke is set to allow uploads of up to 8MB in size. To allow larger file uploads, modifications to this setting are required.

For full information on httpRuntime options, visit the MSDN documentation on httpRuntime at http://msdn.microsoft.com/en-us/library/e1f13641.aspx.

Data Provider

The DotNetNuke data provider configuration section enables individuals to further customize the DotNetNuke database configuration. Typically, modifications to this section are completed *prior* to installing DotNetNuke because of the effects of the settings.

The following code sample shows the default configuration of the data provider section. Table B-3 shows a listing of the available configuration options within it.

```
<data defaultProvider="SqlDataProvider">
    <providers>
      <clear />
      <add name="SqlDataProvider" type="DotNetNuke.Data.SqlDataProvider,
          DotNetNuke.SqlDataProvider" connectionStringName="SiteSqlServer"
          upgradeConnectionString="" providerPath=
          "~\Providers\DataProviders\SqlDataProvider\
          " objectQualifier="" databaseOwner="dbo" />
    </providers>
  </data>
```

Table B-3

Setting Name	Values	Purpose
upgradeConnectionString	String	A second connection string can be provided in this setting that is used *only* for upgrades. This enables users to run DotNetNuke via the standard connection string with a user account that has lower permissions to the database, and then only use an elevated privilege account when completing a site upgrade.
providerPath	String	This is the path to the data provider. If a nonstandard data provider is used, this is where you specify the path to the provider. If you are not changing the data provider, *do not* change this value.
objectQualifier	String	A value specified here will be prefixed to all objects inside your database. This is used to enable multiple DotNetNuke installations inside a single database. If an object qualifier were specified with a value of DNN_, then all objects would contain this prefix. Therefore, the DotNetNuke Users table would become DNN_Users.
databaseOwner	String	Changing this value enables you to modify the owner for individual database objects. By default, an owner of dbo is provided.

It is very important to remember that these settings, if changed after a DotNetNuke installation has been completed, can result in errors when accessing the site or the accidental creation of a new portal.

Further Information

The elements covered in this appendix are the most common settings that are customized by individuals when configuring sites. Additional configuration elements exist, but are beyond the scope of this book. For detailed information, see the documentation available from dotnetnuke.com, as well as the many community resources listed in Appendix A.

C

Distributing Modules

Now that you have created a module, how can these creations be marketed to the greater DotNetNuke community? DotNetNuke has a robust ecosystem for the distribution of modules. Getting into the commercial DotNetNuke module development environment is something that can be aided by having modules reviewed, a process that ensures that the modules adhere to a certain level of functionality. A module can be distributed and supported via an existing communication channel without any external sites needed from the module developer.

This appendix examines various aspects of distributing DotNetNuke modules. The discussion starts with an overview of the DotNetNuke Module Review Program. The discussion continues with information on common distribution channels (including the DotNetNuke Marketplace and SnowCovered), as well as how to get your modules listed there. The discussion concludes with a look at licensing considerations, and provides helpful details on potential license key fields.

DotNetNuke Module Review Program

DotNetNuke Corporation has a Module Review Program whereby module developers can have their modules reviewed by the core team. At the end, if the review process is passed successfully, developers can display the Module Reviewed badge shown in Figure C-1 when marketing the module.

Figure C-1

Review Criteria

Passing the DotNetNuke Module Review Program ensures that the tested module meets a specific list of requirements. The Module Review Program information site (`www.dotnetnuke.com/Programs/Review/Overview/tabid/959/Default.aspx`) contains links to informational documents outlining all criteria that must be met by a tested module. These criteria are designed to ensure that a module meets accepted standards for DotNetNuke development, and that the module functions well within a DotNetNuke environment.

Validation criteria are divided into two categories: required and elective. All conditions of the *required criteria* must be met in order for a module to pass the review process. *Elective criteria* reflect a few different options that might satisfy certain needs. In addition to using the criteria used to determine the pass or fail status of a module review, the DotNetNuke Corporation will also review a few optional elements for informational purposes.

Required Criteria

The following list describes the criteria required in order for a module to pass the Module Review process (as of documentation made available in August 2008):

❑ **Installs without error:** To pass this criterion, if there are any deviations to the standard process, the module must install to the test environment without error following the provided instructions.

❑ **Uninstalls correctly:** A test will be completed to uninstall the module. All installed content and tables must be successfully removed from the system.

❑ **Supports use of** `ObjectQualifier`**:** A test will be completed to ensure that all SQL scripts allow for the use of an optional `ObjectQualifier` value.

❑ **Supports use of** `DatabaseOwner`**:** A test will be completed to ensure that all SQL scripts allow for the use of an optional `DatabaseOwner` value.

❑ **Supports virtual portals:** A test will be completed to ensure that the module properly functions in a multi-portal installation of DotNetNuke.

❑ **Supports globalization:** A test will be completed to ensure that the module does not fail to function when used in a portal with a non-English language enabled.

❑ **Contains an end user license agreement (EULA):** The module must be packaged with an end user license agreement.

These required elements are all very minimal items, and easy for any developer to fully meet. All requirement items have been discussed in previous chapters in this book.

Elective Criteria

To pass the review process, a module must additionally meet requirements for both *support* and *documentation*. Each of these areas has two separate options available for a module to pass the review process.

Criteria for support require that developers either provide support for their modules via a documented channel or optionally provide a source distribution that enables a user to rely upon a third party for issue resolution. This is an important criterion for average DotNetNuke users because it ensures that they will be able to get help when it is needed.

Criteria for documentation require that developers provide online or distributed documentation for installation, uninstallation, and general module usage. Although this is not a very difficult requirement to meet, it is the one item that is most commonly overlooked by module developers, and most desired by end-users.

Optional Criteria

After reviewing a module for support of general functions, a brief review is completed for other common features that are desired in the DotNetNuke community to allow for robust usage. Specifically, the module is checked to determine whether it does the following:

- ❏ **Supports the DotNetNuke localization framework:** A test is performed to determine whether the module supports *static* text localization using the DotNetNuke localization framework. This is a recommended policy to enable developers to design modules for global usage.

- ❏ **Implements the** `IPortable` **interface:** A test is performed to determine whether the module supports importing and exporting of content using the standard import/export options available with an `IPortable` implementation. This is a recommended policy to enable users to move module content from one location to another. It does not always make sense for a module to support this interface.

- ❏ **Implements the** `ISearchable` **interface:** A test is performed to determine whether the module supports the searching of module content via the standard DotNetNuke search system. As with the `IPortable` interface, implementation of `ISearchable` does not make sense for all modules.

- ❏ **Operates in medium trust:** A test is performed to determine whether the module can successfully operate in a medium trust environment. This is a helpful test to ensure that the module can be used in multiple environments. If a module contains Web service or other calls that require elevated permissions, it will *not* be possible to pass this criterion.

- ❏ **Supports standard portal styles:** A test is performed to determine whether the module uses standard DotNetNuke CSS styles. The use of common CSS styles (`Head`, `SubHead`, `Normal`, `NormalRed`, and so on) is key to creating a module that works with multiple skins and systems.

Because of the conditional nature of these elements, DotNetNuke Corporation does not require that these criteria be passed to complete the validation process.

Benefits of Review

The benefits of having a module pass the Module Review process is obvious. This validation demonstrates to potential customers that consideration was given to build a module that can meet the requirements of the DotNetNuke Corporation. Giving customers a little peace of mind can go a long way, especially when marketing a module among many competing modules. It is very possible that review status can be the differentiating factor.

In addition to the benefits of using the Module Reviewed logo, modules that have passed the review process will also be listed in the Reviewed Modules listing on the DotNetNuke website, thus providing more visibility to the module.

Costs

Posted module review prices as of August 2008 were $99 per module, with a current promotion providing reviews for $59. After a module has passed a review, the reviewed status is good for that major version of the module and DotNetNuke, and is considered valid for 24 months.

Distribution Channels

Multiple distribution channels and options are available to new module developers. Custom websites and commercial "module stores" exist that enable users to post their modules for purchase. The two biggest players in this area are the DotNetNuke Marketplace (`http://marketplace.dotnetnuke.com`) and SnowCovered (`www.snowcovered.com`).

Both sites operate similarly, taking a percentage off the retail price of a product sale. DotNetNuke marketplace takes a 25 percent commission and SnowCovered takes a 15 percent commission. Many module developers list products on both sites to ensure the greatest exposure to the community. Selecting the proper distribution channel is important because the channel greatly affects how much exposure your modules get.

Listing your modules on an existing business e-commerce site is also always a valid option. However, given the well-established history of the Marketplace and SnowCovered sites, these are typically the go-to sites for individuals looking for modules.

Licensing Considerations

One of the most difficult items to consider when distributing a DotNetNuke module is how you will protect your intellectual property from unauthorized use. This is something that is always a balancing act, but you should keep in mind a few considerations when evaluating license scenarios for use with a DotNetNuke module.

Ensure the License Can Be Loaded by Admin

One key element that is frustrating to people purchasing modules is when they must manually FTP to their site to load a license file for their recently purchased module. The DotNetNuke framework provides the Module Definitions page, which enables administrator users to quickly upload their content without the need to FTP files to the server. It should be a priority with any licensing scenario to allow the administrator to either use an existing upload facility or provide "license administration" functionality inside the module itself.

Another consideration is that a user must dig up FTP information just to load your module.

Ensure the License Is Not Tied to Hardware

A large number of DotNetNuke installations are on shared hosting hardware. Tying license keys to a specific hardware component such as the Network Interface Card (NIC) address might restrict a user from selecting a different hosting provider, taking a local copy of their site, and it could even render your module unusable after a simple hardware swap by the hosting provider that the administrator is not aware of.

Provide Flexible License Options

Another key consideration when providing a licensed module to users is flexibility — either by offering a flexible default license or by enabling users to select from multiple tiers of service, with options to allow for installation on multiple instances of a site. An increasing number of site administrators are working with multiple sites. These could be development, test, and production environments, or multiple DotNetNuke sites.

Additional .DNN Manifest Options

Several discussions throughout this book have taken a look at the DotNetNuke manifest file in regard to specific scenarios — that is, what does it look like for a module, for a skin object, or for an authentication provider? This appendix dives deeper into the manifest file, and describes the available options, elements, and items that can be included at each level. You will also find direction as to when each option might be of benefit.

Manifest Opening

Listing D-1 shows an example of the manifest opening.

Listing D-1: DotNetNuke Manifest Opening

```
<dotnetnuke type="Package" version="4.0">
  <packages>
```

The beginning parts of a manifest file are always exactly the same: a root `dotnetnuke` element that defines a `type` of package, and a `version` of `4.0`. This `version` information is the version of the manifest type; it is *not* related to the version of any modules or content. For DotNetNuke version 5.x manifests, this value will always be 4.0.

The next element is an opening `packages` tag. Beginning with the new manifest system, it is now possible to install multiple items of different types in a single manifest. Each element is considered a *package*. Therefore, you can have a module package, a skin package, and so on. By using a parent `packages` node, it is possible to bundle these into a single installation.

package Node

As mentioned earlier, the `packages` node holds one or more `package` nodes containing specific packages that are to be installed. The format of this packaging node will be quite similar across the different package types. Taking as an example a form similar to that of Listing D-2, Table D-1 provides detailed information regarding the setup of each potential element and attribute. Overall, the package information is general information that provides package, license, dependency, and developer information to the installing user. The actual package installation items are completed inside the `components` section, which is discussed in the next section.

Listing D-2: Package Node

```
<package name="DNN_LiveIDAuthentication" type=
      "Authentication System" version="01.00.00">
   <friendlyname>DotNetNuke LiveID Authentication
      Project</friendlyname>
   <description>
               The DotNetNuke LiveID Authentication Project is an
        Authentication provider for DotNetNuke that uses the LiveID
               authentication protocol to authenticate users.
   </description>
   <releaseNotes />
   <vendor>
      <name>My Developer</name>
      <organization>MyCompany</ organization >
      <url />
      <email>email@email.com</email>
   </vendor>
      <license src="license.txt" />
   <dependencies>
      <dependency type="CoreVersion">05.01.00</dependency>
   </dependencies>
   <components />
 </package>
```

Table D-1

Element	Attribute	Required	Description
package	name	Yes	This is the unique name of your installation package.
package	type	Yes	This is the type of package you are deploying. Possible values include Authentication System, Module, Skin, SkinObject, and Container.
package	version	Yes	This is the version of your package. It must be in the 00.00.00 format. It is used to control what occurs in various other blocks.
friendlyname	None	Yes	This is the human-friendly name for your package. It should be something descriptive that indicates to users what they are installing.

Element	Attribute	Required	Description
description	None	Yes	This is a description of your package. It is used to provide more information to the user.
releaseNotes	(Optional) src	No	This is where release notes can be placed for users. This is great for notifying users about breaking changes or special considerations. Optionally, a src attribute can define the path to a text document with release note information.
name	None	Yes	This is the name of the company or individual that created the package.
organization	None	Yes	This is the name of the organization that created the module.
url	None	Yes	This is the URL to information about the package or developer.
email	None	Yes	This is the e-mail address for contact.
license	(Optional) src	Yes	This represents the license terms that users must agree to before installing the package. Rather than specify the information in the manifest, an optional src attribute can be used to link to a text file containing the needed information.
dependencies	None	No	Inside the dependencies node, installation dependencies can be created requiring specific types to exist *before* installation can begin.
dependency	None	No	The value provided inside each dependency node is the information needed to enforce the dependency.
dependency	type	Yes	The type attribute defines the type of dependency being reported. Each of the following is a valid type. The note after each type identifies what is to be included inside the actual <dependency> tag.
			CoreVersion: A DotNetNuke version (xx.xx.xx format). Listing D-2 shows an example of the CoreVersion dependency.
			package: The name of a package
			permission: The name of the .NET permission set needed (such as WebPermission)
			type: The fully qualified type that must exist in the application
components	None	Yes	A container node used to hold one of the various components that are to be installed

One of the most powerful items in the new package system is the new dependency feature, shown in Table D-1. This new system provides developers with four key methods to ensure that their modules can properly function in the target environment. Understanding these features is key to creating module packages that ensure users have the proper environment setup *before* installing the module. DotNetNuke 4.x provided similar functionality to the `CoreVersion` and `type` dependencies, although it was a bit more difficult to implement. The `package` and `permission` dependencies make it even easier to set dependencies (for example, between two complementary modules).

component Node

The `component` node is used inside the `components` node of a `package` element. A *component* is a specific function of an installation or a DotNetNuke configuration that must be configured. The general form of a component is outlined in Listing D-3. Depending on the type of component, additional items may be contained inside the `component` element.

Listing D-3: General Form of a component Node

```
<component type="Assembly" installOrder="3">

</component>
```

This information was compiled using resources available in September–October 2008, prior to the release of any formal documentation from DotNetNuke Corporation. Therefore, minor changes in implementation are possible.

Note the optional `installOrder` attribute. This attribute provides developers with the capability to control in which order items are installed. This can be helpful in complex installation scenarios.

assembly Component Type

One of the most common component types is the `assembly` component, which is used to place assemblies into the DotNetNuke system. This is a major improvement from the version 4.x days of module development whereby assemblies were simply placed based on their file extension. Listing D-4 shows a general example of the detailed information for an `assembly` component.

Listing D-4: assembly Component Example

```
<assemblies>
    <assembly>
        <path>bin</path>
        <name>WroxModules.GuestbookCS.dll</name>
        <version>01.00.00</version>
    </assembly>
</assemblies>
```

This example `assembly` component information provides a single assembly that should be loaded to the `bin` directory of the DotNetNuke installation. The name of the assembly is `WroxModules` `.GuestbookCS.dll` and it is version `01.00.00`. This component is a very powerful tool because depending on the specific needs of the installation, `dll` files can be placed in different locations by modifying the path element.

file Component Type

The `file` component is used to add any non-assemblies into the user's DotNetNuke installation. Listing D-5 provides an example `file` component that contains two files to load to the user's system. A base `files` element contains a collection of individual `file` elements, as well as a `basePath` element. The `basePath` element defines the starting point of all file paths. To install a file to the base path location, simply omit the `path` element inside the respective file.

Listing D-5: file Component Example

```
<files>
    <basePath>DesktopModules/GuestbookCS</basePath>
    <file>
        <path>App_LocalResources</path>
        <name>ViewGuestbookCS.ascx.resx</name>
        <sourceFilePath>App_LocalResources</sourceFilePath>
    </file>
    <file>
        <name>ViewGuestbookCS.ascx </name>
    </file>
</files>
```

Given these rules, you can see that the snippet shown in Listing D-5 will place the file `ViewGuestbookCS.ascx` in the folder `/DesktopModules/GuestbookCS`, and the `ViewGuestbookCS` `.ascx.resx` file in the folder `/DesktopModules/GuestbookCS/App_LocalResources`. These path values follow standard Windows path formats, so in order to move one folder up in the hierarchy from the current base path, a file could specify a `path` value of `./`, which refers to the parent directory.

An additional element at the file level, called sourceFilePath, is also available. This allows an alternative source path to be used, which is very helpful when creating combined packages by allowing the package to contain subfolders to isolate files from different package items.

Cleanup Component Type

The `cleanup` component is a method that enables module developers to remove old files that are no longer needed within their modules. This is very helpful for situations in which you might be renaming `dll` files or other actions that require files to be deleted from the file system. This functionality was present in previous versions of DotNetNuke, but it wasn't quite as simple to implement.

Listing D-6 provides a sample implementation of the `cleanup` component. You can see that it is just like the `file` component type. However, rather than indicate the placement of files, it defines the deletion of files. You can use this to remove files from your module path and/or to remove files from the `bin` directory (such as old assemblies).

Listing D-6: Cleanup Component Example

```
<files>
  <file>
    <path>(fullpath)</path>
    <name>(filename)</name>
  </file>
</files>
```

script Component Type

The `script` component type is the method used to control the execution of SQL Server scripts that are needed for installation or uninstallation of a package. This functionality is much improved over the pre-5.x implementation. Prior to DNN 5.0, it was a requirement that files be named using the version number, and you could only have one script per version. This behavior is resolved with the new `script` component type.

Listing D-7 provides an example listing of this component in action, which shows a single installation script for package version 03.01.00. This is determined by looking at the `type` attribute on the `script` element, which has valid values of `Install` and `UnInstall`. Additionally, an uninstall script can be defined for the same version.

Listing D-7: Script Component Example

```
<scripts>
  <basePath>DesktopModules\MyModule</basePath>
  <script type="Install">
    <path>scripts</path>
    <name>03.01.00.sqldataprovider</name>
    <version>03.01.00</version>
  </script>
  <script type="UnInstall">
    <path>scripts</path>
    <name>uninstall.sqldataprovider</name>
    <version>03.01.01</version>
  </script>
</scripts>
```

Note that `basePath` and `Path` values can be used in this component type to reference the proper file locations for all script files.

authenticationSystem Component Type

The `authenticationSystem` component type was introduced in Chapter 17. It can be used only with a package `type` of `Auth_System`. (or `Authentication System` in DNN 4.6.x +). This component is used to define the integration aspects of the authentication provider.

Listing D-8 provides an example of the format for this component type. Note that it has a very fixed format. It can never have more or less elements, and there are no repeating sections that could add to the overall structure. The key thing to remember here is that the `type` is the unique type for the authentication system being created. In addition, keep in mind that the individual `ControlSrc` elements are the full file paths to the respective controls.

Listing D-8: authenticationSystem Component Example

```
<authenticationService>
    <type>LiveID</type>
    <settingsControlSrc>(fullpath)</settingsControlSrc>
    <loginControlSrc>(fullpath)</loginControlSrc>
    <logoffControlSrc>(fullpath)</logoffControlSrc>
</authenticationService>
```

module Component Type

The `module` component type was discussed in earlier chapters when you were creating the installation package for the module, so this section provides only a brief example. Listing D-9 shows an example implementation of this component.

Listing D-9: module Component Example

```
<desktopModule>
  <moduleName>WROX_GuestbookCS</moduleName>
  <foldername>GuestbookCS</foldername>
  <businessControllerClass>WroxModules.GuestbookCS.
      GuestbookCSController</businessControllerClass>
  <supportedFeatures>
    <supportedFeature type="Portable" />
    <supportedFeature type="Searchable" />
    <supportedFeature type="Upgradeable" />
  </supportedFeatures>
  <moduleDefinitions>
    <moduleDefinition>
      <friendlyName>Guestbook CS</friendlyName>
      <defaultCacheTime>0</defaultCacheTime>
      <moduleControls>
        <moduleControl>
          <controlKey />
          <controlSrc>DesktopModules/GuestbookCS/
              ViewGuestbookCS.ascx</controlSrc>
          <supportsPartialRendering>True</supportsPartialRendering>
          <controlTitle />
          <controlType>View</controlType>
          <iconFile />
          <helpUrl />
          <viewOrder>0</viewOrder>
        </moduleControl>
      </moduleControls>
    </moduleDefinition>
  </moduleDefinitions>
</desktopModule>
```

Keep in mind the following:

❑ The `businessControllerClass` is the class that defines the integration point for common DotNetNuke interfaces. The fully qualified namespace to the controller must be specified in order for integration elements to work (such as `IPortable` and `ISearchable`).

❑ The supported `features` element, and its sub-element, `supportedFeature`, are new additions to the module installation process. Historically, DotNetNuke has used reflection during installation to determine the supported features of a module. However, DotNetNuke 5.x has added this optional element collection, thus enabling developers to control the implemented interfaces. It is important to note, however, that you must not list items that are *not* supported in the `businessControllerClass`. Doing so might result in recurring errors on the portal.

❑ A `moduleDefinitions` collection can contain multiple `moduleDefinition` elements. As discussed in previous chapters, each `moduleDefinition` element is a specific view implementation for the module. Multiple `moduleDefinition` elements can be included. Inside each `moduleDefinition` is a collection of `moduleControl` elements. These define each of the individual controls.

SkinObject Component Type

The `SkinObject` component type was introduced in Chapter 16 when the `CurrentTimeSkinObject` was created. This component type is only valid within a package type of `SkinObject`.

Listing D-10 provides a sample implementation of this very simple component type. A single module `control` element is used to store the information needed for the `SkinObject` declaration. First, the `control` key and source are defined, and a Boolean value is declared to indicate support of ASP.NET partial rendering. The `supportsPartialRendering` element is optional; if it is omitted, `false` is the assumed value.

Listing D-10: SkinObject Component Example

```
<moduleControl>
  <controlKey>CurrentTimeVB</controlKey>
  <controlSrc>(fullPath)</controlSrc>
  <supportsPartialRendering>False</supportsPartialRendering>
</moduleControl>
```

container Component Type

The `container` component type is another new feature included with DotNetNuke version 5.x. This container type is valid only inside the `Container` package type, and it simply defines all files associated with a given skin container. A very similar format is used for this component type, starting with a name for the container, a base path declaration, and a collection of `containerFile` elements that define each item to be loaded. Overall, the structure of this component type is very similar to that of the `file` component.

Listing D-11 provides a small sample of a `container` component definition.

Listing D-11: container Component Example

```
<containerFiles>
  <containerName>MinimalExtropy</containerName>
  <basePath>Portals\_default\Containers\MinimalExtropy</basePath>
  <containerFile>
    <path>images</path>
    <name>dnn-minus.png</name>
  </containerFile>
  <containerFile>
    <path>images</path>
    <name>dnn-plus.png</name>
  </containerFile>
</containerFiles>
```

Provider and Library Components

Another two additions to the DotNetNuke 5.x extensions system are the `Provider` and `Library` components. These do not have their own types; they simply utilize other component types to load their information (typically, the `file` and `assembly` component types). These are great additions for module developers because they make it possible to distribute a common library to be shared among multiple modules without worrying about users uninstalling individual modules and causing errors elsewhere.

skin Component Type

New to DotNetNuke 5.0 is the `skin` component type. This is another component that shares its format with the `file` component. It is simply used to provide skin developers with a format to specify all files and installation locations for their skins.

An additional element at the file level is also available called sourceFilePath. This allows an alternative source path to be used, which is very helpful when creating combined packages by allowing the package to contain subfolders to isolate files from different package items.

Listing D-12 provides an example implementation of this component type. Note that this type is valid only with the `Skin` package type.

Listing D-12: skin Component Example

```
<skinFiles>
  <skinName>MinimalExtropy</skinName>
  <basePath>Portals\_default\Skins\MinimalExtropy</basePath>
  <skinFile>
    <path>css</path>
    <name>menu.css</name>
    <sourceFilePath>css</sourceFilePath>
  </skinFile>
  <skinFile>
    <path>images</path>
    <name>body_bg.png</name>
  </skinFile>
</skinFiles>
```

config Component Type

Another new item to DotNetNuke is the `config` component type. This component provides developers with access to the new XML merge functionality that was added to the DotNetNuke core system in version 4.6.2.

For those unfamiliar with this functionality, these are functions within the core system that enable DotNetNuke to successfully manipulate and work with the `web.config` file by using a declarative syntax. Listing D-13 shows an example of the `config` component, here used to insert the `HttpModule` entry needed for the Active Directory authentication provider.

Listing D-13: config Component Example

```
<component type="Config">
    <config>
        <configfile>web.config</configfile>
        <install>
            <configuration>
                <nodes>
                    <node action="update" collision=
                        "overwrite" key="name"
                path="/configuration/system.web/httpModules">
                     <add name="Authentication"
                        type="DotNetNuke.Authentication.ActiveDirectory.
                            HttpModules.AuthenticationModule,
    DotNetNuke.Authentication.ActiveDirectory">
                            </add>
                </node>
         </nodes>
            </configuration>
        </install>
        <uninstall>
            <configuration>
                <nodes>
                    <node action="remove"
        path="/configuration/system.web/httpModules/
            add[@name='Authentication']">
                        </node>
                </nodes>
            </configuration>
        </uninstall>
    </config>
</component>
```

This example demonstrates the simple declarative nature of the `config` component. It starts out with a `config` node that defines which file should be modified (in this case, the `web.config` file). Note, however, that other XML files can be manipulated via this process. An `install` and `uninstall` action are defined inside the `config` node. This enables a module to be a good citizen and remove the elements needed upon uninstallation.

A collection of nodes that define the actual action to handle appears inside the `install` and `uninstall` nodes. Each node element has attributes to handle the desired actions, the `key` element, as well as the `path` and a collision option. This enables developers to pinpoint the area to be modified. The key point to remember here is that the items contained inside the `<node>` tags reflect the value that will actually be inserted into the file. The `uninstall` section works in a similar manner with a `remove` action.

This functionality is a very helpful addition for many third-party developers, as it is now possible to install complex modules that require configuration changes without forcing the end-user to modify the configuration.

dashboardInstaller Component Type

In DotNetNuke versions 4.9.2 and 5.0.1, both due to be released during first quarter 2009, a new component type has been added to install Dashboard Components. Dashboard components are add-ons to a new Host Dashboard that was added in both 4.9.x and 5.x versions. The dashboard is a place to quickly get high-level configuration information from a portal.

An update to this book will be published shortly after the release of 5.0.1 and will include samples of the structure of this component type. At this time the information has yet to be finalized.

Summary

This appendix has provided a general overview of the individual elements that (as of this writing) can comprise a DotNetNuke manifest. Keep in mind that a key benefit of the new package system in DotNetNuke 5.0 is that developers can provide an installation that installs multiple package types at the same time. For example, a skin designer can package a custom skin object and a skin together. A module developer can package a module with a `Library` component. These are key benefits that make adoption of DotNetNuke 5.x for development much more flexible than ever before.

For more information, check out Charles Nurse's blog on `DotNetNuke.com`. He often blogs about new features included in the module installation/package systems well before the information is published in any formal documentation.

Working with DotNetNuke Entities

This book has discussed working with DotNetNuke to create custom modules, skin objects, and authentication providers, and has devoted a fair amount of space to development with custom business processes in mind. This appendix introduces some helpful classes inside the various `DotNetNuke.Entities.____` namespaces that help to provide the custom business logic integration information to the underlying DotNetNuke system.

This appendix is organized by individual namespace. Within each namespace discussion, you will learn about key classes and how they can be leveraged to get application data. This is *not* a comprehensive list of classes, but rather some of the most common classes and namespaces that might be used.

> *Readers looking for a good source of information to dive into the class structure of the DotNetNuke framework might investigate the class browser available at* `http://classbrowser.subzero-solutions.net/home.aspx?tabindex=130.`

DotNetNuke.Entities.Modules

The `DotNetNuke.Entities.Modules` namespace groups together classes that are used when working with modules. Some of these items have been discussed in previous chapters of this book, and are only examined here briefly. The following sections describe the interfaces and classes that exist inside this namespace. Each element description includes information about how and when its usage might be beneficial.

Interfaces

This namespace holds a majority of the interfaces discussed in Chapter 10. These interfaces enable modules to integrate into the core DotNetNuke framework. The `IPortable`, `IActionable`, `ISearchable`, `IUpgradable`, and `IHydratable` interfaces are all contained inside this namespace. The important thing to remember is that in order to implement these interfaces, an `imports` or `using` statement (including the namespace) is required before the interface names will be recognized.

Classes

A number of classes are included in this namespace. These have already been discussed in detail in earlier chapters when you were creating the user interface for the Guestbook module. These classes include `PortalModuleBase` and `ModuleSettingsBase`. They provide the foundation of support needed to create module controls, exposing common DotNetNuke information to the interface code.

The following sections introduce other classes that may have been used in previous discussions throughout the book. The examination here is designed to provide a bit of insight into how these classes might be used, and to provide helpful methods of reference.

ModuleController

The `ModuleController` class provides access to the entire module system, including the capability to add modules, delete modules, and manage module settings. As mentioned in Chapter 18, it is a best practice to work with these controller classes to perform manipulations whenever possible.

Table E-1 shows a helpful static method provided by the controller, and Table E-2 shows helpful public methods that require an instance of the controller.

Table E-1

Name	Return Type	Parameters	Description
SynchronizeModule	None	int ModuleId	This method, which clears the cache for the provided module, is great for ensuring that the user interface is updated after updates to content.

Table E-2

Name	Return Type	Parameters	Description
DeleteModuleSetting	None	int ModuleId	This method removes the setting stored for the provided ModuleId and setting name.
		string SettingName	
DeleteModuleSettings	None	int ModuleId	This method removes all module settings stored for the passed ModuleId.

Name	Return Type	Parameters	Description
DeleteTabModuleSetting	None	int TabModuleId	This method removes the provided tab module setting using the TabModuleId and setting name to locate the value.
		string SettingName	
DeleteTabModuleSettings	None	int TabModuleId	This method will remove all tabmodule settings for the passed TabModuleId.
GetModule	ModuleInfo	int moduleId	This returns the module information for a specific module on a specific tab.
		int tabId	
GetTabModules	Dictionary<int,ModuleInfo>	int TabId	This method returns a dictionary collection with all modules located on a specific page. This is very helpful when modules must communicate with each other directly.
UpdateModuleSetting	None	int ModuleId	This adds or updates the specified module setting using the setting name and setting value provided.
		string settingName	
		string settingValue	

(continued)

Table E-2 *(continued)*

Name	Return Type	Parameters	Description
UpdateTabModuleSetting	None	int TabModuleId	This adds or updates the specified tab module setting using the setting name and value provided.
		string settingName	
		string settingValue	

From Table E-1 and Table E-2, you can see that the primary functions that are useful in general module applications from the ModuleController class are methods to clear the cache, find the modules on a page, and update or remove settings.

ModuleInfo

ModuleInfo is a class that contains information about a specific module. This information includes positioning and other helpful properties regarding the module. This object can help determine where on a page the module was placed, as well as its position within the assigned pane.

DotNetNuke.Entities.Portals

The DotNetNuke.Entities.Portals namespace holds a collection of classes that pertain to portal-specific information. These classes grant users access to common portal information, and allow for easy integration into settings such as the "administrator email" for sending of notifications. No interfaces are exposed inside the namespace. The following sections examine commonly used classes and helpful methods in each class.

PortalSettings Class

The PortalSettings class has many static methods that provide access to various subsets of settings information. When fully instantiated, it contains overall settings information for a specific portal configuration.

Table E-3 shows static methods that are of particular interest to extension developers. Table E-4 shows public properties that are of particular interest once the object has been hydrated.

Table E-3

Name	Return Type	Parameters	Description
GetHostSettings	Hashtable	None	This method returns a hash table with all host settings values. This includes items such as Simple Mail Transfer Protocol (SMTP) configuration.
GetModuleSettings	HashTable	int ModuleId	This method returns a hash table containing all module settings for the specific module.
GetSiteSetting	String	int PortalId	This method returns a single portal setting to the user.
		string SettingName	
GetSiteSettings	HashTable	int portalId	This method returns a hash table containing all portal settings for the supplied portal.
UpdatePortalSetting	void	int portalid	This method updates a portal-level setting with the value specified. It can be used to add portal settings of your own.
		string settingName	
		string settingValue	

Table E-4

Name	Type	Description
ActiveTabId	Integer	ID of the currently active tab
AdministratorId	Integer	User ID of the site administrator
AdministratorRoleId	Integer	ID of the administrator role for the portal
DefaultLanguage	String	Default language for the portal
ExpiryDate	DateTime	Date the portal is set to expire

Table E-4 *(continued)*

Name	Type	Description
GUID	Guid	Globally Unique Identifier (GUID) for the portal. This is helpful if you are working on a licensing plan that requires users to limit by portal.
HomeDirectory	String	Path to the portal home directory
HomeTabId	Integer	Tab ID of the page that is the home page for the portal
RegisteredRoleId	Integer	ID of the registered user's role
UserTabId	Integer	This is the page identified as the user's page, where the user can modify his or her profile.

Table E-3 and Table E-4 provide just a small sampling of the properties and settings information that is available from the `PortalSettings` class. It is also important to consider the information that is exposed by understanding the items in this discussion. For example, knowing the administrator's user ID, it is then possible to look up all the needed information about the administrator.

PortalController Class

Another powerful class contained in the `DotNetNuke.Entities.Portals` namespace is the `PortalController` class. This class is used by the core framework to add, remove, and modify portal-specific information. This class is not often used by extension developers unless they are creating dynamic, multi-portal installations or other items for which portal creation/deletion processes are needed.

DotNetNuke.Entities.Tabs

The `DotNetNuke.Entities.Tabs` namespace groups classes related to tab (or page) management within the portal. The information contained inside this namespace can be very helpful to extension developers because it provides the capability to view all of the pages in a portal, and can be used to allow users to select different tabs for navigation and other purposes.

Two key classes are available inside this namespace:

❑ `TabController`: As with other DotNetNuke controller classes, this class facilitates all communications regarding tabs inside the portal.

❑ `TabInfo`: This class is simply a business object class that holds all information relative to a tab for display.

TabController Class

The `TabController` class provides access to numerous functions that can be beneficial to extensions developers. First and foremost, this controller is the one used by the core team to include Add, Delete, Copy, and Update tabs from the system. Methods supporting these operations are all contained within the controller class, although the use of those methods is not always common when it comes to modules and other extension types.

Table E-5 shows other methods contained inside the `TabController` class. Rather than provide tab management functionality, these methods provide access to view tab information (such as listings of tabs and getting specific tab information objects).

Table E-5

Method	Return Type	Parameters	Description
GetTab	TabInfo	int TabId	Retrieves the settings for a single tab based on the passed `TabId`
GetTabs	ArrayList	int PortalId	Retrieves an array list of `TabInfo` objects that represent *all* tabs created in a portal. (Deprecated)
GetTabsByPortal	Dictionary<int, TabInfo>	int PortalId	New method to retrieve a tab listing for a portal, returning a dictionary of `TabInfo` objects

Using one of these methods, it is easy to get a listing of all available tabs for the portal to create a navigation selection list or other linking reference within your module. This is a very common item to implement in solutions such as shopping carts or payment modules, where a user must be directed to a Success page upon completion.

TabInfo Class

The `TabInfo` class contains all the information that is needed to construct a tab within the DotNetNuke system. Although there are many properties contained in this class, a very small subset of properties are commonly used as integration points. Table E-6 describes these common properties.

Table E-6

Property Name	Type	Description
IsVisible	Boolean	Specifies whether this tab is visible in the menu or hidden from display
ParentId	Integer	ID of the parent tab to which this tab reports
TabId	Integer	ID of the tab, used typically for navigation. The TabId is a key component in all navigation inside DotNetNuke.
TabName	String	Name of the tab as entered in the settings. This is the value that is displayed in the menu.
Title	String	Title of the page as loaded into the browser's title bar

As shown in Table E-6, knowing the tab information can help module developers gain some insight into some the inner workings and configurations of the entities that are commonly used.

DotNetNuke.Entities.Users

The DotNetNuke.Entities.Users namespace groups all classes that relate to user access and expose user functionality to extension developers. There are three classes that are key integration points. Two of them, UserInfo and UserProfileInfo, are simply information object classes that expose developers to the individual items that make up a user, and the user's extended profile information. The following two sections introduce the third class, UserController, and some of its common methods. Following that discussion is a code sample showing how to create a user account using all three of these classes. This example provides additional exposure to a few enumerations that exist inside the namespace to handle authentication events.

UserController Class

The UserController class is the primary conduit for all aspects of working with users, including password changes and updates. A strong majority of the methods commonly used for integration within DotNetNuke are static methods.

Table E-7 shows the commonly used static methods, and provides detailed information about each.

Table E-7

Method Name	Return Type	Parameters	Description
ChangePassword	Boolean	UserInfo user	This method changes the user's password. The first parameter is the user's information, followed by old passwords and new passwords.
		string oldpassword	
		string newpassword	
CreateUser	UserCreateStatus (Enum)	UserInfo newUser	This method creates a user account using the UserInfo information passed to the method. See the example later in this appendix (Listing E-1 and Listing E-2) for the process.
GeneratePassword	String	None	This generates a random password that can be assigned to a user.
GetPassword	String	UserInfo User	This method gets the user's password from the database if passwords are stored encrypted, which is the default action for DotNetNuke. *Note:* By default, Question & Answer is disabled, so passing " " for the password answer allows the password to be retrieved.
		string passwordAnswer	

(continued)

Table E-7 *(continued)*

Method Name	Return Type	Parameters	Description
GetUser	UserInfo	Int userId	This method gets a user based on the user ID and portal. The hydrated method determines whether the full profile information will be returned.
		int PortalId	
		Bool IsHydrated	
GetUserByName	UserInfo	int portalId	This method gets a user based on the portalid and the passed username value.
		string Username	
GetUsers	ArrayList (of UserInfo objects)	int portalId	This method gets all users for the specified portal. The hydration flag controls whether the full information is returned.
		bool IsHydrated	
SetAuthCookie	None	string username	This method creates and sets the authorization cookie, effectively logging in the user with the specified username. A persistent cookie flag controls the "remember me" style functionality.
		bool persistentCookie	

Method Name	Return Type	Parameters	Description
ValidateUser	UserInfo	Int portalId	This method validates the user's login information based on the provided authentication type. To ensure that DotNetNuke validates the user, the authType parameter must receive the value DNN. The UserLoginStatus parameter is passed by reference, and can be checked to determine whether the user's login was successful.
		String Username	
		String Password	
		String authType	
		String VerificationCode	
		String PortalName	
		String IP	
		UserLoginStatus	
		loginStatus	

Creating a User

The best way to understand this in use is to look at an example of creating a user with the default minimum information. Listing E-1 (C#) and Listing E-2 (VB.NET) show the code equivalents for user creation.

Listing E-1: C# User Creation Code

```
UserInfo oUser = new UserInfo();
oUser.PortalID = this.PortalId;
oUser.IsSuperUser = false;
oUser.FirstName = "FirstName";
oUser.LastName = "LastName";
oUser.Email = "Email";
oUser.Username = "Username";
```

(continued)

Listing E-1 *(continued)*

```
oUser.DisplayName = String.Concat(oUser.FirstName, " ",
        oUser.LastName);

//Declare the profile
oUser.Profile = new DotNetNuke.Entities.Users.UserProfile();

//Set profile properties
oUser.Profile.SetProfileProperty("MiddleName","MI");

//Set Membership
DotNetNuke.Entities.Users.UserMembership oNewMembership = new
        DotNetNuke.Entities.Users.UserMembership();
oNewMembership.Approved = true;
oNewMembership.CreatedDate = System.DateTime.Now;
oNewMembership.Email = oUser.Email;
oNewMembership.IsOnLine = false;
oNewMembership.Username = oUser,Username;
oNewMembership.Password = "Password";

//Bind membership to user
oUser.Membership = oNewMembership;

//Add the user, ensure it was successful
if (UserCreateStatus.Success == UserController.CreateUser(ref oUser))
{
    //Success!
}
else
{
    //Failure, check status enum for detail
}
```

Listing E-2: VB User Creation Code

```
Dim oUser as New UserInfo
oUser.PortalID = Me.PortalId
oUser.IsSuperUser = false
oUser.FirstName = "FirstName"
oUser.LastName = "LastName"
oUser.Email = "Email"
oUser.Username = "Username"
oUser.DisplayName = String.Concat(oUser.FirstName, " ", oUser.LastName)

'Declare the profile
oUser.Profile = new DotNetNuke.Entities.Users.UserProfile()

'Set profile properties
oUser.Profile.SetProfileProperty("MiddleName","MI")

'Set Membership
Dim oNewMembership As New DotNetNuke.Entities.Users.UserMembership()
```

```
oNewMembership.Approved = true
oNewMembership.CreatedDate = System.DateTime.Now
oNewMembership.Email = oUser.Email
oNewMembership.IsOnLine = false
oNewMembership.Username = oUser,Username
oNewMembership.Password = "Password"

'Bind membership to user
oUser.Membership = oNewMembership

''Add the user, ensure it was successful
If UserCreateStatus.Success == UserController.CreateUser(oUser) Then
    'Success!
Else
    'Failure, check status enum for detail
End If
```

You can see that this is a very simple process. The code starts out by declaring a new `UserInfo` object, continues to populate its standard properties, and then its profile is set to a new instance of a user profile. The `SetProfileProperty` is used to set the middle initial, and, lastly, the user's membership information is added by using the `UserMembership` object. After fully creating the `UserInfo` object, a single call to the `UserController.CreateUser` method adds the user, and an `enum` value check determines whether the user was created successfully.

Summary

This appendix provided a quick introduction to common classes contained inside the various `DotNetNuke.Entities` namespaces, and showed some important ways that extension developers can utilize these methods to more tightly integrate their applications with the DotNetNuke framework. Ultimately, this creates a better solution — one that is easy to move forward as DotNetNuke continues to evolve as a product and DotNetNuke Corporation modifies various implementations.

Index

U

UI (user interface) base classes, 65–67
uninstall.sqldataprovider file, 101–104
UpdateModuleSetting, 115, 285
UpdatePortalSetting, 287
UpdateSettings, 114
UpdateTabModuleSetting, 286
Upgrade package, 6
upgradeConnectionString, 264
UpgradeModule, 165
Url control, 188–191
Url property, 168
UrlTracking control, 188–191
Use Local IIS Web Server option, 48, 52
UseActionEvent property, 168
UseInstallWizard, 262
UsePortNumber, 262
User Access Control, 20
user control markup. See also controls
  EditGuestbook(cs/vb).ascx control, 129
  Settings.ascx control, 110–112
  SignGuestbook.ascx control, 133–136
  ViewGuestbook(cs/vb).ascx control, 119–121
  ViewSettings.ascx control, 116–117
user interface (UI) base classes, 65–67
User Mapping, 17
"User must change password at next login" option, 17
UserController class, 290–295
UserId, 35, 43, 66
UserInfo class, 66, 290
user-level data isolation, 43
username, 16, 17
UserProfileInfo class, 290
users, 25, 33–35, 37
UserTabId, 288
using statement, 161, 168, 283

V

ValidateUser, 293
ValidationGroup attribute, 136
VB.NET
  code listings. See listings
  templates, installing, 27–28
versions
  DNN, 1–3
  Visual Studio, 13–14
view guestbook control, 39, 40
view settings control, 39, 116
ViewCurrentTimeSkinObject.ascx., 221–224
ViewCurrentTimeSkinObject.ascx.resx, 221
ViewGuestbook(cs/vb).ascx control, 119–128
ViewSettings.ascx control, 116–119
Visible property, 168
Vista (Windows), 19, 20, 154

Visual Studio (Microsoft)
  2005 Professional, 14
  2008 Professional, 14
  Attach to Process option, 154
  Build Events, 150
  Express editions, 14
  Installer packages, 3
  product line overview (online), 14
  versions, 13–14
  WAP and, 13, 14

W

Walker, Shaun, 144
WAP development model. See Web Application Projects model
Washington, Michael, 8, 9, 258
Web Application Framework template, 4
Web Application Projects (WAP) model, 4, 12–13
  debugging and, 154
  "Introduction to Web Application Projects," 13
  Visual Studio and, 13, 14
  WSP v., 13
Web site folder, 5
Web Site Projects (WSP) model, 4, 12–13, 14
web.config
  appSettings section, 261–262
  data provider section, 263–264
  httpRuntime section, 262–263
  modifying, 254
  options, 261–264
  release.config and, 6
  Upgrade package and, 6
[WEBSITE], 127
WebsiteFormat.Text, 141
welcome screen (DNN Installation Wizard), 24
Windows Server 2003/2008, 19, 20, 154
Windows Vista, 19, 20, 154
wizard
  Create Package, 151–153
  Installation, 23–26
WrapUpdatePanelControl method, 212
WroxModules.GuestbookCS, 48
WroxModules.GuestbookVB, 51
WSP development model. See Web Site Projects model

X

XCOPY operations, 150

Z

ZIP files, 145, 149, 150, 151
ZIP utility, 18

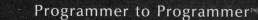